Fundamentals of Curriculum Planning, Development, Implementation, and Evaluation in English Language Teaching

Fundamentals of Curriculum Planning, Development, Implementation, and Evaluation in English Language Teaching

Eman Elturki

Foreword by Jack C. Richards

University of Michigan Press
Ann Arbor

Published in the United States of America by the
University of Michigan Press

ISBN 978-0-472-04009-4 (print)
ISBN 978-0-472-22245-2 (e-book)

First published February 2026

Authorized Representative: Easy Access System Europe, Mustamäe tee 50, 10621
Tallinn, Estonia, gpsr.requests@easproject.com

Contents

List of Figures vii

List of Tables ix

Foreword xiii

Preface xvii

Part I. Curriculum Conception

1. Understanding Curriculum 3
2. Philosophical and Theoretical Foundations of Curriculum 16
3. Curriculum Context and Purpose 51
4. Curriculum Development Models and Approaches 75

Part II. Curriculum Systemization in Practice

5. A Framework to Curriculum 109
6. Curriculum Conceptualization 117
7. Curriculum Planning 130
8. Curriculum Development 175
9. Curriculum Implementation 215
10. Curriculum Evaluation 235

References 255

List of Figures

Figure 1.1	Curriculum as a Multifaceted Phenomenon	6
Figure 1.2	An Illustration of the Relationship between Program, Course, Curriculum, and Syllabus	11
Figure 3.1	Contextual Levels of Curriculum	52
Figure 4.1	A Visualization of Tyler's Curriculum Model	77
Figure 5.1	An Overview of the CPDIE Curriculum Framework	110
Figure 5.2	Decision-Making and the Important Role of the Meso Level	112
Figure 6.1	Sample Features of a Curriculum from a Social Reconstructionist Lens	121
Figure 7.1	Needs Analysis (NA) as a Preliminary, Ongoing, and Evaluative Measure	134
Figure 7.2	Dimensions and Characteristics of Needs	138
Figure 8.1	The Relationship among Curricular Elements	180
Figure 8.2	Curriculum Conceptualization: The Philosophical and Theoretical Bases of ENGL 010	201
Figure 10.1	Framework for Horizontal and Vertical Evaluation of Multi-Level Curricula	242
Figure 10.2	Sample Revision: Progression and Type of Writing Assignments	251

List of Tables

Table 1.1	Sample Syllabus Types and Their Content Focus and Sequencing in ELT	9
Table 1.2	Typologies of Curriculum	13
Table 4.1	CAST's Universal Design for Learning Framework	90
Table 4.2	The UNESCO's Description of a Quality Curriculum	92
Table 6.1	What Informs the Conceptualization Phase	119
Table 6.2	Guiding Questions for the Conceptualization Phase	125
Table 6.3	An Example of the Outcome of a Curriculum-Building Task	127
Table 7.1	Application of Needs Analysis (NA) in an EGP Context	133
Table 7.2	Considerations for Planning Needs Analysis (NA)	135
Table 7.3	Illustrative Example of Common Types of Needs Identified during Curriculum Planning	140
Table 7.4	Application of Task-Based Needs Analysis in an ESP Context	142
Table 7.5	Application I of Critical Needs Analysis in an EAP Context	144

Table 7.6 Application II of Critical Needs Analysis in an EAP Context 145

Table 7.7 Sample Studies Employing Different Needs Analysis Methods and Techniques 150

Table 7.8 Example of Methodological Practices for Improving Needs Analysis Validity and Reliability 153

Table 7.9 Example of a Needs Analysis Activity 154

Table 7.10 Factors to Consider at Various Levels of Curriculum Context in Situation Analysis 160

Table 7.11 Example of a Situation Analysis Process 170

Table 8.1 Using Curriculum Planning Data to Inform Curriculum Development: An ESP Example 177

Table 8.2 Using Curriculum Planning Data to Inform Curriculum Development: An EGP Example 178

Table 8.3 Example I Illustrating the Differences between Goals, Objectives, and Outcomes 183

Table 8.4 Example II Illustrating the Differences between Goals, Objectives, and Outcomes 185

Table 8.5 Bloom's Taxonomy Domains and Corresponding Verbs for Objectives and Outcomes 186

Table 8.6 Considerations for the Articulation of Aims during the Curriculum Development Phase 188

Table 8.7 Sample Assessment Mapping for the EAP Pathway Course 190

Table 8.8 Sample Assessment Mapping for the Adult High-Beginner ESL Course 190

Table 8.9 Sample Chart for Mapping Textbook Contents to Objectives 194

Table 8.10 ENGL 010 Student Learning Outcomes (SLOs) 205

Table 8.11 An Overview of the ENGL 010 Curriculum 205

Table 8.12 Sample Curriculum Development Product I: Summative Assessment, Corresponding SLOs, and Focus of Instruction 207

Table 8.13 Sample Curriculum Development Product II: Summative Assessment, Corresponding SLOs, and Focus of Instruction 208

Table 8.14 Sample ENGL 010 Theme-Related Texts 212

Table 9.1 Guiding Questions for the Planning of Instructional Activities 220

Table 9.2 Curriculum Implementation: A Sample Lesson Plan for ENGL 010 221

Table 10.1 Materials and Data for Curriculum Evaluation, Review, and Revision 239

Table 10.2 Sample Revision: A Preview of the Academic Essay Prompt 250

Foreword

The terms *curriculum* and *curriculum development* mean different things in language teaching depending on whether it involves activities and decision-making at the national and international level (macro), institutional level (meso), or classroom level (micro). Macro-level decisions reflect the socio-political contexts of language teaching such as those related to language policies and the roles and functions of languages in education. Meso-level planning involves turning policies into action plans. It includes goals and standards for primary, secondary, and tertiary education, specifications of the knowledge and skills required of teachers, identification of the teaching resources that will be provided (textbooks, print and digital resources, grammars, dictionaries, etc.), and the teaching methods that are recommended or prescribed. The micro level refers to the classroom level and the teaching and learning processes that teachers and learners make use of, including course design and curricula, teaching techniques and procedures, and the use of tests and assessments.

Curriculum can also be understood as both a ***product*** and a ***process***. When viewed as a ***product***, curriculum is identified with documents that describe the goals, organization, and content of a course, providing the basis for teaching, materials development, and assessment. This framework for teaching may be developed by specialists in a ministry of education or a school or institution, and it reflects current understandings of second language learning and incorporates best practices in language teaching. Such curricula reflect the contexts for which they are designed, whether a national curriculum, an institutional curriculum, or the teacher's curriculum. They require continuous renewal as circumstances change—such as when English is introduced, for example, at the primary rather than the secondary level in English as a Foreign Language (EFL) contexts, when national or school tests and examinations change, and when students' needs change.

Language curricula may also change when the underlying educational philosophies and theories of language and second language learning are questioned or discarded. This was the case when communicative language teaching, process writing, and competency-based instruction replaced earlier teaching approaches. A curriculum may also need to be redesigned due to new modes of delivery, as occurred during the COVID-19 pandemic, when classroom-based face-to-face teaching was often replaced by online instruction. In designing a curriculum from this perspective, decisions must be made regarding the content (e.g., vocabulary, grammar, texts, skills), the learning outcomes it aims to achieve (such as the ability to write an argumentative essay), the roles of teachers and learners, and the methods of teaching and assessment to be used. These decisions will depend on where and how the curriculum will be implemented, as well as the constraints and affordances provided by the context, often identified through what is referred to as *situational* or *environmental analysis*. The mode of implementation may be face-to-face, blended, or online, each of which will impact different aspects of the curriculum design.

When viewed as a *process*, the focus shifts to the micro level of the curriculum, which refers to how teachers implement it and the processes that arise as teachers and learners engage in the day-to-day aspects of classroom teaching. The classroom is viewed as a setting where learning is not necessarily predetermined but arises out of the learners' participation in classroom activities. Consequently, a process-oriented understanding of the curriculum views the classroom as a site where teachers and learners participate in tasks and activities, adapt and extend teaching materials based on moment-to-moment incidents that arise during the teaching process, and negotiate their identities through the interactional processes involved. This is sometimes referred to as the "lived" or "enacted" curriculum, which emerges through the processes that drive teaching and learning—processes such as investigation, decision-making, reflection, discussion, interpretation, critical thinking, making choices, and cooperating with others. Content is selected based on how it promotes the use of these processes and outcomes. Other features of the curriculum as a process include an emphasis on guiding principles for the teaching-learning process, a recognition of learners as active participants in shaping their own learning, acknowledgment of the uniqueness of each teaching-learning context, a focus on the development of the learner as an individual, and a view of learning as a creative, problem-solving activity.

In this timely and important book, Dr. Eman Elturki offers a superb account of the macro, meso, and micro dimensions of language curriculum development, exploring how curriculum is realized both as a product and as a process. The book provides a comprehensive overview of various approaches to curriculum development in educational planning and language teaching. It traces the evolution of curriculum models, from early language-based approaches to a more holistic view of curriculum as a "comprehensive, context-dependent phenomenon composed of interrelated processes grounded in philosophy and theory (. . .) and informed by a clear understanding of the educational context as well as the needs and beliefs of the different stakeholders" (p. 5, this book). Throughout, the book moves seamlessly from theory to practice and from practice to theory, fully realizing the aims suggested by the book's title: ***Fundamentals of Curriculum Planning, Development, Implementation, and Evaluation in English Language Teaching.***

This book will be welcomed by a wide range of those involved in developing and implementing language curriculum, both those involved with curriculum at the national and institutional level, to teachers developing curriculum and materials for their own teaching contexts. Written in a clear and engaging style, the book effectively uses discussion questions, examples, and follow-up activities. It provides educational planners, teachers, material designers, and student teachers with the knowledge and skills necessary to review, adapt, and create curricula and materials, thus better preparing them to respond to the current realities of language teaching and the needs of today's learners.

Jack C. Richards
University of Sydney

Preface

Effective curriculum practices can result in a curriculum that is purposeful, relevant, meaningful, and tailored to the intended student population. Such practices look at the teaching and learning experience comprehensively to ensure its readiness, coherence, effectiveness, and consistency in optimizing student learning. Curriculum planning, development, implementation, and evaluation are closely tied together. They complement and inform one another, leading to a quality curriculum. Developing conceptual knowledge and practical understanding of these areas is essential both at the program level and for teachers, whether they are curriculum developers, planners, or users.

This book covers fundamental topics related to curriculum conceptualization and practice to maximize the effectiveness of English as a second/foreign language (ESL/EFL) teaching and learning. It draws largely on knowledge from the field of education, particularly curriculum studies, to complement what we know about second language (L2) teaching and learning from Applied Linguistics, Second Language Acquisition (SLA), and English Language Teaching (ELT). Despite the rich history of curriculum theory and practice in general education, ELT has often remained "isolated from mainstream developments" and has instead been informed primarily "by research in linguistics and applied linguistics" (Finney, 2002, p. 70). Historically, ELT has focused on specific teaching methods (e.g., Grammar-Translation Method, Direct Method, Total Physical Response, Communicative Language Teaching) and syllabus types (e.g., Structural Syllabus, Situational Syllabus, Notional Syllabus), which often neglect the totality of the teaching and learning experience (H. D. Brown, 2002; J. D. Brown, 2012; Finney, 2002; Richards, 1984). This narrow focus on methodology and the overlook of the different interrelated elements that constitute a learning experience have been criticized for lacking rigor and failing to align with advancements in curriculum development (Richards, 1984; Rodgers, 1989). These concerns have resulted in works that take a comprehensive approach to language curricula, extending beyond the lens of a single teaching method or approach (e.g., Brown, 1995; Graves, 2000; Macalister & Nation, 2020; Nation & Macalister, 2010; Richards, 2001, 2017). A comprehensive approach considers learners' needs and the teaching context to identify meaningful curriculum objectives, learning experiences, and evaluation means.

This book offers conceptual and practical knowledge grounded in curriculum studies and ELT research to guide the planning, execution, and revision of the ESL/EFL curriculum to ensure its interconnectedness and overall effectiveness. It is important to note that this book is not about what to teach or how to teach. As Nicholls and Nicholls (1972/2018) emphasized, "decisions such as these are best made by the teachers in the schools on the basis of a complete set of evidence which only they are in a position to collect" (p. 13). Instead, this book offers a framework to support a systematic and informed navigation of the phases of the curriculum cycle, from inception to evaluation. The framework is generic in nature so that it can be adapted by programs and teachers as found suitable to their unique educational contexts and circumstances.

Fundamentals of Curriculum Planning, Development, Implementation, and Evaluation in English Language Teaching is intended for ELT teachers, teachers-in-training, and language programs. Conceptualized initially for a Teaching English to Speakers of Other Languages (TESOL) master's course on curriculum planning and development, this book addresses a gap identified in many TESOL programs, which often lack dedicated courses on this essential topic. Hansen (1995) observed that teacher education often focuses on how to teach to enable teacher candidates to transmit knowledge and skills in a specific subject area effectively. However, as they become practitioners, the realization hits that "successful practice in the classroom is inextricably linked to curriculum development—the everyday decisions about both what to teach and how to teach" (Hansen, 2015, para. 1). I firmly believe that equipping teachers-in-training in TESOL/TEFL with an understanding of curriculum is as important as knowledge of language pedagogies and SLA. Since curriculum is central to teaching, as Print (1993) stressed, teachers "need to be knowledgeable about curriculum and understand the processes by which curricula may be developed" (p. 1). Understanding curriculum conceptualization, planning, development, and evaluation can lead to informed and rational practices that take careful consideration of the totality of the teaching and learning situation.

This book is also intended for programs or schools offering ESL/EFL instruction. At the program level, it provides guidance for developing new curricula as well as evaluating and revising existing ones. The book includes processes, measures, and tools to help establish a rigorous curriculum and strengthen the connection between instruction and curriculum at both the classroom (micro) and program (meso) levels. The content of this book is based on my experience as an instructor and administrator with hands-on experience in curriculum planning, development, review, and revision. At my previous institution, a U.S. university-based intensive English language program, I led the development of new curricula, revitalized existing ones, and established procedures to enhance curriculum effectiveness and meet accreditation standards. Similar programs can benefit from the guidelines and tools provided in this book, particularly ESL/EFL institutions seeking quality assurance or undergoing accreditation.

In the EFL context, drawing from my personal experience as a student and a teacher in such environments, I found that curriculum and instruction were predominately textbook-based. Language institutes often adopt specific EFL textbook series without a clearly established curriculum outlining skills and knowledge to be taught at a given level. In such cases, the textbook practically becomes the curriculum. In fact, recent ELT research also highlights that textbooks continue to be the primary source shaping EFL teaching and learning (e.g., Cabrera, 2014; Ibrahim, 2022; Zhang, 2020). While many well-designed EFL textbooks provide essential knowledge, skills, and activities, it is crucial to recognize that a textbook is not the curriculum and should not solely drive instruction. Commercial textbooks often fail to account for the local sociocultural context, which can lead to ineffective learning or resistance from teachers and students (Hilliard, 2014; Xiong, 2012). A textbook, like technology, is a tool to support teaching and learning and should not be equated with curriculum. Similarly, adopting curricula that were not specifically designed for the context of their implementation—without scrutiny or consideration of their suitability—can also pose challenges to teaching and learning (Nicholls & Nicholls, 1972/2018). Chapter 3 discusses how these factors affect teaching and learning.

In summary, this book provides knowledge and resources to systematize and optimize the L2 teaching and learning experience. The book is divided into two parts. Part I focuses on building conceptual and theoretical knowledge of curriculum topics, including educational philosophies, learning theories, curriculum contexts, and curriculum models. Part II offers practical guidance on curriculum conceptualization, planning, development, implementation, and evaluation. The chapters follow a consistent organizational pattern: Each draws on literature from the field of education and transitions to discuss its relevance in the ELT field. Chapters start with pre-reading questions to stimulate thinking and conclude with post-reading questions for review and reflection to encourage connections to the readers' context. By the end of the book, the reader will be able to:

- Define curriculum and related concepts. (Chapter 1)
- Differentiate between educational philosophies, learning theories, and L2 teaching approaches. (Chapter 2)
- Identify factors at different contextual levels that influence curriculum development and implementation, and differentiate between the purposes of the language curricula. (Chapter 3)
- Distinguish between models of curriculum development in education and ELT curriculum development approaches. (Chapter 4)
- Identify the different phases of curriculum development and organize curriculum practices. (Chapter 5)
- Articulate the underlying philosophical and theoretical basis for decision-making. (Chapter 6)
- Determine ways to gather data about the targeted student population and the curriculum context in preparation for curriculum development activities. (Chapter 7)
- Identify the components and procedures involved in curriculum development. (Chapter 8)
- Facilitate effective curriculum implementation. (Chapter 9)
- Determine procedures and materials for curriculum evaluation, review, and revision. (Chapter 10)

Part I

Curriculum Conception

Chapter 1

Understanding Curriculum

Before you read, reflect on the following questions:

1. What is your definition of curriculum?
2. How do you think our views of the curriculum are shaped?
3. Are curricula and syllabi the same or different? Why?
4. What are some potential challenges teachers might face when implementing a curriculum prescribed by administrators or policymakers?

This chapter surveys how the term *curriculum* is defined and clarifies related concepts. It also explores different typologies of curriculum and approaches to curriculum decision-making.

Defining Curriculum

What Is Curriculum?

- "Curriculum is any *document* that exists in a school or school system that defines the work of teachers, at least to the extent of identifying the content to be taught [. . .] and the methods to be used" (English, 2000, p. 2).
- Curriculum is a "totality of *courses* that constitute a course of study offered by an institution or followed by a student" (Wood & Davis, 1978, p.16).
- Curriculum is "a *plan* for a sustained process of teaching and learning, actual teaching and learning is not curriculum, for curriculum refers to plans for instructional acts, not the acts of instruction themselves" (Pratt, 1994, p. 5).

- "Curriculum is a systematic and intended packaging of *competencies* (i.e. knowledge, skills and attitudes that are underpinned by values) that learners should acquire through organised learning experiences both in formal and non-formal settings" (UNESCO's International Bureau of Education, 2012, p. 30).
- Curriculum is "all the *experiences* that a learner has under the guidance of the school" (Kearney & Cook, 1961, p. 358).
- Curriculum is "an interrelated set of *plans* and *experiences* which a student completes under the guidance of the school" (Marsh, 1997, p. 5).
- "The curriculum is *all* of the *experiences* that individual learners have in a program of education whose purpose is to achieve broad goals and related specific objectives, which is *planned* in terms of a *framework* of theory and research or past and present professional practice" (Hass, 1987, p. 5).
- "A curriculum is an attempt to communicate the essential principles and features of *an educational proposal* in such a form that it is open to critical scrutiny and capable of effective translation into practice" (Stenhouse, 1975, p. 4).

In the field of education, and more specifically curriculum studies, there seems to be no shared understanding of what curriculum is. The snapshot of definitions listed above demonstrates a range of perspectives on what curriculum entails, from narrow (e.g., as a document) to broad (e.g., as experiences). Perceiving curriculum merely as courses or subjects can be problematic because this view presents it as a product or package ready to be consumed, disregarding the process. It fails to address how and why a curriculum exists, how it is executed, and how effective it is. Endeley and Zama (2021) also argued that viewing curricula solely as courses or subjects is narrow, as such definitions do not account for "all other facets of the teaching-learning process that take place within and outside the classroom" (p. 1). Similarly, defining curriculum exclusively as a plan or document implies abstraction and overlooks the actual teaching and learning experiences. Definitions of curriculum as experiences also vary; some emphasize actual learning experiences and deemphasize written plans (Kearney & Cook, 1961), while others stress the interconnectedness between planning and experiences (Hass, 1987).

These varied perspectives highlight the intricate nature of curriculum, with each definition revealing a specific facet or characteristic of what curriculum is. Our views on the term *curriculum* are shaped by various factors, including one's educational context, experiences, as well as beliefs and philosophies about teaching and learning.

So, What Is Curriculum?

Despite the complexity of defining *curriculum*, it is crucial to establish a common understanding of what the term entails within an educational context to ensure clarity of curriculum goals and consistency in learning experiences. The definitions listed at the beginning of this chapter highlight important aspects of curriculum that cannot and should not be ignored. Curriculum is indeed a plan, a document, a framework, courses, competencies, and experiences. These dimensions are inseparable; they complement one another and should be considered in curriculum planning and development. Therefore, in this book, curriculum is viewed as a comprehensive, context-dependent phenomenon composed of interrelated processes grounded in philosophy and theory. It is also informed by a clear understanding of the educational context as well as the needs and beliefs of the different stakeholders.

Viewing curriculum as a cyclical process of conceptualizing, planning, developing, and reviewing ensures a logical and meaningful connection among its objectives, content, learning experiences, and assessments. Like puzzle pieces, each element of the curriculum requires careful consideration to create a complete and coherent picture. In short, curricula comprise a framework that describes the teaching and learning experience, shaped by the overall goal of the educational program, the local context, student needs, and the philosophies of the stakeholders. This framework guides practice and is translated into experiences. Once these experiences are "lived," they inform and guide the refinement of the framework. The relationship between the planned curriculum and the implemented curriculum is reciprocal; the plan informs the process, and the process informs the plan. Periodic review and revision of the curriculum are crucial to maintaining this reciprocal relationship.

Figure 1.1 displays *curriculum* as a comprehensive term encompassing three interrelated components that operate in a cyclical manner, emphasizing the interplay between its constituents. It is important to note that in this book, the term *curriculum* refers to the overall teaching and learning experience and is occasionally used in a

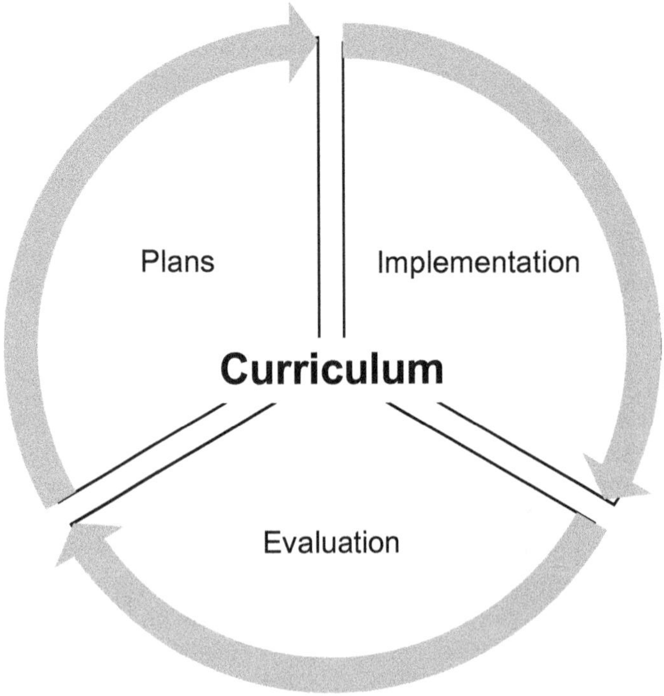

Figure 1.1. Curriculum as a Multifaceted Phenomenon

narrower sense when referring to a specific course. The use of *curriculum* and *a curriculum* is intentional to distinguish between these two meanings.

Clarification of Curriculum-Related Terms

Curriculum Planning, Design, Development, and Course Design

Do curriculum planning, curriculum development, curriculum design, and course design refer to the same activity? In the *Longman Dictionary of Language Teaching and Applied Linguistics*, *curriculum design* is presented as a synonym for *curriculum development.* It is defined as "the study and development of the goals, content, implementation, and evaluation of an educational system" (Richards & Schmidt, 2011, p. 152). The dictionary also lists *language program design* and *curriculum design* as synonyms for the *course design* entry. Based on these definitions, it appears that these terms can be used interchangeably, at least within ELT, to refer to language curriculum development or course design.

In the glossary of terms provided in Murray Print's (1993) *Curriculum Development and Design*, *curriculum development* and *curriculum design* are listed as two separate concepts. *Curriculum design* is defined as "the process of conceptualizing and arranging the elements of curriculum into a coherent pattern" and *curriculum development* as "the process of planning learning opportunities intended to bring about certain desired changes in [students], and the assessment of the extent to which these changes have taken place" (p. xvii). Print (1993) also included a definition for *curriculum planning* as:

> the process whereby curriculum developers conceptualize and organize the features of the curriculum they wish to construct. This involves a broad analysis of the curriculum intent and context (what you wish to achieve), conceptualizing the curriculum's design (what it will look like), organizing the sequencing of developmental tasks (how to construct the curriculum) and arranging for the process of implementation and evaluation. (p. xviii)

At first glance, these definitions may seem similar. However, a closer look reveals that curriculum design and planning lay the groundwork for curriculum development. The first two are concerned with curriculum theorizing or conceptualizing and gathering information to prepare for the curriculum development process.

Since this work is teacher-oriented, the term *curriculum development* is used instead of *curriculum design* or *course design* (except when citing other works). This choice is simply because *curriculum development* sounds less technical and is more teacher-friendly, as developing lesson plans, activities, and materials is second nature to teachers. The terms *conceptualizing* and *planning* are used in the subsequent chapters in the same sense as Print's (1993) definitions to refer to the tasks that precede the actual curriculum development phase.

Curriculum Versus Syllabus

Before discussing the difference between curriculum and syllabus, let's first tackle whether syllabus design and curriculum development in ELT refer to similar or different activities. Nunan (1988a) noted that "there are several conflicting views on just what it is that distinguishes syllabus design from curriculum development. There is also some disagreement about the nature of 'the syllabus'" (p. 5). This was particularly true in earlier ELT works (e.g., Allen, 1977; Brumfit, 1979; Munby, 1978; Wilkins, 1976; Valdman, 1978). Historically, syllabus design focused on specifying and sequencing the content of an ESL course (Mackey, 1967). This led to various types of syllabi aimed at specifying the language focus of ELT curricula, including published ESL/EFL textbooks (Brown, 1995). The content specification and sequencing reflected specific views on L2 teaching and learning. For example, the structural syllabus, one of the earlier types, emphasized grammatical knowledge and was based on methods like audio-lingual and grammar-translation. With the rise of communicative teaching approaches in the 1970s and 1980s, other types of syllabi emerged, such as the situational and functional syllabi, which aimed to promote communication in the target language (Ellis, 1993). Table 1.1 lists sample syllabus types, their curricular focus, and sequencing criteria, which are typically determined by frequency of use, difficulty level, progression from basic to advanced, usefulness to the learner, and/or the likelihood of occurrence.

The traditional approach to syllabus design has been criticized as narrow and prescriptive. Richards (1984) argued that "what is understood by curriculum development in language teaching has often been rather narrowly conceived. The focus has primarily been on language syllabuses rather than on the broader processes of curriculum development" (p. 1). Over time, curriculum development in ELT has shifted from focusing solely on content specification and sequencing to adopting a more comprehensive approach. This approach encompasses processes such as conducting needs analysis, setting curricular goals, formulating objectives and outcomes, and identifying assessment methods (e.g., Brown, 1995; Graves, 2000; Nation & Macalister, 2010; Richards, 1984).

Going back to the question of whether *syllabus* is the same as *curriculum*, there is no straightforward answer. The two terms are sometimes used interchangeably by practitioners and researchers to refer either to the narrower perspective of curriculum (i.e., a plan or a document) or the more comprehensive view (i.e., a process or experience). In this work, a distinction is made between curriculum and syllabus as two separate but interrelated entities. A syllabus is a sub-component of a curriculum, typically presented as a document shared with students to communicate curriculum expectations and course policies. It is derived

Table 1.1 Sample Syllabus Types and Their Content Focus and Sequencing in ELT

Syllabus Type	Curricular Focus	Curricular Sequencing
Structural syllabus	Grammatical forms and structures	Difficulty, frequency, or usefulness (e.g., tenses and sentence types)
Topical syllabus	Topics and themes (often societal)	Usefulness or difficulty (e.g., unemployment, tourism, and pollution)
Situational syllabus	Language use in situations or meaningful contexts	Likelihood or chronology (e.g., in the restaurant or at the doctor's office)
Functional Syllabus	Semantic use/ language functions	Usefulness or frequency (e.g., greeting, interrupting, agreeing/disagreeing, asking for directions)
Notional syllabus (or notional-functional syllabus)	Abstract concepts and functions	Chronology, frequency, or usefulness (e.g., time, size, location, or quantity)
Skills-based syllabus	Language or academic skills	Usefulness, chronology, or frequency (e.g., identifying main ideas vs. supporting details)
Task-based syllabus	Language use through task performance	Usefulness (e.g., making appointments)

from and grounded in the curriculum. In the field of curriculum studies, a syllabus is defined as follows:

> A detailed and operational document for teaching and learning derived from curriculum goals and focused on one subject or one theme. A syllabus indicates goals and objectives, content, and strategies for teaching, learning and evaluation according to subject areas or themes. (Endeley & Zama, 2021, p. 268)

Standard components of a syllabus often include the instructor's information (e.g., office hours and location), course description (e.g., goals, objectives, and outcomes), schedule of topics (i.e., content and sequence), required and recommended materials, assessments (e.g., assignments and exams), grade allocations, and policies (e.g., attendance and academic integrity). The content, length, and structure of a syllabus can vary significantly. For example, syllabi for college courses tend to be lengthy and include detailed descriptions of major assignments and grading criteria. In addition to informing students about course logistics and content, a syllabus sometimes functions as a contract between the course instructor and students, defining responsibilities and expected behaviors (Parkes & Harris, 2002). As Jenks (2016, para. 1) described, the repetitive use of "it's on the syllabus!" by many instructors, particularly in North America, underscores this implicit function of a syllabus.

The Educational Program

In this work, the term ***program*** refers to the educational setting in which the ELT curriculum operates. This could be a stand-alone ESL/EFL language institute or a part of a larger institution such as a school, college, or university. A program's mission, goals, scope, philosophy, and policies typically shape and influence the purpose and structure of the ELT curriculum. A program often consists of a set of courses, each representing a curriculum that contributes to the overall curriculum. In this sense, "the term curriculum [is] used to refer to the curriculum of a particular course as well as the holistic curriculum of a program or an institution" (Elturki, 2022, p. 38). A syllabus, as previously explained, is the specific plan that captures and conveys the curriculum content of a given course along with other course- and program-related information.

As an example, an English for Academic Purposes (EAP) curriculum might be offered by a university-based English language center that is part of a larger educational institution. This English language program would consist of different levels of English language proficiency, with each level offering multiple courses in different language skills. As illustrated in Figure 1.2, the term *curriculum* (in capital letters) is used in a comprehensive, holistic sense to refer to the entire program curriculum and in a more specific manner to refer to individual courses. The comprehensive curriculum is often documented in a written format—such as within the program or faculty handbook, or as a separate manual—containing all the information for the various levels and courses. This document is valuable because it typically covers different aspects of the curriculum, including what the curriculum objectives are

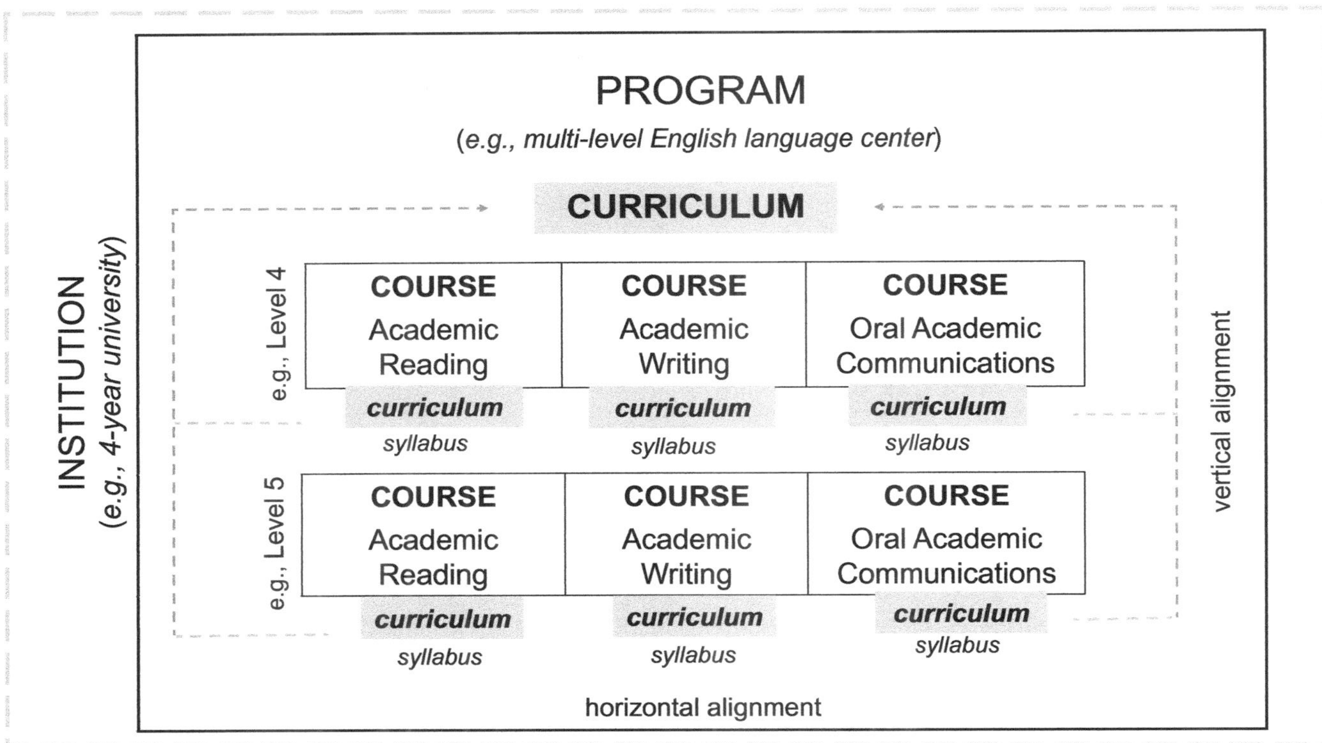

Figure 1.2. An Illustration of the Relationship between Program, Course, Curriculum, and Syllabus

and how they progress within (i.e., horizontal alignment) and across (i.e., vertical alignment) levels. Consequently, this holistic document becomes the source from which the curriculum for each course is extracted and presented in the syllabus.

Curriculum Typology and Decision-Making

Curriculum Typology

Due to the complex and dynamic nature of curricula and the fact that they operate at different levels of context (e.g., program and classroom) and involve various stakeholders (e.g., developers, administrators, teachers, and students), a developed curriculum can manifest in different forms, either intentionally or unintentionally. The fundamental premise is that a curriculum is typically designed with specific intentions (curriculum plan). These intentions might be altered or realized differently during implementation (teaching), and what is actually learned from the implementation may vary (learning). A range of distinct and synonymous terms have been used in curriculum studies to describe the different forms that a curriculum can take. Some examples of these curriculum types are summarized in Table 1.2 (Eisner, 1979; Endeley & Zama, 2021; Flinders et al., 1986; Goodlad, 1979; Null, 2011; Van den Akker, 2007).

Understanding curriculum typology and recognizing that a curriculum can evolve in different directions helps inform effective curriculum development and implementation. Although some of these manifestations are difficult to control, it is crucial to minimize the gap between the intended, implemented, and learned curricula. A shared vision and understanding of curriculum requirements are essential to ensure consistent implementation. Developing a curriculum that considers students' factors (e.g., needs, prior knowledge, attitudes, and personalities) as well as the local context and involves teachers in its development is vital for creating a coherent curriculum that can be meaningfully translated into the classroom.

Top-Down and Bottom-Up Curriculum Processes and the Teacher Role

Curricula come into existence through either top-down or bottom-up processes. In a top-down approach, the curriculum (or aspects of it) is decided by an external entity or the upper administration of an institution. This

Table 1.2 Typologies of Curriculum

Curriculum Type	Brief Description
• Intended curriculum • Planned curriculum • Written curriculum • Formal curriculum • Overt curriculum • Explicit curriculum	Goals and objectives typically articulated in a written format
• Implemented curriculum • Taught curriculum • Actual curriculum • Delivered curriculum • Operational curriculum	The actual teaching of goals and objectives, which may vary due to instructor interpretation
• Attained curriculum • Learned Curriculum • Received curriculum	The learning outcomes; what students actually learned
• Hidden curriculum • Implicit curriculum • Unintended curriculum • Covert curriculum • Implicit curriculum	Learning that is not explicitly specified or planned, which may include norms, attitudes, beliefs, and values
• Null curriculum • Ignored curriculum • Excluded curriculum	Information intentionally or unintentionally excluded from or overlooked in the intended and/or implemented curriculum

process often involves policymakers, administrators, and curriculum specialists, with minimal or no input from teachers. Conversely, a bottom-up approach incorporates teachers' input and takes into account the needs and interests of the intended student population. Such considerations may be overlooked in a top-down approach. Smith (2018) remarked that "teachers often find themselves caught in the middle between the constraints imposed by pre-specified curricular guidelines and the needs and interests of their students" (p. 38). Miller and colleagues (2021) also noted that "current research is demonstrating that top-down decisions often do not take students' language proficiency into account, resulting in unsuccessful implementation of such programmes" (p. 217). Another factor that can lead to unsuccessful implementation is that a curriculum reflects someone's reasoning on what should be learned (Jackson, 1992).

If this does not align with what teachers perceive as students' true needs, the planned curriculum may be compromised.

Therefore, teachers' involvement in curriculum decision-making is considered a crucial factor for ensuring curriculum effectiveness and fidelity (Ellili-Cherif & Hadba, 2017; Glatthorn et al., 2019; Troudi & Alwan, 2010). Curriculum fidelity refers to "the degree to which teachers or stakeholders abide by a curriculum's original design when implementing it" (Bumen et al., 2014, p. 220). Kelly (2004) argued that teachers play a "make or break" role in curriculum implementation and that they "have been known to sabotage attempts at change; certainly it is clear that such attempts can succeed only when the teachers concerned are committed to them and, especially, when they understand, as well as accept, their underlying principles" (p. 9). Establishing clear processes that involve teachers in decision-making or, at the very least, helping them understand the reasons behind a top-down curriculum is vital for curriculum effectiveness and fidelity. It can reduce the gap between the intended, implemented, and learned curricula and ensure a meaningful and cohesive curriculum that can be effectively implemented. It also goes without saying that teacher participation in curriculum activities can foster professional development and collaboration, serving as a valuable "vehicle for continuing education" and enhancing "professionalism in teachers" (Nicholls & Nicholls, 1972/2018, p. 18). This last point is discussed further in Chapter 9.

After you read, consider the following questions:

1. Draft your own definition of curriculum. Then, write a brief commentary explaining why you chose this definition, its underlying basis, and what it emphasizes. Include a visual representation of your thinking process.
2. Locate an ESL/EFL syllabus and examine its components. What information is listed in the syllabus? Does this information offer sufficient details about the curriculum type and its goals?
3. As discussed in this chapter, the same curriculum can manifest in different types (see Table 1.2). Review and research these types further, and then respond to the following:

a. What are some possible ways to maintain an alignment between the planned, taught, and learned curriculum?

b. What constitutes a hidden curriculum? Recall your teaching and/or schooling experiences. Can you identify specific encounters with the hidden curriculum? What are they? How can issues related to the hidden curriculum be addressed?

Chapter 2

Philosophical and Theoretical Foundations of Curriculum

Before you read, reflect on the following questions:

1. What is the relationship among curriculum, philosophy, and theory?
2. From your perspective, what should be the primary aim of education in society? What should teaching look like in the classroom? What roles should teachers and students play?
3. Why is it important to explore different beliefs about teaching and learning and to develop and articulate your own perspective?
4. Reflecting on your own educational experience, can you identify a subject or topic you understood clearly and one you found challenging? In each case, how was the teaching conducted, and what was your role as a learner?
5. In your opinion, what is the most effective way to learn a second language?

This chapter aims to build a general understanding of philosophical and theoretical foundations that ground educational practices and shape curricula. It will first preview different philosophical orientations to teaching and learning and then highlight major learning theories and their impact on curriculum and instruction. The chapter will conclude with a historical and conceptual overview of major paradigms in L2 teaching and learning, highlighting how shifting theoretical, pedagogical, and sociocultural perspectives have shaped curriculum and instructional practices over time.

Philosophy, Theory, and Curriculum

One's personal philosophy shapes their way of thinking, guides their practices, and impacts their decision-making. While our philosophies influence how we define issues, our knowledge of theories helps us rationalize how to approach those issues. As Himes and Schulenberg (2013) explained, "philosophy and theory are perpetually linked; philosophy influences how one sees the world, theory shapes how one intentionally interacts with that world" (para. 7). Both philosophy and theory play a crucial role in all aspects of teaching and learning, whether consciously or subconsciously. They provide the basis for rationalizing how the curriculum is devised, the learning activities we choose for our students, and the methods we use to assess their learning. In this subsection, we will explore several educational philosophies, including perennialism, essentialism, progressivism, social reconstructionism and critical pedagogy, indigenism, and posthumanism. We will then survey different theoretical trends and their impact on curriculum and instruction.

Educational Philosophies

An educational philosophy represents the beliefs and assumptions of an individual, group, community, or society regarding the fundamentals of education, such as what knowledge is worth teaching and how this knowledge can be transmitted through curricula and pedagogical practices. Philosophy provides the basis of curriculum development, serves as the starting point for the process, and aids in rationalizing decision-making (Ogwora et al., 2013; Ornstein & Hunkins, 2018). Philosophy drives different aspects of teaching and learning. Teacher's choices in the classroom, for example, are influenced by their personal beliefs and values, including when making smaller decisions such as how to best group students. Curriculum development is a collective effort that necessitates coming to an agreement on what the purpose of the curriculum is and how best to achieve it.

Besides articulating one's own philosophy, it is equally important to develop some understanding of other philosophical perspectives on teaching and learning. Ornstein and Hunkins (2018) maintained that "mature people are more capable of examining their philosophy and appreciate other points of view, especially when facts or trends challenge their original beliefs and values" (p. 47). The subsequent discussion explores some philosophical orientations that shape the aims of education. It is important to note that while there are distinct philosophical paradigms within the field of philosophy of education—a branch of practical philosophy—elements from these established philosophies may be blended to form an eclectic philosophy of education. As you read, consider how these schools of thought translate into the ESL/EFL context.

Perennialism

Perennialism is a traditional educational philosophy that emphasizes the ideas and works of earlier thinkers and writers (Ornstein & Hunkins, 2018). These are seen as ideals that are eternal and universally relevant, thus worthy of study in any era. Consequently, any educational system, regardless of time or place, should disseminate those universal truths to nurture rational thinking, problem-solving, and intellectualism. The curriculum is subject-centric focusing on teaching subjects such as mathematics, literature, and rhetoric through the study of seminal works by prominent philosophers and thinkers. Students are expected to study established knowledge under the guidance of the teacher, who serves as an intellectual authority. The curriculum prioritizes enduring ideas over individual student preferences, emphasizing intellectual discipline and critical reasoning. Notable proponents of perennialism include the educational philosophers Robert Hutchins and Mortimer Adler. Hutchins and Adler established curricula for adult education programs and college courses in the United States based on influential Western books and were also the editors of *Great Books of the Western World* (Mayer & Hicks, 1993; "The Great Ideas," n.d.).

Essentialism

Essentialism is another traditional educational philosophy that emphasizes moral and intellectual values, similar to perennialism. However, while perennialism believes that knowledge construction stems from studying classical texts, essentialism prioritizes the teaching of "essential" knowledge and skills in areas such as math, reading, writing, and science. Essentialism advocates for a systematic and disciplined approach to teaching, with the goal of preparing students to become effective participants in society. For essentialists, "a curriculum that takes students' interests or social issues into account is regarded as wasteful, as are teaching methods that rely on psychological theories" (Ornstein & Hunkins,

2018, p. 54). The primary aim of education in essentialism is the transmission of core academic knowledge to students. Social or psychological considerations are often de-emphasized, as they are believed to weaken academic rigor. The teacher assumes an authoritative role and is expected to possess in-depth knowledge of the core curriculum. Students are required to work diligently and demonstrate discipline. Homework and periodic assessments are integral to maintaining accountability and progress. According to Ornstein and Levine (1993), competency exams mandated by many U.S. states reflect "contemporary essentialist thinking" (p. 467). Curriculum revisions occur only when there is a clear need, typically determined by policymakers or educational authorities. Prominent proponents of essentialism include William Bagley, Theodore Sizer, and E. D. Hirsch Jr.

Progressivism

Progressivism is a contemporary and liberal educational philosophy that values student-centered education, experiential learning, collaborative learning, and real-world problem-solving. Unlike perennialism and essentialism, progressivists advocate for a democratic approach to education in which the teacher acts as a facilitator and students participate actively in the learning process (Dewey, 1938). Within this paradigm, the focus of education shifts away from the teacher, the subject matter, textbooks, and rote memorization, centering instead on the student as a whole. The curriculum development process takes into account students' interests and incorporates opportunities for real-world applications of curriculum objectives. Through engaging in practical projects, students identify significant problems and work collaboratively to solve them using the scientific method, which involves experimentation and systematic observations to test hypotheses or answer questions. The aim of education in progressivism is to teach students "how to think, not what to think" (Ornstein & Hunkins, 2018, p. 58). John Dewey (1938), a leading figure in progressivism, argued that curriculum content, regardless of what the subject is, should incorporate topics, materials, and activities that connect with students' everyday experiences.

Social Reconstructionism and Critical Pedagogy

Social reconstructionism is a modern educational philosophy that views education as a means to address social problems and reconstruct a better society. Both progressivism and reconstructionism are philosophies centered on students. However, progressivism emphasizes individual growth, while reconstructionism aims to develop problem-solvers who can positively impact the world. Earlier reconstructionists such as George Counts (1932) and Theodore Brameld (1965) believed in the power of education to bring about a new social order and transform society. According to reconstructionist philosophers, curriculum and instruction should "educate 'the masses of humanity' to critically analyze themselves in relation to their society, understand the ills of their society, develop a vision of a better world based on a conception of social justice, and actualize that vision" (Schiro, 2012, p. 133).

Critical pedagogy is a movement that aligns with social reconstructionism in its view of education as a tool for empowerment and for challenging the status quo to address social inequities. Paulo Freire, a prominent Brazilian philosopher and educator in critical pedagogy, argued that education can be emancipating to oppressed, marginalized, and less privileged communities. This emancipation occurs when curriculum and instruction focus on instilling critical consciousness, generating social awareness, and promoting ongoing dialogues between teachers and students (Freire, 1970). Freire explored these ideas in his seminal book, *Pedagogy of the Oppressed*, originally published in Portuguese in 1968 and later translated into various languages.

Both social reconstructionist and critical pedagogical approaches to curriculum and instruction employ inquiry, critical and reflective analyses, group discussions, and community-based projects. Course topics often tackle social, economic, political, environmental, and/or global issues such as racism, injustice, inequality, oppression, illiteracy, hunger, pollution, violence, colonialism, and war. In this framework, the teacher functions as "an agent of change" and "a project director and research leader," assisting students in becoming conscious of challenges facing humans (Ornstein & Hunkins, 2018, p. 89). Teachers are also expected to be "transformative intellectual[s]," analyzing their "own social and cultural history, question[ing] the contents of education, and reveal[ing] its 'hidden tensions,' i.e., 'the hidden curriculum' (Giroux 1997/2000)" (Bertrand, 2003, p. 242). Influenced by social reconstructionism and critical pedagogy, various educational paradigms with a social justice emphasis have emerged, including bell hooks' (intentionally uncapitalized) ***engaged pedagogy*** (hooks, 1994). Engaged pedagogy views teaching and learning as a participatory praxis within an inclusive learning community (i.e., the classroom), emphasizing that teachers' well-being and self-actualization are prerequisites for empowering their students.

Indigenism

> We find it pedagogically tragic that various indigenous knowledges of how action affects reality in particular locales have been dismissed from academic curricula. Such ways of knowing and acting could contribute so much to the educational experiences of all students; but because of the rules of evidence and the dominant epistemologies of Western knowledge production, such understandings are deemed irrelevant by the academic gatekeepers. (Semali & Kincheloe, 1999, p. 15)

In the field of philosophy of education, the educational philosophies highlighted above represent dominant philosophical orientations concerning the nature and aims of education. Many aspects of these philosophies, including earlier ones, are present in today's educational systems and instructional practices in different parts of the world (Alemdar & Aytaç, 2002; Corcoran, 2014; Danner & Ofuani, 2022; Kooli, 2019). The spread of these Western philosophies of education could be attributed to globalization, colonialism, and imperialism. As argued in the quote by Semali and Kincheloe (1999) above, it is unfortunate that Indigenous philosophical perspectives on the nature of teaching and learning are often overlooked. These perspectives reflect the values and beliefs of native populations in various countries such as the United States, Canada, Australia, and New Zealand. They also encompass the experiences of nations historically affected by colonization, such as South Africa, India, Algeria, the Philippines, and Portugal, as well as the diverse linguistic and cultural communities that represent minorities within different societies. Of course, this broad categorization results in diverse forms of indigeneity, each with unique circumstances, values, and beliefs that shape their philosophical understandings of education in distinct ways. As such, this makes it beyond the scope of this book to dive into and capture these distinct schools of thought in depth. However, what follows aims to highlight some philosophical perspectives on teaching and learning among Indigenous communities as well as post-colonial educational thoughts.

While recognizing the plurality and diversity in the epistemologies of different Indigenous communities on teaching and learning, Antoine and colleagues (2018) pinpointed three commonalities among the Indigenous schools of thought. These include (1) ***relationality***, which emphasizes interconnectedness among human relations and with the environment; (2) ***holism***, which views human development as a multidimensional endeavor encompassing spiritual, cognitive, emotional, physical, and ancestral aspects; (3) ***spirituality*** and ***secularity***, which are interwoven and thus inseparable from one another. Grounded in these principles, relevant and meaningful learning for Indigenous students should be personal, holistic, experiential, intergenerational, and place-based (Antoine et al., 2018). To briefly illustrate, curriculum and instruction should build relationships among students, teachers, family, and community members. They should also incorporate place-based learning opportunities to enable students to learn about and in relation to their local communities. Additionally, curriculum and instruction should create opportunities for self-reflection, integrate the knowledge and wisdom of elders, and encourage students to make connections between their learning and spiritual thoughts and feelings. In fact, several scholars have called for the naturalization and integration of Indigenous thinking in education as a means of empowerment for marginalized communities and a valuable intellectual resource for all students and society (Battiste, 2009; Jacob et al., 2018; Kanu, 2011; Semali & Kincheloe, 1999).

In the same vein, ample voices in nations that have suffered from colonialism, such as South Africa and other African countries, have been calling for the reconceptualization of their local philosophy of education. This reconceptualization seeks to decolonize the curriculum by developing a conscious awareness of self, the local language, and the cultural heritage and placing these fundamentals at the center and not the side of the curriculum (Mbembe, 2015; Mheta et al., 2018; Sebbowa & Majani, 2021; Thiong'o, 1986; Wawrzynski & Garton, 2023). In the words of the Kenyan writer and post-colonial scholar Thiong'o (1986), "education is a means of knowledge about ourselves. Therefore, after we have examined ourselves, we radiate outwards and discover peoples and worlds around us" (p. 94). In brief, a post-colonial perspective on education seeks to restore and center Indigenous forms of knowledge production.

Posthumanism

Posthumanism is a relatively new philosophical orientation that challenges human-centered approaches to education and knowledge (Le Grange & Du Preeze, 2023; Weaver, 2020; Yan et al., 2020). As a philosophy of education, posthumanism interrogates the foundational values, assumptions, and purposes of education in the context of rapidly evolving technological and ecological conditions. It signifies a philosophical shift away from anthropocentrism, which places human beings at the center of the world, and toward a more inclusive, non-anthropocentric view by recognizing the agency of non-human entities—such as animals, machines, and the environment—alongside humans. This perspective critiques the core assumptions of humanism, a tradition that has long dominated Western educational thought by privileging human autonomy, rationality, and individuality (Weaver, 2020). Whereas humanism emphasizes the individual learner's personal growth and self-actualization (discussed in the subsequent section as a learning theory), posthumanism urges educators to consider the broader network of human and non-human forces that shape learning environments. Le Grange and Du Preeze (2023) illustrate this shift by emphasizing that the entanglement of human lives with advanced technologies and the urgency of environmental crises present unprecedented challenges to how we learn and what we value in education:

> We live in unparalleled times. Human lives have become entangled with advanced technologies to an extent that it is difficult to know what human now is, what it means to be human. These technologies are growing at a rapid rate. Concurrently, environmental problems have reached unprecedented levels, to the extent that planet Earth is on the threshold of ecological catastrophe. (p. 61)

The central concept of posthumanism is that learning is not solely a human endeavor. Instead of viewing students as isolated individuals, this perspective recognizes them as interconnected beings who interact with a network of both human and non-human agents, such as technology, animals, and the environment (Le Grange & Du Preeze, 2023). Posthumanist educational practices may involve incorporating technology in ways that extend beyond traditional tools and resources. For instance, the curriculum might examine how humans interact with artificial intelligence (AI) or how environmental issues, such as climate change, are perceived from non-human perspectives. These practices require a more open-ended and flexible curriculum that recognizes the multiplicity of learning and the intricate ways in which knowledge is created and shared. Furthermore, posthumanism critiques traditional ethical frameworks that often prioritize human interests over those of other species or ecological systems. In posthumanist education, there may be a greater emphasis on environmental sustainability, animal rights, and the ethical implications of emerging technologies. This shift encourages students to move beyond human-centered values and to consider the well-being of the planet and all its inhabitants, human and non-human.

While still an emerging area in educational philosophy, posthumanism provides a new perspective that addresses the challenges posed by technological advancement, environmental crises, and the evolving role of humans in a more-than-human world. As an educational philosophy, it encourages us to rethink what it means to learn, to be human, and to educate in an increasingly interconnected and interdependent environment. It compels educators to critically consider how curricula can evolve to reflect these realities and how to incorporate non-human perspectives and technologies to create more inclusive, ecologically responsible, and ethically aware learning spaces.

To wrap up this subsection, the philosophical thoughts of individuals, communities, or nations on curriculum and instruction are shaped by diverse factors. These include personal, historical, political, sociocultural, ethical, and/or spiritual/religious influences (e.g., the influence of Confucian ideals on Chinese education), which result in a wide range of philosophical thoughts that extend beyond what is discussed in this chapter. Many aspects of the educational philosophies highlighted earlier can be observed in the context of language teaching and learning. For example, there is an increased interest in curricula and classroom practices that address learner needs and promote student-centered education, active learning, collaborative learning, self-reflection, place-based and community-based projects, and social justice issues (in line with aspects of progressivism, reconstructionism, and critical pedagogy). Nonetheless, there are also ESL/EFL classrooms that remain teacher-centered and textbook-driven, with an emphasis on memorization and drilling of language items (reflecting elements of perennialism and essentialism). These ELT approaches will be explored later in this chapter.

Theories of Learning

An array of theories has emerged over the years to explain human learning. Early contributions, particularly from educational and cognitive psychology, have significantly influenced teaching and learning (e.g., Piaget, 1952; Piaget & Inhelder, 1969; Vygotsky, 1962, 1978). Because human learning is a complex and multifaceted phenomenon that cannot be confined solely to psychology and cognition, valuable insights into intellectual development also come from fields such as education, sociology, and anthropology (e.g., Freire, 1970; Illeris, 2016; Jarvis, 2006; Lave & Wenger, 1991). This subsection captures some theoretical trends from behavioristic, cognitive, social, and humanistic standpoints. These theoretical perspectives provide various insights into how knowledge is acquired, what types of knowledge and skills are emphasized, which instructional methods are considered effective, and the roles of teachers and students.

Behavioristic Theoretical Perspectives

Behaviorism is a traditional theory from psychology that views learning as an observable behavior that can be shaped by the environment. This is based on the premise that human behaviors are primarily learned rather than inherited and can, therefore, be controlled (Skinner, 1965; Watson, 1924). Regulating the environment is considered crucial for conditioning behaviors and achieving the desired outcomes. Key constructs within this theory include stimulus (i.e., the interaction or input that evokes the learner's behavior), response (i.e., the output or learner's response to the stimulus), and reinforcement (i.e., a follow-up interaction or input to reinforce or redirect the behavior). Other aspects of behaviorism include rewards and punishments.

Early experimentations by behaviorists such as Thorndike (1911) involved animals to investigate the association between stimuli and responses. Thorndike's behaviorist learning theory, known as connectionism, views learning as a complex system of "habit formation," with "knowledge result[ing] from the accumulation of these stimulus-response associations within this complex structure" (Ornstein & Hunkins, 2018,

p. 113). Several theories under the behaviorist tenet have been developed and refined over the years by psychologists such as Watson (1913), Tolman (1925), Pavlov (1927), and Skinner (1938). These theories share the essential principle of conditioning human behavior but emphasize or expand on different aspects of behaviorism, such as Skinner's research (1938), which further distinguished between different types of reinforcements and punishments.

Behaviorism has had a direct impact on the classroom. Although behaviorists focus more on the classroom environment and instructional methods than on the curriculum itself, a behaviorist-based curriculum is typically prescriptive, specifying what students need to learn and in what order (Ornstein & Hunkins, 2018; Perez, 2022). The teacher's role involves planning step-by-step tasks following the stimulus-response-reinforcement formula to transmit knowledge and achieve mastery of the objectives (Cunningham et al., 2007; Perez, 2022). The teacher sets instructional objectives, prepares appropriate stimuli, such as lectures and drills, and prompts students to respond to these stimuli. If the learner's performance yields the desirable response, the teacher reinforces the information and rewards the student (through grades or verbal encouragement). This signals an observed change in behavior and the achievement of lesson objectives. If the learner fails to respond appropriately, the teacher attempts to reinforce the stimulus by redirecting or eliciting further response and may resort to punishment. Failure to produce the desirable response indicates that learning has not taken place, which necessitates repeating the cycle. Major features of a behaviorist classroom include teacher-centered instruction, lectures, memorization, imitation, modeling, repetition, monitoring, corrective feedback, testing, and the use of rewards and punishments (Endeley & Zama, 2021; Ornstein & Hunkins, 2018).

While various aspects of behaviorism are still prevalent in modern education, this theory has been criticized for its exclusive focus on observable behaviors and neglect of mental processes (Brau et al., 2022). Critics argue that concentrating solely on observable behaviors oversimplifies the complexity of learning, which involves numerous internal variables such as cognition, motivation, and emotion. Another issue with behaviorism is the generalization of findings from animal research to human learning. Instructional methods that focus purely on memorizing and recalling information are also criticized for depriving learners of opportunities to develop critical thinking and problem-solving skills.

Additionally, students have limited agency in the learning process due to the teacher's control over behavior through the stimulus-response-reinforcement method.

Cognitive-Constructivist Theoretical Perspectives

Cognitivist learning theories view knowledge construction as an internal mental process rather than simply an observable behavior. These theories seek to understand mental capabilities and cognitive growth. The shift to cognition was motivated by the limitations of behaviorism, which reduced human knowledge acquisition to observable behaviors. The cognitivist movement encompasses a wide spectrum of theoretical and empirical efforts to understand the human mind and intellectual growth. These efforts evolved and shifted over time from basic and narrow understandings of mental mechanisms to more complex interpretations of cognitive development (Grider, 1993). Knowledge gained from such efforts transformed teaching and learning from a mechanical to an active process. It informs how to plan and sequence curricula, equip learners with strategies for processing and retaining information more effectively, and create a classroom environment that nurtures meaningful knowledge construction.

One of the pioneers in theorizing how humans develop knowledge was the Swiss psychologist Jean Piaget, who put forward a theory of cognitive development. Piaget (1952) suggested that knowledge construction is a biological process that goes along a gradual path and is influenced by the environment. Following children from birth to maturation, Piaget identified four age-specific developmental stages through which intelligence evolves (Piaget, 1952; Piaget & Inhelder, 1969):

1. Sensorimotor stage (birth–2 years old): Developing an understanding of senses, movements, and objects (e.g., sucking, touching, and listening)
2. Preoperational stage (2–7 years old): Utilizing gestures, symbols, and words (e.g., engaging in pretend play, drawing, and using basic language)
3. Concrete operational stage (7–11 years old): Displaying rational thinking about concrete ideas (e.g., performing numerical operations)

4. Formal operational stage (12 years old and up): Employing logical reasoning to abstract concepts (e.g., tackling probability questions or political topics)

Piaget (1952) proposed that children actively construct knowledge about the world through assimilation (i.e., integrating new information into existing mental structures or *schema*) and accommodation (i.e., expanding or adapting existing schema when encountering new knowledge). As a child grows older and interacts more with their environment, knowledge continues to be organized while their mental processes evolve and become more complex. Piaget (1952) also noted that while cognitive development follows a sequential order, a child's environment plays an important role in accelerating or slowing down the chronology of this development.

Another influential figure is Russian psychologist Lev Vygotsky (1962, 1978), who theorized knowledge construction from both cognitive and sociocultural perspectives. Vygotsky and Piaget share similar deductions about cognition and the environment. However, Piaget emphasized stages of cognitive growth, whereas Vygotsky focused on the social and linguistic influences on intellectual development. In his commentary on Piaget's ideas, Vygotsky (1962) wrote:

> Thought [cognitive] development is determined by language, i.e., by the linguistic tools of thought and by the sociocultural experience of the child. Essentially, the development of inner speech depends on outside factors; the development of logic in the child, as Piaget's studies have shown, is a direct function of [her/his] socialized speech. The child's intellectual growth is contingent on [his/her] mastering the social means of thought, that is, language. (p. 51)

Vygotsky (1962, 1978) argued that rich social interactions and experiences can significantly influence a child's cognitive abilities, allowing them to acquire certain skills earlier than Piaget suggested, given proper guidance and support. This idea brought to us the well-known concept of the zone of proximal development (ZPD), defined by Vygotsky (1978) as "the distance between the actual developmental level as determined by independent problem solving and the level of potential development as determined through problem-solving under adult guidance or in collaboration with more capable peers" (p. 86). Simply put, ZPD represents the gap between what a learner already knows and can do independently and what they do not yet know or are unable to do. This gap in knowledge or skills can be bridged through appropriate support and collaboration.

American psychologist Jerome Bruner also made significant contributions to cognitive learning theories with profound implications for curriculum and instruction. Bruner (1960) extended Piaget's stages by introducing three modes of representation: enactive (action-based), iconic (image-based), and symbolic (language-based). Unlike Piaget, Bruner argued that cognitive stages are not necessarily age-linked or a "clock-work sequence of events" (p. 39). He believed that a child could "forge ahead in [his/her] development" (p. 39) through challenging learning opportunities and proper support, especially in the school environment. In a later publication (Wood et al., 1976), Bruner and his colleagues described instructional support as *scaffolding*; a process that helps learners navigate tasks that demand cognitive abilities beyond their current level. This concept aligns with Vygotsky's ZPD (1978). Bruner (1966) also advocated for a *spiral curriculum design*, where curriculum content revisits important concepts repeatedly and builds on existing knowledge, allowing for discovery learning and continuous mental acquisition of knowledge. Objectives in a spiral curriculum are organized on a concrete-abstract continuum and reinforced throughout the course of study with increased knowledge complexity over time.

Collectively, these theorists laid the groundwork for the emergence of constructivist theories of learning, which emphasize active, social, and individualized knowledge construction (Ertmer & Newby, 2013; Fosnot & Perry, 2005; Yilmaz, 2011). While cognitive constructivism sees knowledge construction as an internal mental process where new information is continually reconstructed and integrated into an existing schema, social constructivism emphasizes the central role of social interactions and experiences in facilitating cognitive growth. These socio-cognitive perspectives on how humans come to know marked a paradigm shift in education, transforming learning from a passive reception of information to an active, socially mediated process. Fosnot (1996) noted that "rather than behaviors or skills as the goal of instruction, concept development and deep understanding are the foci" (p.10). Teachers play an instrumental role not only as the deliverers but also as the developers of curricula. Brooks (1987) emphasized this role by stating:

> The success of constructivist approaches to curriculum development and delivery is contingent on the thoughtful mediation of the teacher.

> Although written curriculums are valued as general guides denoting what students should learn, the cognitive abilities of students often force teachers to shift direction. This requires teachers to think on their feet and reflect on their practice [. . .]. If students are not constructing knowledge as anticipated by the teacher, the teacher must quickly analyze the reasons and alter the curriculum or develop a new curriculum. (p. 66)

A constructivist curriculum typically targets higher-order thinking skills, such as analyzing and evaluating information critically, rather than just understanding and recalling information (Jonassen, 1991). A constructivist approach to instruction gives agency to the learner in the pursuit of knowledge and considers individual differences and multiple perspectives. Teachers nurture cognitive development by engaging students in dialogues about their learning, promoting metacognition (i.e., monitoring and regulating one's thinking), implementing real-world tasks, and fostering social interactions. Teachers also collect data on individual students through observations. The curriculum and instructional methods involve schema building, problem-solving, inquiry-based tasks, reflective learning, and collaborative group work (Jonassen, 1991, 1994; Murphy, 1997).

Another theory that has impacted education is Gardner's (1983, 1993) theory of multiple intelligences. Instead of viewing cognitive development as universal, Gardner proposed that humans possess different types of intelligence that may operate independently of one another and vary in degrees. These intelligences include linguistic, mathematical, spatial, musical, kinesthetic, and personal. Gardner (1987) criticized Piaget's universal view of the intellect, arguing that "Piaget thought he was studying all intelligence, but I believe he was basically studying logical mathematical intelligence, one kind of intelligence" (p. 28). Like cognitivist theories of learning that account for individual differences and development, Gardner's theory advances this by identifying multiple ways humans process information. Its educational implications include incorporating varied teaching methods and strategies, using different modalities to present curricular content, and differentiating instruction and assessment to accommodate diverse learning styles.

The knowledge gained from these theories has positively influenced teaching and learning, but it has also introduced some challenges. One concern is that developing and implementing a curriculum that addresses individual differences, provides strategic scaffolding, integrates authentic tasks, and fosters meaningful collaboration can be time-consuming and may not always result in efficient or targeted learning outcomes (Wilson, 2012). Since learning within this paradigm is socially situated, there are concerns about the effectiveness of peer work and collaborative learning. Factors such as insufficient prior knowledge, poor communication skills, or dominating personalities in group settings might hinder the learning process (Moskal et al., 2016). Despite these challenges, which can be mitigated through thoughtful planning and targeted professional development, the cognitive-constructivist movement has offered valuable insights into nurturing intellectual growth.

Social Theoretical Perspectives

A spectrum of distinct social learning theories has emerged over the years, drawing from diverse fields such as psychology, education, sociology, and anthropology. Early social learning theories, rooted in psychology, extended previous theoretical perspectives by emphasizing the interplay of behaviors, cognition, and the social environment in acquiring new knowledge and skills. Bandura's (1977) social learning theory, for example, presents learning as a social construct resulting from both direct and indirect observations of behaviors and interactions within one's environment (e.g., people, media, and literature). This theory recognizes the role of personal and cognitive factors such as attention, motivation, and attitudes and emphasizes the crucial role of self-regulation in managing and directing one's learning. Although Bandura's social learning theory emphasized behavior and imitation, it rejected the behaviorist learning theories' portrayal of learning as a passive mechanical procedure and their lack of attention to mental processes. Instead, learning is presented as a dynamic process in which learners play an active role and can regulate their learning through self-efficacy (Bandura, 1997). As opposed to cognitivist theorists who underscored the importance of social interactions in supporting cognitive growth, Bandura (1977) highlighted observation as central to knowledge acquisition. Educational practices grounded in this perspective position teachers as role models and emphasize observational learning, modeling, imitation, and feedback. Instructional activities provide social opportunities for students to observe, imitate, process, retain, and apply knowledge. Engaging methods such as collaborative tasks, games, and self-reflection are essential for maintaining learners' attention and motivation. Despite its contributions, particularly in bringing attention to the importance of self-regulation in (re)directing one's learning, the overemphasis on observation as a primary element of knowledge acquisition has been criticized as overly simplistic given the complexity of the learning process (McLeod, 2024; Muro & Jeffrey, 2008).

While traditional social perspectives expanded on earlier assumptions about knowledge, behavior, cognition, and the environment, they often treated the social dimension in a limited or abstract way. In contrast, later theories placed the social nature of learning at the forefront. In the 1990s, social learning theorists like Lave and Wenger (1991) and Wenger (1998) conceptualized learning as a social act occurring within a community of practice. Given that humans by nature are social beings, Wenger (1998) rationalized that knowledge and identity are co-constructed through social interactions in one's sociocultural contexts. Wenger (1998) identified four interrelated elements of social learning: meaning (learning as meaningful experience), practice (learning as doing), identity (learning as becoming), and community (learning as belonging). For effective teaching and learning, knowledge construction should not be individualistic; instead, it should develop through students' active participation in social learning systems or communities of practice (Lave & Wenger, 1991; Wenger, 1998). For effective communities of practice, curriculum and instruction must be thoughtfully planned to support mutual interests and goals and foster rapport and a sense of belonging. Through collaborative and cooperative learning, students work together to uncover new concepts, teach each other, negotiate ideas, and solve problems. Providing students with meaningful experiences that are socially and culturally embedded helps develop their competence in the subject matter and contributes to their evolving identities. Hence, situating learning within students' social and cultural contexts is a crucial aspect of this social perspective on learning (Lave & Wenger, 1991; Stein, 1998). Curriculum content and instructional activities should create authentic opportunities for students to apply and acquire knowledge relevant to their everyday lives. The teacher-student dynamic shifts from a traditional model, where the teacher is the sole expert, to one with more equal roles as co-participants in a community of practice (Li et al., 2009).

This theoretical perspective represents a shift from viewing learning as an individualistic cognitive process to a collective social activity (Irving et al., 2020), emphasizing participation, belonging, and identity development. While learning through cooperation and collaboration can be applied across various age groups, implementing the concept of a community of practice with younger learners may present challenges. This difficulty may stem from the fact that the concept was initially developed to study learning in apprenticeship contexts (Lave & Wenger, 1991) before being adapted to educational and workplace settings. There is a substantial body of literature on the application of this theoretical framework to promote social learning in face-to-face and online settings, primarily within higher education (e.g., Ching, 2021; Irving et al., 2020; Trenholm & Peschke, 2020) and for professional development (e.g., Feldman, 2020; Nkambule & Tang, 2023; Wang & Lu, 2012). Despite limited research on applying the community of practice theory with younger learners, Berman et al. (2016) reported successful implementation of this framework at a U.S. elementary school serving underrepresented populations. They employed this socially mediated approach to support the 5th-grade science curriculum and study the impact of community formation on learning. Given the reported benefits (see Berman et al., 2016), the researchers advocated for addressing curriculum and instructional constraints that may prevent making this social approach to learning "a sustainable practice as opposed to singular, independent" sessions (p. 9).

Social learning theories also encompass critical perspectives focused on empowering, transforming, and creating conscientious individuals and societies. Rooted in social reconstructionism and critical pedagogy, critical social learning theories (Freire, 1970; Giroux, 2001; McLaren, 2016; Shor, 2002) place the development of personal consciousness and critical thinking at the core of learning. While their foci may vary, curriculum and instruction within this paradigm generally aim to achieve the following objectives: generating awareness among students of social, cultural, political, and/or ecological issues within their society; cultivating critical thinking skills, and equipping students with critical language (Bertrand, 2003). Regardless of the subject matter, a critical curriculum integrates knowledge into students' lives as a problem to be negotiated and worked out (Shor, 2002). To facilitate this integration, the community in which a school is situated "becomes a central point of reference for curriculum development" (Smyth et al., 2014, p. 117). Knowledge (re)creation in the classroom happens through a dialogical method of instruction, making learning participatory, collaborative, and reflective (Shor, 2002; Shor & Freire, 1987). This method "invites students to think critically about subject matter, doctrines, the learning process itself, and their society" (Shor, 2002, p. 24). A critical teacher is thus seen as a classroom researcher, problem-poser, transformative intellectual, cultural worker, politician, and artist (Bertrand, 2003; Giroux, 2002; Shor, 2002; Shor & Freire, 1987).

Despite the emphasis of critical social theories on the empowering aspects of learning and their goal of developing socially responsible individuals, critics point out several conceptual and practical challenges (Evans, 2010; Joseph Jeyaraj & Harland, 2016; Tinning, 2002). These challenges include difficulties teachers face in understanding the literature, as well as concerns about ideological imposition, indoctrination, and subjectiveness. Additionally, the effective design and implementation of a socially critical curriculum may also be compromised by a lack of clear understanding of its practical features, as well as insufficient institutional support, resources, and training. Given the diversity in today's classrooms, there is also concern that emphasizing dialogue as the primary means for students to communicate opinions, negotiate alternatives, and reconcile differences in collaborative problem-solving tasks may lead to exclusion, marginalization, or domination, particularly for multilingual students and those with disabilities (Gabel, 2002; Burbules, 2000). Addressing these challenges requires a focused effort to bridge theory and practice in teacher education programs, along with targeted training and action research. Furthermore, collaborative efforts among teachers and administrators are crucial for developing and implementing a socially critical curriculum that is context-specific and suitable for diverse student backgrounds.

Humanistic Theoretical Perspectives

Although rooted in broader philosophical traditions, humanism is most commonly understood in educational contexts as a learning theory that emphasizes personal growth, intrinsic motivation, and the development of the whole learner. From this perspective, humanistic learning theories posit that humans are born with intrinsic desires for personal growth and improvement and that teaching and learning should focus on helping individuals realize their full potential. Humanism in education builds on Maslow's (1943) hierarchy of needs, which classifies human needs into two categories. Lower-level needs consist of fundamental basic needs, progressing from physiological needs (e.g., water, food, shelter), to safety needs (e.g., security, job, health), and finally to love and belonging needs. Higher-level needs encompass self-esteem (e.g., respect, confidence, achievement) and self-actualization (e.g., purpose, creativity). Humans strive to satisfy these needs, and what distinguishes us from other species is our drive to fulfill higher-level needs, particularly the pursuit of self-actualization "to become more and more what one is, to become everything one is capable of becoming" (Maslow, 1943, p. 383).

Instead of looking at learning primarily as a behavioristic, cognitive, or social activity, humanism is concerned with what a learner experiences, needs, and feels. Rogers' (1969) perspective on experiential learning emphasizes that education should nurture the whole learner, not merely promote the acquisition of academic knowledge. Curriculum and instruction should attend to learners' unique needs, personal interests, values, emotions, and psychological well-being. In a humanistic classroom, the emphasis is on learner autonomy, creativity, positive relationships, and active engagement. Students take an authoritative role, driving the curriculum and initiating their own learning. They determine topics, materials, and amount of work, and they engage in self-assessment. The humanistic curriculum is practical in nature and serves as a tool for providing "a way of life centered upon human interests and values" (Goodlad, 1967, p. 91). Teachers facilitate the learning experience, nurture students' emotional and intellectual development, and guide them toward their goals. The Montessori approach exemplifies curriculum and instruction grounded in humanistic learning theories (D'Emidio-Caston & Crocker, 1987).

Despite its emphasis on the humane aspects of education, humanistic learning theories have faced criticism (Stewart, 2021). One critique centers on the principle of self-directed learning as not all students possess the intrinsic motivation necessary for intellectual growth and self-actualization. Others pointed out that such theories as the experiential learning theory lack a scientific basis and are more ideological than theoretical. Regardless of these concerns, the significant benefits of humanizing teaching and learning and addressing the whole individual cannot be denied.

To conclude this subsection, it is important to note that human learning is influenced by numerous internal and external factors that a single theory cannot fully capture. Beyond what has been highlighted in this chapter, there is a diverse body of learning theories that have (a) extended or expanded on some of the theoretical concepts discussed above (e.g., cognitive load theory, Sweller, 1988, 1994, 2022), (b) shed light on specific dimensions of learning (e.g., theory of growth mindset, Dweck, 2006), (c) addressed aspects of adult learning (e.g., transformative learning theory, Mezirow, 1997, 2018), and (d) explored facets of modern learning related to multimedia and online environments (e.g., connectivism learning theory, Siemens, 2005; cognitive theory of multimedia learning, Mayer & Moreno, 1998; Mayer, 2014; collaborativism, Harasim, 2012).

Evolving Views on L2 Teaching and Learning

This subsection offers a brief historical account of trends in ELT and their impact on L2 curriculum and instruction. More specifically, it sheds some light on major L2 teaching approaches, their underlying assumptions, and relevant teaching methods. In ELT, an approach provides the theoretical basis for the practice (Anthony, 1963; Clarke, 1983; Richards & Rodgers, 1982). It is defined as "the philosophical orientation to instruction that serves as a guide for choosing among methods that are considered to be consistent with the tenets of the theory and scientifically based research that ground the philosophy" (Herrera & Murry, 2011, p. 189). Essentially, an approach reflects one's philosophical and theoretical assumptions about L2 teaching and learning and informs their instructional methods (i.e., teaching techniques and procedures). Many ELT approaches are influenced, directly or indirectly, by the theories of learning discussed earlier, as well as theories of SLA, which attempt to describe how second languages are acquired and learned.

A Classical Approach

Traditional foreign language teaching and learning practices primarily utilized the grammar-translation method. This approach focuses on learning the grammatical rules of the target language to translate and read foreign texts, with little or no emphasis on developing oral skills. This method was originally used in the 17th and 18th centuries to enable individuals to read foreign classical texts for intellectual development (Howatt, 1984), consistent with the perennial philosophy of that time. It lacks a theoretical basis for its instructional techniques (Richards & Rodgers, 2001) since it was never intended for learning to communicate in a foreign language. Nevertheless, it was adapted for use in schools to teach foreign languages by applying similar grammar and translation techniques at the sentence level and incorporating behaviorist elements such as repetition, memorization, and drills.

One of the earliest EFL curricula based on what would later be known as the grammar-translation method was developed by Johann Christian Fick in 1793 and published as a course book for German speakers learning English as a foreign language (Howatt, 1984). The course book employed a deductive approach by starting with explicit explanations of grammar rules and sentence examples, followed by translation exercises. The approach to instruction is teacher centric. It uses the native language as a medium of instruction and emphasizes accuracy of grammar and sentence structure.

The grammar-translation method has been criticized for its ineffectiveness in language learning due to its focus on rote memorization of grammar rules and neglect of communication skills. Despite the criticism, a quick Google Scholar search reveals that this approach is still employed in some EFL classrooms in the 21st century (e.g., Aqel, 2013; Khan et al., 2016; Kurniawan et al., 2021; Mart, 2013; Milawati, 2019). Its continued use is often attributed to institutional traditions, teacher familiarity, exam-oriented education systems, and a lack of access to training in more communicative methodologies.

A Naturalistic Approach

In response to the grammar-translation method, a naturalistic approach to teaching foreign languages emerged in the mid-19th century. This approach advocated for a more natural way of learning a second language, similar to how one acquires their native language. One of the methods that is based on this premise is the direct method. Gouin (1892), one of the founders of the direct method, argued in his book, *The Art of Teaching and Studying Languages*, that if a child can learn to speak and think in a language within 6–12 months, then both youth and adults should also be able to learn the target language "without trouble" within the same timeframe, "since [they] already know how to think" (p. 6). In order to learn in a naturalistic manner, the direct method uses the target language as the medium of instruction. Oral production and aural comprehension are prioritized in the curriculum to connect learners "directly" with the target language. Reading and writing are introduced later, akin to the process of acquiring a native language, and grammar is learned inductively. Translation and the use of the native language are discouraged. Gouin's method (1892)—which was later known as the direct method—included specific techniques for its implementation. The teacher directs learners to listen to and recite a series of logically sequenced, simple statements related to a specific theme or situation. These statements maintain the same subject and use a consistent tense but incorporate varied concrete action verbs. Visual aids and physical activities help learners form a direct association between meaning and language items. Another important contributor to the direct method is Maximilian Berlitz, who founded several language schools and published textbooks based on this method (Stieglitz, 1955). Despite its innovative techniques and novel approach to language learning, the direct method faced criticism for its lack of clear theoretical foundations (Brown & Lee, 2015) and its emphasis on oral skills at the expense of reading, writing, and a systematic understanding of language structure.

It is important to note that calls for fostering a naturalistic L2 teaching and learning environment have emerged at various times in the ELT field. Terrell (1977) and later Krashen and Terrell (1983) advocated for a natural approach to L2 teaching and learning. This approach differs in application from the direct method but shares the assumption that L2 learning can benefit from a process similar to native language acquisition. Key differences between the direct method and the natural approach include their handling of grammar, the teacher's role, and the characteristics of the learning environment. In the natural approach, grammar is acquired implicitly through exposure to comprehensible input without explicit instruction, and the teacher fosters a relaxed environment rich in meaningful interactions with an emphasis on understanding rather than accuracy (this will be discussed further in the subsection "A Communicative Approach"). In contrast, the direct method teaches grammar inductively through practice and repetition, with the teacher actively directing learning, utilizing repetition and structured drills, and focusing on accuracy.

A Structural Approach

Several teaching methods that focused on a systematic study of language structure emerged in the 20th century. Drawing upon structural linguistics (Bloomfield, 1935, 1942), behavioral psychology (Skinner, 1938), and the contrastive analysis hypothesis (Lado, 1957), Fries (1957) underlined "that the fundamental purpose or objective of language teaching is to achieve an understanding, as complete as possible, between people of different linguistic backgrounds" (p. 267). To accomplish this objective, Fries explained that teaching methods should focus on building knowledge of the target language's sound system, grammatical patterns, lexical units, and cultural norms. Fries (1945, 1957) called this the oral approach to L2 teaching and learning. While this approach might resemble the direct method—particularly in its goal of achieving oral fluency—the processes involved differ. The direct method focuses exclusively on teaching listening, speaking, and vocabulary with no explicit teaching of grammar. In contrast, the oral approach prioritizes teaching grammatical patterns, providing learners with language formulas that enable them to get started with communicating in the target language. Knowledge of these formulas would eventually allow them to expand their language production by substituting or manipulating words within a given language frame. Reading longer texts, writing extensively, and learning specialized vocabulary take place only later, after learners have mastered the sound system and grammatical structures.

This approach is based on the rationale that, in first language acquisition, individuals develop subconscious knowledge of grammatical structures, allowing them to produce language automatically without thinking about forms or word order. Hence, the earlier stages of L2 acquisition necessitate learning basic language patterns until they become part of the learner's repertoire, and their use becomes an automatic habit (Fries, 1945; Lado & Fries, 1958). This approach also accounts for learners' linguistic backgrounds in curriculum development because, in Fries' (1945) words, "the most efficient materials are those that are based upon a scientific description of the language to be learned, carefully compared with a parallel description of the native language of the learner" (p. 9). During the 1950s and 1960s, contrastive analysis studies, which compared native and target languages to predict potential errors, were popular for informing instructional materials (Lado, 1957). The audiolingual method was developed based on these assumptions, and its teaching techniques involve modeling, dialogues, memorization, inductive learning, and pattern drills (Lado, 1964).

The audiolingual method started to lose its popularity as researchers (e.g., Ausubel et al., 1978; Harmer, 1983; Rivers, 1964; Valdman, 1968, 1970) expressed concerns regarding the lack of evidence supporting its effectiveness in achieving language proficiency. Chomsky (1964) also criticized the stimulus-response approach to language acquisition in general because it presents language as a script learned through imitation and memorization. He argued that the performance of memorized utterances does not necessarily indicate linguistic competence (i.e., one's underlying knowledge of linguistic structures and grammatical rules). Concerns about this teaching approach being rooted in behaviorist practices led to an interest in teaching strategies that target learners' cognition.

A Cognitive Approach

Unlike the structural approach, which viewed L2 learning as habit formation and emphasized the mechanical learning of structural patterns, the cognitive approach posits that the brain is capable of generating novel utterances based on acquired linguistic knowledge of the target language. Influenced by the mid-20th-century cognitive movement, the cognitive approach to L2 learning focuses on mental aspects such as information processing, problem-solving, and comprehension. Carroll (1965) described language learning in this approach as "a process of acquiring conscious control of the phonological, grammatical, and lexical patterns of a second language, largely through study and analysis of these patterns as a body of knowledge" (p. 278). The aim is to supply L2 learners with "a proper degree of cognitive control over the structures of the language" so they can use them automatically in meaningful contexts (Carroll, 1965, p. 278). Within this paradigm, L2 instruction involves explicit teaching of linguistic features and learning strategies that help learners notice, analyze, and interact with the target language meaningfully. Chastain (1971) suggested that the explanations of language forms should precede practice, emphasizing that cognition involves moving "from mental understanding and awareness to practice; from studying a structure to seeing it used in context" (p. 48).

In addition to drawing from various cognitive theories, the cognitive approach to L2 teaching and learning also incorporates insights from linguistic theories. Among these linguistic theories are Chomsky's generative grammar (1964, 1978) and universal grammar (1986), which described first language (L1) acquisition processes as innate and universal. He (1986) hypothesized that all languages share similar structures and grammatical rules and that the human brain is equipped with an abstract language acquisition device that facilitates syntactic development through experience. Research in the 1980s began exploring these concepts in relation to SLA, including L2 learners' access to universal grammar, language transfer, and the differences and similarities between L1 and L2 acquisition (Schwartz & Sprouse, 1998; Rothman & Slabakova, 2018).

Viewing SLA as a universal process of developmental sequences and as a purely mental linguistic operation has been critiqued for overlooking the impact of sociocultural factors and individual differences (Breen, 1985; Firth & Wagner, 1997; Lantolf, 2000; Lantolf & Appel, 1994; Skehan, 1991). In his discussion of a theory of language cognition, Nick

Ellis (2019) argued that individual cognitive processes, along with human interactions, are crucial in shaping language acquisition. He emphasized the need to understand the interplay between cognitive mechanisms, language use, and cultural context. N. C. Ellis (2019) stated that "language cognition is shared across naturally occurring, culturally constituted, communicative activities. Usage affects learning and it affects languages, too. These are essential components of a theory of language cognition" (p. 39). Ellis highlighted the significance of frequency of experience and usage in aiding learning and memory, noting that repeated exposure to language input and opportunities for meaningful output help learners form neural connections between linguistic patterns and their usage.

This shift in focus in ELT reflects the broader educational progression from an emphasis on behavior to cognition and, subsequently, to the interplay between cognition and the social environment. This evolution has given rise to a socio-cognitive approach to L2 learning, which perceives SLA as a simultaneous mental and social activity happening "both 'in the head' and 'in the world'" (Atkinson, 2002, p. 525). The socio-cognitive approach to L2 extends Vygotsky's (1978) theoretical perspective by emphasizing the role of language use and the social environment in influencing second language development (e.g., Lantolf, 2000; Lantolf & Appel). Theories and research in cognition and socio-cognition have profoundly impacted language curriculum and pedagogical practices. This includes acknowledging individual differences in cognitive abilities, tailoring instruction to diverse needs, providing rich input and meaningful practice, and equipping learners with cognitive and metacognitive strategies. Further practices within this paradigm aiming to enhance the efficiency and effectiveness of L2 learning include schema building, discovery learning, instructional scaffolding, collaborative learning, task-based language teaching, explicit and implicit instruction, and constructive feedback.

A Communicative Approach

Most traditional ELT approaches had a similar goal, building learners' grammatical competence in the target language. They differed, however, in their assumptions about how best curriculum and instruction can foster this knowledge. Should L2 linguistic structures be taught implicitly to allow learners to acquire them as units of knowledge similar to L1 acquisition? Or should they be taught explicitly so that learners are cognitively able to generate novel language based on the learned L2 syntactic rules?

Although some earlier methods, such as the direct method, emphasized oral language skills after the dominance of the grammar-translation method, the 1970s marked a major shift toward building L2 learners' communicative competence. In response to Chomsky's (1964) construct of linguistic competence, Hymes (1972) argued that competence involves not just knowledge of language forms but also knowledge of language functions, which is acquired through social interactions. While Chomsky (1964) distinguished between competence and performance, suggesting that performed utterances might not always reflect a learner's underlying linguistic knowledge, Hymes (1972) viewed competence and performance as inseparable. For Hymes, competency in the target language involves not only grammatical correctness but also social acceptability, which he encapsulated in his notion of communicative competence. Wilkins (1973) further argued that mastery of grammatical rules does not always translate into effective communication. In fact, Wilkins' 1973 publication was one of the first to advocate for a communicative approach to L2 curriculum and instruction. He criticized the approach of grounding courses, materials, and lessons primarily in grammatical topics, with only occasional focus on pronunciation or vocabulary. He stated that "the grammatical content [. . .] is thought of as the core of a course[,] and the essence of learning a language is taken to be the learning of its grammar" (Wilkins, 1973, p. 1). This grammar-driven approach to L2 teaching and learning, as Wilkins described, is artificial and irrelevant to real language use, insufficient for developing communication skills, and inadequate for addressing learners' professional, social, and leisure needs, as well as sustaining their motivation. Wilkins (1973) further explained that unlike a grammar-based curriculum, which is derived from form, the development of a communicative curriculum centers on content, aiming to identify "the types of language interaction in which the individual is going to engage and with what purpose" (p. 4).

The communicative approach emphasizes designing curricula based on learners' needs and meaningful language use. It seeks to build fluency in L2 by incorporating opportunities for interactions, using authentic materials, creating meaningful tasks, and contextualizing the learning of grammar. ELT methods grounded in these principles include task-based language teaching (TBLT), content-based instruction (CBI), and communicative language teaching (CLT). The communicative movement to language teaching and learning has also been influenced by various theories and hypotheses, including the affective filter hypothesis and the input hypothesis (Krashen & Terrell, 1983). To optimize learning and facilitate communication, these hypotheses emphasize the importance of creating a relaxed atmosphere to lower learners' affective filter and providing comprehensible input slightly beyond their current level: "i + 1," similar to Vygotsky's (1978) ZPD concept and Bruner's notion of instructional scaffolding (Wood et al., 1976).

Although the communicative approach has transformed L2 teaching and learning by making the process more meaningful and less mechanical, it is not without its criticisms. One early criticism was its heavy focus on language functions and the neglect of grammatical structures. Swan (1985) argued that some complex grammatical structures are difficult to pick up without explicit instruction so that learners are eventually able to use them communicatively. He further described the principles of the communicative approach as overly theoretical and practically confusing, causing teachers to feel guilty when incorporating grammar explanations, translation, or rote learning. While acknowledging the value of authentic materials and real-life language use, Swan (1985) defended the use of quality ESL materials for effective linguistic learning, recognizing that "a certain amount of artificiality is inseparable" due to the nature of classroom discourse (p. 82). Another criticism concerns the lack of clarity regarding the principles and practices of the communicative approach (Harmer, 2003; Spada, 2007; Littlewood, 2011; Swan, 1985). Littlewood (2011) noted ambiguity about whether the term *communicative approach* refers to curricular objectives focused on communicative skills or to teaching methodologies that consistently engage learners in communication. Furthermore, research on classrooms that claim to follow a communicative curriculum has identified discrepancies between the curriculum's principles and actual classroom practices (Kumaravadivelu, 1993, 2006a). A key finding was the absence of authentic activities and meaningful interactions. Some challenges that can hinder the effective implementation of communicative methods, as reported by Littlewood (2007), include large class sizes, learners' reluctance to use the target language, difficulties in preparing students for standardized testing, and mismatches with local educational practices and values. Another critique of the communicative approach is its emphasis on using the target language while neglecting L1 as a valuable tool for supporting L2 learning (Cook, 2001; Hall & Cook, 2012; Turnbull, 2001).

A Critical Approach

A critical approach to language curriculum and instruction challenges the monolithic approaches that idealize native-speaker-like competence (Hall et al., 2013) and confine learning to specific teaching methods, often incompatible with the local educational context (Canagarajah, 2002; Kumaravadivelu, 2001). With English serving as a lingua franca (i.e., a medium for global communications) and the spread of World Englishes (Kachru, 1984, 1992a) (i.e., the existence of different varieties of English), the notion of Standard English and native-speaker norms (Fang, 2018) has been contested, resulting in a more pluralistic view of English teaching and learning (Galloway & Numajiri, 2019; Hall et al., 2013). Such a critical lens has brought increased attention to issues like linguistic prejudice toward "non-standard" accents and dialects (Baratta, 2018; Zuidema, 2005), linguistic imperialism found in some ELT materials (Canagarajah, 1999; Zhang & Song, 2022), and the limitations of imported curricula and teaching methods that fail to account for the local linguistic, social, cultural, and political contexts (Canagarajah, 2002; Kumaravadivelu, 2001).

Critical ELT practices do not favor a specific teaching method and resist or question dominant norms. Curriculum development and implementation are context-dependent and embrace linguistic and cultural diversity. Critical practices invite "teachers to consider the deficit model of learning and teaching associated with monolithism, [. . .] acknowledge the multiple, locally-modulated outcomes of learning and teaching that actually occur in real classrooms, [and] value the diversity of Englishes" (Hall et al., 2013, p. 6). Galloway and Numajiri (2019) added that the principles of *real* and *authentic* language use, traditionally associated with native-speaker norms in communicative language teaching, have evolved to represent "real and authentic use of English [. . .] as a lingua franca with speakers from diverse lingua-cultural backgrounds" (p. 119). Within this paradigm shift, language curricula, as outlined in Galloway and Numajiri (2019), should:

- incorporate World Englishes,
- expose learners to English as a lingua franca,
- equip learners with strategies for multilingual communications,
- instill respect for linguistic and cultural diversity,

- encourage learners to utilize their full linguistic repertoire,
- and assess language proficiency based on "intercultural communicative competence" rather than "native English norms" (pp. 122–123).

Unlike the traditional practices of communicative language teaching that suppressed the use of L1 in the classroom, the critical approach to ELT views translanguaging (i.e., moving between one's L1 and L2) as an important means for supporting communication and constructing meaning (Canagarajah, 2011). Research has shown that translanguaging benefits learners in monolingual contexts, bilingual education, and multilingual classrooms (De Los Reyes, 2018; García & Lin, 2017; García-Mateus & Palmer, 2017; Rabbidge, 2019). It facilitates communication and comprehension in classrooms that use communicative curricula such as content-based instruction (CBI), content and language integrated learning (CLIL) (Sohn et al., 2022), and task-based language teaching (TBLT) (Bui & Tai, 2022; Seals et al., 2020).

Critical EFL/ESL classrooms extend beyond mere language acquisition to become spaces for social transformation and environmental awareness. In order to bring consciousness to social justice as well as political and ecological issues among ESL/EFL learners, Morgan (1998) advocated for language curricula relevant to learners' immediate sociocultural context and existing political conditions to develop both their linguistic abilities and identities. He (1998) argued that language curriculum should extend beyond mere linguistic structures to address "how language is used to *structure* expectation, participation, and exclusion in our society. Such an approach actively encourages social advocacy and critical thinking as central to language curricula" (pp. 5–6). This can be facilitated by focusing on themes, topics, readings, and activities that bring awareness of these issues and provide opportunities for "dialogic critical thinking" (Benesch, 1999b, p. 573).

Similarly, using a posthuman lens, Karthika (2024) described today's ESL/EFL "classrooms as ecosystems of learning where multiple assemblages are formulated" (p. 164). This perspective highlights the interconnectedness of human and non-human elements—such as teachers, students, emotions, materials, and technology—within the learning process, where these elements interact in fluid, non-hierarchical ways. Knowledge is no longer the sole domain of the teacher, but it is co-constructed through collaboration, translingual communication, and technology-mediated interactions to allow learners to become active agents in both their learning and the broader world. Posthuman teaching practices consider how current technological advancements such as AI tools bring in new dynamics and interactions in the classroom, engage with critical global and social issues such as climate change and gender equity through discussions and project-oriented learning, and encourage the use of multiple languages and perspectives. Karthika (2024) remarked that "when English language education is seen through a posthuman lens, it is a turn towards social justice, equitable practices and increased sensitivity about the planet itself" (p. 164).

Developing critical language awareness among L2 writers is another pedagogy within this critical orientation to language curriculum and instruction. Shapiro (2022) described Critical Language Awareness (CLA) pedagogy as "an approach to language and literacy education that focuses on the intersections of language, identity, power, and privilege, with the goal of promoting self-reflection, social justice, and rhetorical agency among student writers" (p. 4). CLA pedagogy challenges the focus of writing curriculum and instruction on norms of academic language and Standard English, but at the same time, it acknowledges that these cannot be entirely disregarded. Instead, CLA pedagogy seeks "to demystify, critique, and—at times—resist those norms and standards" (Shapiro, 2022, p. 14). CLA-based writing curricula use texts by multilingual authors, promote understanding of how identity influences language and vice versa, encourage code-meshing (i.e., writers utilizing their full linguistic repertoire to communicate ideas), engage students in critical text analysis, and nurture an inclusive writing environment that values linguistic diversity (Shapiro, 2022).

The discussion above captures bits and pieces of orientations of criticality in language curriculum and instruction. These range from practices that draw on Freire's critical pedagogy (e.g., cultivating critical consciousness) to those that take a postmodernist skeptical stance toward norms claiming to be true for all backgrounds and under all circumstances (Kubota, 2018). Some scholars, such as Hyland (2018), advised proceeding cautiously with critical pedagogy and the critical take on academic writing, particularly in English for Academic Purposes (EAP). Hyland argued that "many of the canonical texts in Critical EAP and Critical pedagogy more generally are too remote from everyday practice, favoring impenetrable jargon over classroom approaches, and therefore offering poor guides to pedagogy" (p. 392). Besides the critiques concerning the obscure concepts in critical literature, several works have raised further concerns (e.g., Ellsworth, 1992; Ewald, 1999; Harwood & Hadley, 2004; Haque, 2007; Jeon, 2009; Johnston, 1999; Usher & Edwards, 1994).

These concerns include the lack of accessible and realistic classroom applications, especially when it comes to constructs such as empowerment, voice, emancipation/liberation, consciousness, transformation, and resistance. Another issue involves barriers to dialogue and opinion expression, which may arise due to students' limited language abilities and the inherent unequal power dynamics in the classroom.

Additionally, because one of the main principles of criticality is resisting or questioning the status quo, Hyland (2018) noted that EAP has been criticized for perpetuating dominant norms by "uncritically filling obedient students with disciplinary norms and ideologies" (p. 392), which can lead to conformity and a passive learning approach where students "mimic expert practices rather than engage as active learners in questioning and understanding them" (p. 387). Hyland (2018) countered these claims by arguing that the main goal of EAP is to help students succeed in their fields of study. To help learners navigate academic writing demands, efficient and effective time use necessitates attention to writing conventions, linguistic patterns, and discourse features specific to their disciplines. Central to the EAP curriculum design is addressing students' learning needs and their communicative goals. This can only be accomplished by providing students with purposeful language relevant to real-world contexts (Hyland, 2018). This is often facilitated through genre analysis, a common practice in the EAP classroom that helps students develop an analytical perspective by recognizing both similarities and variations in language use. In his concluding remarks, Hyland (2018) acknowledged the benefits of incorporating critical practices into the EAP curriculum. He supported the idea of providing students with "the best of both worlds" (p. 396) by integrating elements of criticality, such as attention to social and global issues, encouraging dialogue, fostering critical thinking and reflection, and raising awareness of linguistic diversity. This approach can indeed make learning more meaningful and impactful.

To sum up this subsection, the ELT field has witnessed different orientations and foci in L2 teaching and learning, including:

- focusing on the memorization of grammatical rules,
- emphasizing the development of learners' oral language skills in a naturalistic manner,
- prioritizing reading skills through a reading approach, with speaking and writing following naturally (West, 1937),
- emphasizing subconscious learning of linguistic structures for automatic language production,

- shifting to conscious learning of grammar to enable cognitively controlled language production,
- focusing on building communicative language skills to enable effective communication in the target language,
- and instilling opportunities that cultivate critical awareness and embrace linguistic diversity.

Whether to emphasize accuracy over fluency, build linguistic competence or communicative competence, and teach grammar deductively or inductively have been among the major conflicting views over the focus of L2 curriculum and instruction.

After you read, consider the following questions:

1. As was demonstrated in this chapter, educational philosophies make varied assumptions about what is worth teaching and how it should be taught. In the chart below, summarize the beliefs held by each philosophy on the aim of education, core principles of curriculum and instruction, and the roles of teachers and students. In the last two columns, identify theories and ELT approaches that align with or support each philosophy's beliefs. If needed, conduct further research or consult sources from the References.

Philosophy	**Aim of Education**	**Core Principles**	**Teacher vs. Student Role**	**Corresponding Learning Theory**	**Corresponding ELT Approach**
Perennialism					
Essentialism					
Progressivism					
Social Reconstructionism and Critical Pedagogy					
Indigenism					
Posthumanism					

2. Identify aspects from the educational philosophies and theories of learning discussed in this chapter that align with your values and beliefs about teaching and learning. Draft a reflective statement exploring your philosophy, using concrete examples from your own teaching or learning experiences that reflect your values and beliefs.
3. Different ELT methods have emerged over the years, such as Total Physical Response, Community Language Learning, the Silent Way, Suggestopedia, the Reading Method, and Task-Based Language Teaching, among others. Select one method to research its theoretical basis, techniques, and procedures. Determine whether this method promotes fluency or accuracy, fosters linguistic or communicative competence, generates knowledge of grammar deductively or inductively, and considers any affective factors.
4. Examine each of the educational enterprises provided in the links below. Identify their core principles, educational philosophies, and underlying theories. Describe how you determined these aspects based on the information provided.
    a. *Maria Montessori Academy* https://mariamontessoriacademy.net/montessori/philosophy/
    b. *Community Engaged Learning* https://www.rrcc.edu/hub/servicelearning
    c. *Core Knowledge Foundation* https://www.coreknowledge.org/curriculum/
    d. *Coalition of Essential Schools* http://essentialschools.org/common-principles/
    e. *University of Chicago's Basic Program of Liberal Education for Adults* https://graham.uchicago.edu/programs-courses/basic-program
5. Reflect on the role of technology, AI, and other non-human elements in the learning process based on your own experiences. How could a posthumanist approach reshape the traditional roles of teaching and learning in the ESL/EFL classroom? What implications does this have for learner agency, curriculum design, and classroom dynamics?

6. Explore the CLA Collective [https://cla.middcreate.net/], an "online resource hub" for Shawna Shapiro's book *Cultivating Critical Language Awareness in the Writing Classroom* (2022). This hub serves as a "gathering space for teachers committed to promoting Critical Language Awareness (CLA) in our writing, literacy, and language classrooms and curricula." Select three materials from the "Teaching Resources" section (e.g., a syllabus, handout, reading, or student work) to describe how each material exemplifies or promotes the principles of CLA pedagogy.
7. Bonus task! Interview an ESL teacher (or a classmate) about their educational philosophies, views of L2 learning, and teaching practices. Use the discussion from this chapter to formulate interview questions centered around educational philosophy, theory, L2 teaching approaches, and curriculum and instruction. After the interview, reflect on how the interviewee's beliefs compare to your own.

Chapter 3

Curriculum Context and Purpose

Before you read, reflect on the following questions:

1. What does *context* mean in relation to curriculum design and implementation?
2. Why is it crucial to understand and define the specific context of a curriculum?
3. In what ways can the context affect the development and delivery of a curriculum?
4. What are the different objectives of a language curriculum? How can the purpose of a curriculum be determined?

The first part of this chapter explores the complexity of curriculum by examining the multiple layers of context in which it operates and the various factors that can impact its effectiveness. The second part delves into the broad and specific purposes of ESL/EFL learning, illustrating how language curriculum and instruction are shaped by these contexts.

Contextual Levels of Curriculum

Curricula operate within a complex, multilayered context. Here, *context* refers to the environment, setting, time, and conditions in which a curriculum is executed. Understanding this context is crucial for developing an effective curriculum, as it helps identify factors that could influence its success. Cornbleth (1990) described curriculum as a "contextualized social process [that] cannot be understood adequately without attention to its setting and context" (p. 6). Wedell and Malderez (2013) emphasized that key elements of context, such as individuals, location, and time, are often overlooked in curriculum planning and implementation.

Researchers differentiate between various contextual levels. Fien (1992) identified two primary levels: the *micro* context, which includes the classroom and the program, school, or institution, and the *macro* level, which encompasses national and sociocultural factors. Van den Akker (2007) and Thijs and van den Akker (2009) highlighted the *meso* level, which also involves the program, school, or institution but within a broader context that bridges the micro and macro levels. Additionally, these two works introduced two more levels: the *supra* level, representing international factors influencing curriculum, and the *nano* level, focusing on individuals directly interacting with the curriculum, such as teachers and students.

Figure 3.1 illustrates the various contextual levels in which the curriculum is embedded, including their constituents and potential factors

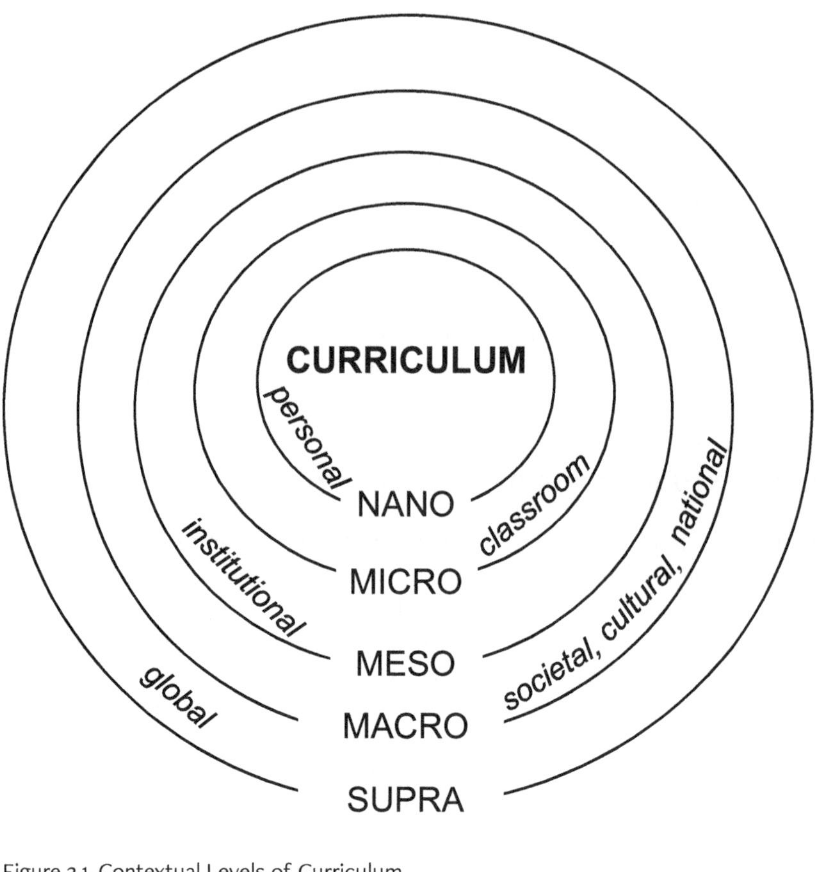

Figure 3.1. Contextual Levels of Curriculum

that can impact curriculum effectiveness. Building on these concepts, the following discussion will explore each level of context and its potential impact on curriculum development and effectiveness.

Nano and Micro Contexts

At the core of the micro context is the classroom where the curriculum unfolds. Within this context, the implementers and users of the curriculum present nano-level factors that can impact its implementation. The effectiveness of curriculum implementation and delivery is influenced by various factors related to students, teachers, the school, and other circumstances. Student-related factors can be broadly categorized into:

- demographic, linguistic, cultural, and socioeconomic backgrounds
- cognitive abilities
- mental and emotional well-being
- personality traits
- learning styles and preferences
- motivation and attitudes
- prior learning experiences and knowledge
- personal goals, interests, and needs

These intricate and fluid factors at the nano level necessitate top-down and bottom-up measures for effective curriculum implementation within the micro context. Top-down measures include systems in place at the meso level (i.e., program, school, or institution) related to curriculum development, such as analyzing the target student population, selecting and designing materials thoughtfully, and involving teachers in curriculum decision-making. Collecting comprehensive student-related data through surveys, interviews, observations, and assessments (e.g., diagnostic, formative, and summative) is crucial for planning a curriculum suited for its learners (discussed in Chapter 7). For effective teaching and learning, top-down measures also encompass teacher collaboration, professional development opportunities, and student support services such as advising and counseling. Ongoing needs assessment at the micro level is essential to ensure that curriculum implementation remains responsive and adaptable (discussed in Chapter 7).

Teachers play a pivotal role in the success of curriculum implementation at the micro level, as documented in the literature (e.g., Cheung & Man Wong, 2012; Gouëdard et al., 2020; Roehrig & Kruse, 2005; Roehrig et al., 2007; Wang & Cheng, 2009). Teacher-related factors influencing curriculum delivery include attitudes and beliefs about teaching and learning, instructional methods, and levels of experience and expertise. Issues arising from these factors can lead to inconsistent horizontal implementation of the planned curriculum across subjects or courses within the same grade or language proficiency level. For example, it is common to hear that Teacher A's class differs significantly from Teacher B's class, even though they are teaching the same curriculum. Shawer (2017) noted that "individual teacher interpretations of the same (formal) curriculum drive teachers to transform a single curriculum into multiple (taught) curricula" (p. 296). This horizontal misalignment (Wiles & Bondi, 2014) can result from differing instructional styles and philosophies or a lack of understanding of the curriculum's purpose. For this reason, Stenhouse (1975) argued that "each classroom should not be an island" (p. 157) and advocated for teacher collaboration, communication, and involvement in curriculum development. He also emphasized that, given the unique context of each classroom, even within the same school or program, a curriculum "needs to be tested and verified and adapted by each teacher in his [or her] own classroom" (p. 143) to address nano/micro-level factors and optimize its effectiveness.

In addition to the impact of student- and teacher-related factors on curriculum success and student achievement, the larger contexts of the meso and macro levels can optimize or impede curriculum effectiveness at the nano/micro levels. These effects may be due to factors related to (Altinyelken, 2010; Ham & Dekkers, 2019; Jones, 2016; O'Sullivan, 2002; Ssentanda et al., 2019; Tromp & Datzberger, 2019; Yan & He, 2012):

- the location and environment of the school, program, or institution
- available funds, resources, and facilities
- leadership and management style
- classroom setting and physical resources
- class size and composition

- teachers' workload, pay, and incentives
- national policies on curriculum reform, testing, and standards

These overlapping contextual influences underscore the complexity of curricula. The following discussion will highlight how factors at the meso and macro levels can impact curriculum development and implementation. Although some variables may be beyond control, Part II of this book explores procedures, such as situation analysis and needs analysis, to help address potential barriers to effective curriculum implementation.

Meso Context

The classroom and its constituents are situated within the meso level, which encompasses the program, school, or institution. At this level, curriculum development and implementation are influenced by various factors, including program design and infrastructure; mission, values, and goals; institutional and departmental policies; program budgets and resources; teaching qualification requirements; support for faculty and students; stakeholder beliefs; and administration and leadership style. Careful planning, consideration, and alignment of these elements are crucial for creating a coherent and consistent curriculum that effectively translates into the micro context.

Curriculum decision-making at the meso level must account for the perspectives and needs of those directly impacted at the micro level. Teachers' participation in or buy-in of curricular decisions has been shown to play a significant role in the success or failure of curriculum initiatives (Hübner et al., 2021; Obilo & Sangoleye, 2010). For instance, Nevenglosky and colleagues (2019) reported inconsistencies in the implementation of a phonics program purchased by a U.S. K-12 private school administration. These inconsistencies negatively impacted the achievement of learning objectives and left students unprepared for the next grade level. Teachers in the study expressed concerns and reported barriers that hindered the effective implementation of the phonics curriculum. These barriers included inadequate training, lack of peer collaboration, and insufficient support resources. Additionally, some teachers felt that the new curriculum did not address students' needs as effectively as the previous phonics program (Nevenglosky et al., 2019).

Top-down decisions without sufficient training or buy-in from instructors can create a disconnect between the meso, micro, and nano contexts, leading to reduced curriculum fidelity and inconsistencies in student learning. This underscores the close interconnectedness of the meso, micro, and nano levels and highlights the importance of procedures and practices that ensure a mutual understanding of curriculum decisions, rationales, and expectations. Effective curriculum development and implementation require ongoing communication and alignment across all contextual levels to achieve desired educational outcomes.

Macro Context

The intersecting nano, micro, and meso levels of context are nested within a larger macro context comprised of community, society, culture, and nation. Baykut and colleagues (2022) explained that "the cultural traditions, political ideologies and elements of other socio-economic contexts of the macro level shape the meso, or organizations" (p. 160), which regulate teaching and learning practices within the micro context. At the macro level, a curriculum can be influenced by various factors, such as geographical location, sociocultural norms, traditions, ideologies, historical events, political and economic conditions, and national standards. Curricula thus function not only as a tool for cognitive, linguistic, academic, and/or professional development but also, as Cornbleth (1988) described, "an ongoing social activity shaped by various contextual influences within and beyond the classroom" (p. 89).

This perspective highlights why ESL and EFL are often treated as distinct contexts in the ELT literature (Graves, 2008) and necessitate different considerations in curriculum planning and development. ESL typically refers to teaching English in countries where English is the primary or predominant language (e.g., a Saudi student studying English in Canada), whereas EFL refers to teaching English in countries where it is not the dominant language (e.g., a Saudi student studying English in Saudi Arabia). Graves (2008) categorizes EFL as "target language-removed contexts" and ESL as "target language-embedded contexts" (p. 155).

However, the distinction between ESL and EFL is more complex due to varied sociocultural, political, and historical factors influencing language use and formation. The spread of English as a lingua franca and the development of World Englishes further complicate this distinction. Kachru's (1982) three-circle model illustrates the different forms of English within a macro context. The inner circle includes countries where English is the primary language (e.g., the United Kingdom and the United States). The outer circle consists of nations historically colonized by inner-circle countries where English functions as an official language (e.g., India and South Africa). The expanding circle encompasses countries using English for international communication and increasingly for work and study purposes (e.g., China, Japan, Italy, and Sudan).

Supra-context factors such as globalization, ease of mobility, and advances in communication have blurred the boundaries between these circles and challenged the notion of Standard English and the traditional view of the inner circle as "the norm provider" (Kachru, 1992b) for English language curricula. Local languages, sociocultural practices, and political contexts further complicate the norms of English usage and teaching within a macro context. For these reasons, language curricula are perceived as "sociocultural artifacts that reflect local values and local beliefs about language and language learning" (Christison & Murray, 2014, p. 1).

When developing or adopting language curricula and materials at the macro level, it is essential to consider factors such as individual learning goals, geographical and historical circumstances, and stakeholders' sociocultural beliefs and values. Research shows that curricula and textbooks designed for other contexts are often not implemented as intended or face resistance because they do not align with the target population's background or local context (Christison & Murray, 2014; Richards, 2017). Since ELT textbooks often serve as primary linguistic resources or as the curricula, particularly in EFL contexts (Richards, 1993), several studies have evaluated how imported textbooks align with local beliefs, norms, traditions, and values in various contexts, including Iran (e.g., Abdollahzadeh, & Baniasad, 2010; Seidi et al., 2016), the Arab Gulf (e.g., Ahmed, 2011), Turkey (e.g., Köksal & Ulum, 2021), and South Korea (e.g., Kim, 2011; Lee, 2009).

Concerns about imported textbooks have included minimal or lack of representation of the local culture, promotion of Western ideologies and social practices, linguistic imperialism, and cultural stereotypes. Content in such textbooks may also be unappealing, irrelevant, or insensitive, potentially contributing to the hidden curriculum (discussed in Chapter 1), which involves implied learning that occurs in a biased, stigmatized, or stereotyped manner (Baykut et al., 2022). As noted by Li (2016), "policymakers and educators are often alarmed by the hidden risk that the cultural values imported by the English language may threaten national cultures and political, economic, and social systems" (p. 130). Li analyzed cultural values embedded in national EFL textbooks for Chinese primary education, produced under the supervision of China's Ministry of Education. The analysis found that these textbooks aligned with the Chinese national curriculum by reinforcing moral education grounded in the Confucian philosophy, emphasizing traditional values related to collectivism, patriotism, diligence, and respect. Additionally, the analysis revealed that the textbooks included themes aimed at introducing foreign cultures in an ideologically acceptable manner, featuring topics on costumes, food, landmarks, and modern perspectives on gender roles and social inclusion. This example illustrates how macro-level decisions shape meso-level materials to align with local values and sociopolitical goals, often serving not only as a form of cultural preservation but also as a tool of soft power.

National education standards (e.g., the U.S. Common Core State Standards, which offer a framework for the K-12 English language arts and math curricula) and government policies and initiatives for curriculum reform are also macro-level factors influencing curricula in the meso and micro contexts. These policies and initiatives are often driven by supra factors, which will be explored in the subsequent discussion.

Supra Context

External global trends and events, political climate, technological advancements, and international job demands can have a direct or indirect impact on curricula. The disruption caused by the COVID-19 pandemic in 2020 is a basic example of how a global factor can affect various contextual levels of teaching and learning. The pandemic abruptly forced educational systems worldwide to find alternative modes of instruction to avoid school closures, which opened a Pandora's box of technical and instructional challenges. This included adapting curricula designed for face-to-face instruction to a virtual setting and addressing barriers related to digital access and skills that limited the participation of less advantaged students in online education (Gottschalk & Weise, 2023). Despite these challenges, such a supra-level factor has had a significant and continuing impact on educational practices and opportunities in the post-pandemic era. It has generated more interest in integrating digital technologies and implementing varied models of in-person and online learning to meet the demands of the 21st century and enhance accessibility (Tso et al., 2023).

Furthermore, national curriculum reforms and education policies, previously identified as macro factors, are often motivated by supra-level influences. Given the status of English as a lingua franca, many countries in various EFL contexts have undertaken curriculum reforms to keep pace with globalization. In the Chinese context, for example, Li (2016) highlighted China's efforts over the past two decades to reform their EFL national curriculum. These reforms aimed at fostering "cross-cultural communicative competence" through curricular objectives promoting "communicative English in specific sociocultural contexts" (p. 132). According to Li (2016), the motivation behind these reforms is to enhance international communication and, most importantly, drive economic growth.

International standards, such as the Common European Framework of Reference for Languages (CEFR), are also utilized in different ESL and EFL contexts as frameworks outlining language abilities at different levels of English proficiency to guide the ELT curriculum. In her discussion of curriculum reform efforts in Turkey, Kirkgöz (2019a) described how the Turkish Ministry of National Education implemented CEFR standards and the European Language Portfolio (ELP), a tool developed by the Council of Europe to help learners document and reflect on their language learning progress, to ensure that the national foreign language curriculum is in line with international standards and current educational research. This reform also emphasizes nurturing communicative competence across all grade levels and is motivated by global changes (Kirkgöz, 2019a).

Another illustration of the influence of the supra level on national educational decisions is the spread of the English as the medium of instruction (EMI) educational model. EMI refers to the use of the English language to teach academic subjects like mathematics and science in countries where English is not the primary language. This model has been adopted by a growing number of academic institutions in various EFL contexts, in countries such as Turkey, Afghanistan, Kuwait, Saudi Arabia, Spain, Germany, China, and Japan, and across all levels of education in both public and private sectors (Dearden, 2014; Doiz et al., 2012; Kırkgöz, 2019b). According to a British Council report (Dearden, 2014), the implementation of EMI is motivated by several factors. These include the desire to develop students' English language skills, foster bilingualism, improve international communications and relations, provide less privileged students with the opportunity to learn English, prepare students for study abroad and global job markets, diversify research efforts, improve world university rankings, and gain financial benefits.

It is important to point out that curriculum decisions that are made at the macro level and motivated by supra-contextual factors sometimes do not translate as planned at the meso, micro, and/or nano contexts. For example, in Bangladesh, Rahman, Islam, and colleagues (2019) noted that "given the significance of English in the global world, English language teaching in Bangladesh has become subject to a supreme concern in maintaining economic growth and developing a skilled workforce" (p. 1). Consequently, the Bangladeshi government, with support from the United Kingdom, mandated the implementation of a communicative language-teaching-based curriculum in primary and secondary education, replacing the previous grammar-translation method. Nonetheless, several publications on this reform have reported that the new curriculum has not been implemented as intended at the micro level (e.g., Ali & Walker, 2014; Rahman, Islam, et al., 2019; Rahman, Johan, et al. 2019). Reasons for this include insufficient teacher training and support, especially in rural areas, and a lack of collaboration among stakeholders.

Similarly, Mustafawi and Shaaban (2019) reported on the 2002 implementation of EMI in Qatar for K-12 science, mathematics, and technology education. They found that the initiative faced ideological reservations and concerns about its feasibility from the outset. National exam data revealed that the reform did not enhance student performance, which led to the reinstatement of Arabic as the language of instruction for grades K-12 and for social science courses at Qatar University in 2012. The lack of success of the EMI initiative in Qatar was attributed to factors such as "attitudes of stakeholders; teachers' qualifications and preparedness to take up such a daring task; the complexity of the context of teaching; and the manner of introducing the reform agenda" (Mustafawi & Shaaban, 2019, p. 209).

In addition to the influence of supra-level factors on a country's curricular reform decisions and the adoption of educational models like EMI, there has been growing interest in incorporating global dimensions into curriculum development to foster global competencies and citizenship, particularly in higher education (Caniglia et al., 2018; Ramaswamy et al., 2021; Valcke, 2020). Although the precise components of a global or internationalized curriculum in higher education are debated, Leask (2014) emphasized that learning should "occur within the context of the different cultures and practices of knowing, doing, and being in the disciplines" so that students "develop their international and intercultural perspectives as global professionals and citizens" (p. 6). Beyond higher education, international organizations have made collective efforts to promote globally oriented education for all ages. The Organisation for Economic Co-Operation and Development (OECD), for example, introduced the "Future of Education and Skills 2030/2040" project in 2015. This global initiative aims to help students worldwide develop the skills, knowledge, values, and attitudes necessary to thrive as responsible global citizens by 2030 (OECD, n.d.). Part of this project is "The OECD Learning Compass 2030" framework, which provides a common language and a set of competencies deemed crucial for advancing teaching and learning (OECD, 2019). The project also involves comparative analyses of curriculum projects worldwide to monitor progress toward achieving the goal of a better future (OECD, n.d.).

In the same direction, The United Nations Educational, Scientific and Cultural Organization (UNESCO) launched the "2030 Agenda for Sustainable Development" in 2015, comprising of 17 goals targeting social, environmental, and economic issues. Among these goals, Goal 4 aims to improve the quality of education for all students. Target 4.7 of this global goal directly impacts curriculum, instruction, and educational policies as it aims to achieve the following (United Nations, 2015):

> By 2030, ensure that all learners acquire the knowledge and skills needed to promote sustainable development, including, among others, through education for sustainable development and sustainable lifestyles, human rights, gender equality, promotion of a culture of peace and non-violence, global citizenship and appreciation of cultural diversity and of culture's contribution to sustainable development.

Progress toward this target is monitored by evaluating how national educational policies, teacher education, curricula, and assessments reflect aspects of sustainable development and global citizenship (United Nations, n.d.). The Global Education Monitoring Report (UNESCO, 2023) indicated that many countries have taken substantial steps "in mainstreaming climate change in the curricula at all levels of education" (p. 3). However, only 38% of countries have specific strategies or policies for the Climate Change Communication and Education (CCE) initiative (UNESCO, 2021). To support the development of curricula with global dimensions, UNESCO provides guidelines and resources (e.g., *Sustainable Development Goals–Resources for Educators*, UNESCO).

In addition to the growing calls for internationalized curricula aimed at fostering global competencies and citizenship, there is increasing support for the concept of a borderless curriculum, particularly with the advancements in technology that made this approach more feasible (Dube et al., 2023a, 2023b). In the context of teacher education, Dube and Campbell (2023) described a collaborative project between a university in the United States and one in South Africa that leveraged technology to pursue a borderless curriculum. The authors argued that nationalized curricula restrict teaching and learning by limiting access to best educational practices from beyond national borders. In contrast, a borderless curriculum can promote awareness of global educational trends and practices while also preparing teachers for today's increasingly diverse classrooms. Dube and Campbell (2023) explained that this is particularly achievable in the posthuman era as technological platforms and virtual spaces now enable global connections regardless of geographical location. By taking advantage of these opportunities, a borderless curriculum can facilitate initiatives like dual degrees and cross-border teacher training programs. Such initiatives can expand the educational experience, foster engagement between students and teachers in different countries, broaden knowledge beyond national contexts, promote global collaboration, and reduce the need for costly physical exchanges.

Moreover, in today's digitally interconnected world, a borderless curriculum can bridge social and cultural divides by addressing not only educational gaps but also global crises and existential threats to humanity, such as war, political conflict, inequality, and climate change (Dube & Campbell, 2023; Dube et al., 2023b). Just as the use of technology during the coronavirus pandemic provided students with distance and continuous access to education, a borderless curriculum with online options can offer sustainable learning solutions (Dube et al., 2023a), providing students in conflict zones and refugee settings with opportunities for education. Such curricula can transcend national borders and offer flexible and accessible learning for students worldwide.

In the context of ELT, the British Council (2022) highlighted the efforts of Hà Ánh Phượng, a high school teacher in Vietnam who successfully implemented a borderless classroom model. By leveraging online platforms and conferencing tools, Phượng provided her students with opportunities to connect with classrooms in various parts of the world. This allowed them to collaborate on projects, engage in discussions, participate in virtual field trips, and invite guest speakers. Through action research, Phượng (2022) identified several challenges in implementing a borderless classroom model, including time zone differences, unreliable Internet connectivity, the risk of cyberbullying, and varying levels of English proficiency. Despite these hurdles, Phượng found that borderless classrooms offer significant benefits for ESL/EFL teaching, including enhanced language learning, greater intercultural awareness, and increased student engagement.

In summary, this section demonstrates that curricula are not isolated entities; rather, they are embedded within complex, multilayered contexts. They are influenced by a range of interconnected factors, including those related to students, teachers, classrooms, or programs, as well as broader macro and global trends and circumstances. Thus, understanding the curriculum context and examining the factors that could shape curriculum development and/or impact its implementation is essential. Chapter 7 offers suggestions for gathering context-specific information to inform and enhance curriculum development.

The Purposes of Language Curricula

The design of a language curriculum is generally influenced by the context it operates within, the purpose it intends to fulfill, the student population it serves, and the philosophies its stakeholders hold. Fundamentally, the goal of any language curriculum is to enable effective communication in the target language. However, this goal must be further specified to offer targeted learning experiences that help students achieve specific communicative objectives. Are students learning English as a foreign or second language for general purposes? If so, what exactly are these "general" purposes? Alternatively, are they learning English to address more specific needs, such as pursuing study or work in the target language? In the ELT field, these distinctions are typically categorized into two main areas: English for General Purposes (EGP) and English for Specific Purposes (ESP). ESP encompasses several branches, including one of particular interest: English for Academic Purposes (EAP). The following discussion will provide an overview of EGP and ESP/EAP.

English for General Purposes

EGP in Theory

EGP is a broad domain within ELT that covers foundational aspects of language learning, in contrast to ESP and EAP, which focus on specific professional or academic language needs. EGP courses are typically designed to provide learners with the language skills necessary for general communication. These courses are commonly offered as part of an English language program or institute in ESL or EFL contexts or as a compulsory school subject, especially in EFL settings. An EGP course might focus on specific language skills, such as reading, writing, listening, or speaking, or on individual language components like grammar, pronunciation, or vocabulary. Alternatively, it may provide an integrated skills curriculum where these areas are taught concurrently. The ultimate goal of an EGP course, in theory, is to develop learners' general language proficiency rather than skills tailored to professional or academic contexts.

EGP in Practice

Although labeled as "general," the nature of an EGP course can vary widely depending on its purpose, target audience, design, and other context-specific factors. For instance, an EGP course may aim to develop basic English language skills or serve as a foundation for learners before they transition to ESP courses. In addition, as mentioned previously, it could be taken as a mandatory school subject.

In practice, how an EGP curriculum unfolds in the micro context is often shaped by nano-level factors, such as teachers' backgrounds, beliefs, and approaches to instruction. For example, studies examining EGP as a compulsory school subject (e.g., Akbari, 2015; Ghorbani, 2009; Huang & Yang, 2020) have found that some teachers tend to focus on specific language skills or areas, such as grammar, reading, or vocabulary, while neglecting or downplaying others, particularly listening and speaking. Additionally, teachers may prioritize preparing students for standardized national exams or teach only what the textbook has to offer.

The design of an EGP curriculum is also shaped by its meso and macro contexts, which can affect its "general" nature and blur the distinction between EGP and ESP/EAP. As an example, consider the overall goals of the General English curriculum for secondary students, as designed by the Madhya Pradesh Board of Secondary Education (MPBSE) in Madhya Pradesh, India (MPBSE, n.d., p. 9):

a. to enable the learner to communicate effectively and appropriately in real life situations
b. to use English effectively for study purposes across the curriculum
c. to develop interest in and appreciation of Literature
d. to develop and integrate the use of the four language skills[,] i.e. Reading, Listening, Speaking and Writing
e. to revise and reinforce structure already learnt

In addition to these goal statements, the MPBSE curriculum guide lists an extensive set of specific objectives related to reading, writing, listening, and speaking skills. These objectives range from general competence (e.g., being able to comprehend text) to academic and study skills (e.g., drawing inferences and conclusions, note-taking, summarizing, and consulting graphs and charts). Other objectives also target attitudinal change to foster "ethical, moral, national and cultural values through various forms of literature" as well as creative expression to enable students to "write an original, dialogue, story one-act play, poems etc." (MPBSE, n.d., p. 10). The specified assignments also vary from writing formal and informal letters; to reading, analyzing, and responding to literary texts; to completing grammar translation exercises from the native language into English. This EGP curriculum targets more than just "general" English language skills for everyday communication. Given that this curriculum is designed for secondary school students, it makes sense to have some focus on academic language and study skills. The literary element of the EGP curriculum can perhaps be explained by digging deeper into the specific sociocultural context of the curriculum, including the stakeholders' values and beliefs.

EGP Limitations and Challenges

General English language courses face the risk of failing to address specific student needs. The general approach or lack of focus may lead to teaching "too much, e.g., vocabulary, skills, registers or styles some learners do not need, and too little, e.g., omitting lexis and genres that they do" (Long, 2005, p. 19). As a result, when learning does not translate into real-world applications, it becomes ineffective and meaningless. Identifying learners' communicative goals is essential for tailoring an EGP curriculum to better meet their specific needs. For this reason, many scholars in ELT reject the one-size-fits-all approach, emphasizing that any language curriculum should be designed to serve specific purposes (Basturkmen, 2024; Belcher, 2009; Hutchinson & Waters, 1987; Long, 2005). This is accomplished through a comprehensive approach to curriculum development that prioritizes students' needs (e.g., Graves, 2000; Macalister & Nation, 2020; Richards, 2017), resulting in targeted and meaningful learning experiences (approaches to language curriculum development are discussed in the following chapter).

English for Specific Purposes

Overview of ESP

In contrast to "general" English, English for Specific Purposes (ESP) focuses on teaching and learning English for "specific" academic or professional purposes. ESP is typically divided into two broad categories: English for Occupational Purposes (EOP) and English for Academic Purposes (EAP) (Hutchinson & Waters, 1987; Strevens, 1977; Dudley-Evans & St. John, 1998). EOP is often subcategorized into specialized areas of English to meet specific occupational or professional needs such as English for Legal Purposes, English for Business Purposes, and English for Medical Purposes (Belcher, 2009). EAP generally involves language curricula or programs designed to prepare students for academic studies in English and/or to support their navigation of disciplinary language and discourse. Thus, EAP courses may be taken prior to or alongside academic studies. With the rise of educational models such as EMI (Galloway & Rose, 2021; Wingate, 2022) and pathway or bridge programs (Agosti & Bernat, 2018, Elturki, 2021a), EAP has become a vital component of many colleges and universities worldwide.

In their discussion of the origin and nature of ESP, Hutchinson and Waters (1987) noted that post-WWII economic and technological developments, along with English being the lingua franca of technology and commerce, created a demand not only for basic language skills but also for the ability to use and understand English in specialized contexts. This necessitated investigating learners' language needs and the specific demands of the target situation to inform ESP course design, including materials and instruction. The focus and content of ESP courses and materials have evolved over the years in five stages, as described by Hutchinson and Waters (1987):

- Stage 1: Using register analysis to identify and prioritize salient grammatical forms and vocabulary specific to different registers (e.g., medicine versus business) (e.g., Ewer & Latorre, 1967)
- Stage 2: Shifting from analyzing language at the sentence level to analyzing language at the discourse level through rhetorical or discourse analysis to uncover organizational patterns common within specific fields (e.g., Allen & Widdowson, 1974; Trimble, 1985)
- Stage 3: Analyzing the target situation to identify language structures and functions commonly encountered in specific communicative situations (e.g., Munby, 1978)
- Stage 4: Emphasizing a skills-centered approach to equip students with strategies applicable to any information processing, regardless of the register or discourse of the target situation (e.g., Frydenberg, 1982)
- Stage 5: Taking a learner-centered approach that considers learners' needs, the learning environment, and the target situation throughout the course design and implementation process (e.g., Hutchinson & Waters, 1987)

These developments reflect the syllabus design era in ELT, which resulted in the creation of various types of syllabi, as detailed in Table 1.1 of Chapter 1. They illustrate a shift in the assumptions about what constitutes an ESP curriculum, evolving from a narrow focus on grammatical forms, lexical items, and communicative functions to a more comprehensive approach that considers a range of factors affecting curriculum and instruction.

Current Research and Practice in ESP/EAP

ESP/EAP has become central to ELT due to increased mobility for study and work as well as growing linguistic diversity in academic institutions and the workplace. Current research and pedagogy in

ESP/EAP are supported by extensive literature and draw on various approaches and tools. Needs analysis remains crucial for understanding learners, teaching contexts, and target situations (Brown, 2009; Basturkmen, 2010; Dudley-Evans & St. John, 1998; Flowerdew, 2012). Common methods for needs analysis involve interviews, questionnaires, surveys, observations, and analysis of language samples and other artifacts (Serafini et al., 2015) (needs analysis is discussed further in Chapter 7). Genre analysis and corpus analysis are widely used in ESP/EAP as research methodologies, means of needs assessment, and instructional approaches. These methods help to understand how language is constructed within specific discourse communities. Consequently, they aid in identifying the linguistic features, language functions, and genres typical of a particular discipline or profession. This information can then be incorporated into ESP/EAP curriculum and instruction.

Genre Analysis

Genre analysis examines how writers and speakers within specific disciplines or rhetorical situations communicate their ideas to their intended audience and achieve their purpose. Swales (1990) introduced the CARS (Create A Research Space) model for analyzing research article introductions, revealing that scholars use specific rhetorical moves to establish authority, justify their inquiry, and articulate their research purpose. Similarly, Bhatia (1993) proposed a comprehensive framework for genre analysis that begins with broad steps, such as contextualizing texts and reviewing relevant literature, and progresses to a detailed analysis of linguistic features and expert insights. He applied this framework to genres such as sales letters and job application letters, demonstrating how rhetorical moves like establishing credentials and introducing offers are used to persuade and achieve specific communicative goals.

The study of rhetorical moves and strategies, which builds on the seminal works of Swales and Bhatia, has become a significant area of ESP/EAP research (Casal & Kessler, 2023) that offers useful insights into language use and variations across disciplines and types of communication (e.g., Basturkmen, 2009, 2012; Connor, 2000; Fryer, 2012; Kanoksilapatham, 2005; Kessler, 2020; Kuteeva & McGrath, 2015; Parkinson, 2017; Yoon & Casal, 2020). In addition to its importance as a research tool and means for needs assessment, genre analysis as a pedagogy is suggested to enhance learners' genre awareness, enable them to develop genre-specific knowledge and skills, and improve their ability to communicate effectively within particular genres (Hyon, 2018; Tardy, 2019).

Corpus Analysis

The study of corpora—large collections of texts—using concordance software has also been instrumental for ESP/EAP. Corpus tools and methodologies help identify recurring language patterns such vocabulary, multiword sequences, grammatical structures, and discourse markers within similar and across different contexts (Biber, 2006; Hyland, 2022; Thompson, 2022). Corpus-based research has revealed variations in multiword patterns across disciplinary writing (e.g., Hyland, 2008) and in both spoken and written discourses (e.g., Biber, 2009), including textbooks and university instruction (e.g., Biber et al., 2004). It has also shed light on disciplinary practices, such as how arguments are constructed within specific fields (e.g., Hyland, 2011).

Furthermore, corpus data has been important for creating educational materials and informing curriculum development. Staples (2019), for example, utilized corpus methodologies in the context of healthcare communication to assess the pronunciation needs of international nurses and develop a tailored curriculum. Corpus data has also been used to produce wordlists, including the Academic Word List (AWL) (Coxhead, 2000), as well as specialized vocabulary lists such as the marine engineering wordlist (Đurović, 2021) and the plumbing wordlist (Coxhead & Demecheleer, 2018). Moreover, corpus applications extend into the classroom to support learning (Römer, 2011). Indirect applications involve teachers using or compiling corpora to create instructional materials, such as vocabulary lists or collocations, and designing exercises for students, such as analyzing concordance lines to identify specific language patterns. A more hands-on approach to corpus pedagogy allows students to interact directly with corpus tools. This has become more accessible with free online corpus platforms such as the Michigan Corpus of Upper-Level Student Papers (MICUSP) and the Michigan Corpus of Academic Spoken English (MICASE). The practice of students working with corpus data is commonly known as data-driven learning (Johns, 1994).

Integrated Genre and Corpus Analysis

Combining genre and corpus analyses provides a comprehensive approach to text analysis, offering both bottom-up and top-down insights into language use (Flowerdew, 2005). For instance, Zhang (2023) employed corpus- and genre-based discourse analysis to examine citation patterns and authorial stances in engineering research articles written by students and expert writers. The quantitative and qualitative data obtained from this integrated approach revealed "not only the connections between the citation and stance patterns and the key rhetorical moves of a part-genre [Introduction-Methods-Discussion] but also the variations in student and expert writers' presentation of authorial stance in citations across part-genres" (Zhang, 2023, p. 146). For ESP/EAP pedagogical implications, this research suggested that instruction on citation styles should extend beyond formatting, quoting, and paraphrasing strategies. It should also include training students on how to effectively express their authorial stance when incorporating sources into their own texts.

This integrated approach to text analysis is also applied in the classroom to help students develop a deeper understanding of linguistic patterns and rhetorical structures. Dong and Lu (2020), for example, describe a set of corpus-based genre analysis activities that students engaged in to explore rhetorical structures. These activities were found to be effective in enhancing students' competence in discipline-specific genres.

Limitations of Textual Focus and Alternatives

While there is no doubt that corpus and genre research and pedagogies have been valuable for ESP/EAP, there are also critical voices concerned that these approaches place excessive emphasis on textual knowledge while disregarding contextual knowledge (Bhatia, 2010, 2019; Dressen-Hammouda, 2013; Hyland, 2002, 2003; Huhta et al., 2013). Contextual knowledge refers to an understanding of the social and cultural practices surrounding language use within specific academic or professional settings. Huhta et al. (2013), for instance, maintained that ESP should pay attention to "the dynamic communication practices of particular professional discourse communities rather than the language associated with a particular professional group" (p. 36). Along the same lines, Bhatia (2019) argued that "professional communication is not simply a matter of putting words together in a grammatically accurate and rhetorically coherent text, but, more importantly, a matter of performance by members of specific professional communities in relevant contexts of their everyday practice" (p. 37). These perspectives are supported by findings in Warren (2014), which examined meeting-related communication in Hong Kong. The study identified challenges professionals faced during meetings, including understanding diverse accents, presenting persuasive arguments, and interrupting speakers in a professional manner (Warren, 2014).

In order to align "with the demands of global professional communication in the 21st century" (p. 285), Le (2021) summarized key competencies that the ESP/EAP curriculum should address beyond linguistic knowledge. These include "knowledge of the workplace culture [or the academic setting] and interlocutors, strategic communicative competence, pragmatic competence, or pragmalinguistic and sociopragmatic skills" (p. 284). This brings us to ethnography as a growing area of ESP research that goes beyond the analysis of texts and genres (Hyland, 2022). Simply put, an ethnographic approach allows for a sustained and deeper examination of the sociocultural context in which language is used by integrating various methods such as observations and interviews, alongside text analysis (Dressen-Hammouda, 2025; Hyland, 2022). As a research approach to ESP/EAP, ethnography has been utilized to study different aspects of professional and disciplinary communicative events and discourse processes (e.g., Dahm et al., 2022; Huang & Wible, 2024; Flowerdew & Wan, 2006, 2010; Fraiberg, 2018), as well as academic writing (Guillén-Galve & Bocanegra-Valle, 2021; Paltridge et al., 2016).

Emerging Trends in ESP/EAP Curriculum and Instruction

ESP/EAP curriculum development and implementation can draw on elements of genre and corpus analysis, as well as other ELT approaches such as communicative language teaching, project-based learning, and task-based learning (Hyland, 2022). Gvelesiani (2023) highlighted additional methods and strategies for ESP to better address the needs of 21st-century classrooms. She rationalized that macro-level factors, such as mobility and permanent migration due to regional conflicts, wars, and natural disasters, have led to "different minority groups [settling] in new countries and [making] attempts at being incorporated into a mainstream society" (p. 25). Consequently, this has increased the number of multilingual students around the globe. To support and leverage multilingualism, Gvelesiani (2023) proposed integrating translation, heteroglossia (i.e., the coexistence and interaction of multiple languages within the classroom), code-switching, and translanguaging into ESP curriculum and instruction. In brief, translation assists students in deconstructing and comprehending specialized texts. Additionally, incorporating practices such as heteroglossia, code-switching, and translanguaging into tasks and discussions promotes engagement, inclusion, and learning, while enhancing learners' proficiency in the target language (see Gvelesiani, 2023 for sample activities).

To conclude, effective language curriculum development and implementation—whether focused on EGP or ESP/ESP—depends on understanding and addressing the specific needs of learners, along with considering potential contextual factors that may impact curriculum effectiveness. The research methodologies and pedagogical practices highlighted above can be applied to any language curriculum, whether general or specialized, to enhance its relevance and success.

After you read, consider the following questions:

1. Identify and reflect on factors at various levels that may have impacted your experience as a student or teacher. Consider factors at the nano (individual), micro (classroom), meso (institutional), macro (community/society), and supra (global) levels. How did these factors influence your educational experience or teaching practices?
2. Explore how the United Nations Sustainable Development Goals [https://sdgs.un.org/goals, *Sustainable Development Goals,* hereafter SDG] can inform language curriculum development, and then address the following questions:
    a. How can integrating the SDGs into language curricula enhance the "supra" dimension and engage students with their broader "macro" context, such as community, society, or culture? How might you use the SDGs to promote awareness of global issues?
    b. Which educational philosophies discussed in Chapter 2 best align with the goals of the SDGs?

c. What instructional methods would be most effective in supporting teaching and learning within this paradigm?

3. How might the concept of a borderless curriculum influence curriculum development in your educational context, and how can technology and online tools be leveraged to support its goals? What potential challenges might arise in implementing a borderless curriculum, and how could these be addressed?

4. Select at least two articles from the list below. Summarize the main context and issues discussed in each article. How do these issues relate to the topics covered in this chapter?

   a. Soliman, R., & Shaker, H. S. (2022). The embedded ideology in English and history textbooks at the public high schools in Egypt. *Port Said Journal of Educational Research*, *1*(1), 60–112. https://psjer.journals.ekb.eg/article_260704_46f6ee02ad1378cb87f719420c02d16d.pdf

   b. Bümen, N. T., Çakar, E., & Yildiz, D. G. (2014). Curriculum fidelity and factors affecting fidelity in the Turkish context. *Educational Sciences: Theory and Practice*, *14*(1), 219–228. https://files.eric.ed.gov/fulltext/EJ1038715.pdf

   c. Ali, M. M. (2010). Revisiting English language teaching (ELT) curriculum design: How appropriate is Bangladesh higher secondary level national ELT curriculum as a learner-centred one? *IIUC Studies, 7,* 283–296. https://banglajol.info/index.php/IIUCS/article/view/12494

   d. Wang, H. (2010). Translating policies into practice: The role of middle-level administrators in language curriculum implementation. *Curriculum Journal*, *21*(2), 123–140. https://doi.org/10.1080/09585171003802637

   e. Ellili-Cherif, M., & Hadba, H. M. (2017). Fidelity to and satisfaction with prescribed curriculum in an Arab educational context: ESL teachers' perspective. *The Curriculum Journal*, *28*(3), 367–388. https://doi.org/10.1080/09585176.2016.1240885

5. Choose one of the following tasks based on what is available to you:
    a. Conduct an interview with at least two international students at your institution to explore their experiences with EAP/ESP. Your questions should include nano-level inquiries about their goals for studying English and how their experiences at the micro and meso levels support these goals. Share your findings with a classmate.
    b. Interview at least two ESL/EFL teachers about their experiences teaching English. Your interview questions should focus on their experiences with teaching EGP, EAP, and/or ESP, including questions about the specific contexts of their teaching. Share your findings with a classmate.
    c. Find 1–2 syllabi for EGP, EAP, and/or ESP courses and conduct a syllabus analysis. Identify the purpose of the course and evaluate how the syllabus content supports this purpose. Share your findings with a classmate.

Chapter 4

Curriculum Development Models and Approaches

Before you read, reflect on the following questions:

1. What is a curriculum model? What does a model of curriculum development specify?
2. How would you approach a curriculum development task (e.g., course, unit, lesson, or activity)? What specific steps would you take to complete the task? Why do you choose this approach?
3. What role do you believe teachers should play in curriculum development at the program level?
4. Based on your own perspective, which do you think is more ideal for guiding teaching and learning: (a) a curriculum plan that outlines specific objectives and related elements, or (b) a curriculum plan that evolves from the actual teaching situation? Why do you prefer the approach you selected?

Chapter 4 begins with a historical account of curriculum development models that have established the fundamentals of curriculum making and continue to influence contemporary practices. It also highlights efforts to improve the accessibility and inclusion of curricula. The chapter then explores historical and current approaches to language curriculum development.

Curriculum Development Models in Education

Curriculum development is the process of thoughtfully planning and piecing out curricular elements to create a meaningful, coherent whole. It involves identifying the knowledge and skills students need, determining the necessary experiences for effective teaching and learning, and establishing assessment means to measure the effectiveness of these experiences. Various models exist to guide curriculum planning, implementation, and evaluation. Curriculum models or paradigms, as explained by Wheeler (1976), "imply decisions about what variables and what interrelationships are important" (p. 52). While many models share common elements and procedures—such as defining goals and objectives, selecting and organizing content, and determining assessment practices—there are differences in the emphasis and prioritization of these elements, the interrelationships among them, and the decision-making processes involved (Taba, 1962). The role of the teacher in curriculum development also varies among models.

The discussion below highlights six models of curriculum development from the field of education. These models have significantly contributed to the practice of curriculum development and laid the foundation for contemporary efforts. Many of these models consider curriculum development a scientific endeavor. In 1918, the American educationist Franklin Bobbitt advocated for treating curriculum development as a scientific undertaking. His seminal book, *The Curriculum* (1918), followed by *How to Make a Curriculum* (1924), argued for the development of scientific-based techniques that would guide curriculum creation. Bobbitt (1918) criticized the education system of his time for lacking clear objectives to direct teaching and learning. He stated:

> So long as objectives are but vague guesses, or not even that, there can be no demand for anything but vague guesses as to means and procedures. But the era of contentment with large, undefined purposes is rapidly passing. An age of science is demanding exactness and particularity. (Bobbitt, 1918, p. 41)

Bobbitt (1918, 1924) emphasized that curricula should have well-defined objectives based on an understanding of the knowledge and skills needed by students in a given society. As will be demonstrated, many of the highlighted models are based on this premise. However, there are also models that advocate for curriculum emerging organically from the teaching and learning process. This subsection highlights the features of six curriculum development models proposed by pioneer scholars in curriculum studies.

Tyler's Model: Simple and Rational

Influenced by Bobbit, Ralph Tyler (1949/2013) was one of the earliest curriculum scholars. He put together a simple yet systematic framework for curriculum development in his influential book, ***Basic Principles of Curriculum and Instruction***. The model consists of four guiding questions (p. 1):

1. What educational purposes should the school seek to attain?
2. What educational experiences can be provided that are likely to attain these purposes?
3. How can these educational experiences be effectively organized?
4. How can we determine whether these purposes are being attained?

Visually, Tyler's model can be represented as four sequential steps, as demonstrated in Figure 4.1.

The first fundamental step in Tyler's model is to communicate the overall educational purposes of a given program and formulate objectives accordingly. To emphasize the importance of objectives as the starting point of the curriculum development process and their role in shaping all subsequent curricular elements, Tyler (1949/2013, p. 3) elaborated that:

> These educational objectives become criteria by which materials are selected, content is outlined, instructional procedures are developed, and tests and examinations are prepared. All aspects

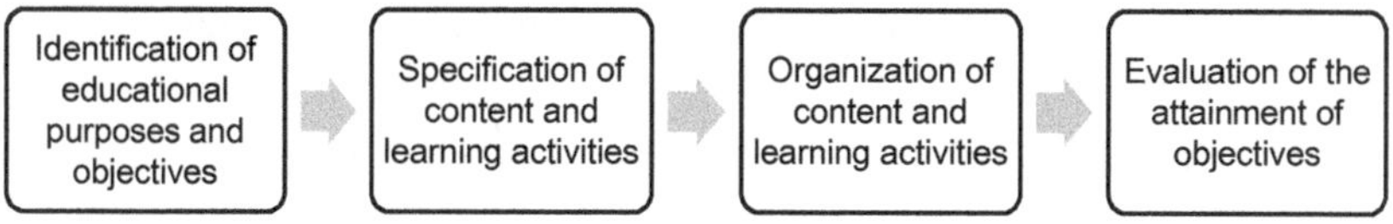

Figure 4.1. A Visualization of Tyler's Curriculum Model

> of the educational program are really means to accomplish basic educational purposes. Hence, if we are to study an educational program systematically and intelligently we must first be sure as to the educational objectives aimed at.

This approach is characterized as deductive since the curriculum process starts with general premises (i.e., objectives) from which specific conclusions (e.g., content and activities) are drawn. Tyler suggested that the data sources for identifying school objectives include studies of learners' needs and how to meet these needs, contemporary life to identify relevant knowledge and skills, and information from subject matter specialists. After defining the desired objectives using these sources, Tyler advised refining and filtering the initial list by evaluating their usefulness and values according to the institution's philosophy of education and the literature on the psychology of learning (i.e., learning theories). To illustrate how philosophical perspectives influence curriculum developers, Tyler noted that a progressivist educator would use data on students' interests, goals, and problems to guide objective selection, whereas an essentialist educator would derive objectives from established bodies of knowledge.

Following the refinement of objectives, the next steps are to specify and organize instructional materials and learning activities in a meaningful way. Learning experiences for Tyler extend beyond content and activities to include "the external conditions in the environment" (p. 63) where learners interact. To achieve the desired objectives, learning experiences must be practical, meaningful, and engaging. They should foster logical thinking, problem-solving, information acquisition, and social attitudes. Additionally, they should be appropriate to students' backgrounds and levels of knowledge and designed to address or reinforce multiple objectives. Tyler proposed three guiding principles for effective organization of learning experiences:

1. Continuity: Implanting recurring opportunities to practice objectives
2. Sequence: Arranging objectives mindfully so learning experiences build progressively on one another
3. Integration: Connecting similar objectives across different subjects

The final stage in this framework is evaluation, which involves "finding out how far the learning experiences as developed and organized are actually producing the desired results" (p. 105). This includes collecting evidence on student performance or, as Tyler put it, "evidence about behavior changes in the students" (p. 107), reflecting the behavioral focus prevalent in U.S. education at the time. The ultimate goal of the evaluation phase is to analyze assessment data to identify strengths and weaknesses in the curriculum and make necessary improvements.

Although Tyler's model is widely accepted as a rational framework offering logical and practical steps for curriculum development, some critics argue that it constrains the teaching and learning process by enforcing predesignated objectives (Kliebard, 1970; Pinar, 1978). These views reject the idea of governing the curriculum with a fixed list of objectives, arguing instead that curricula should emerge from the actual teaching and learning experiences (Stenhouse, 1975). Despite these criticisms, Tyler's model has had a profound and lasting impact on education worldwide. In the foreword to the 2013 edition of Tyler's book, Peter Hlebowitsh noted:

> [The Tyler Rationale] put Ralph W. Tyler's name in permanent and powerful association with the concept of curriculum development. [It] gave curriculum developers an enduringly useful way to plan the conduct of the school. Tyler never conceived of it as the only way to do curriculum development work. But it was his way and it has, for five decades now, proven to be a valuable way for others as well. [The Tyler Rationale] has traveled far and wide, having found a readership across the world and having advanced curriculum development efforts in a variety of school settings, ranging from preschools to medical schools. (Tyler, 2013, p. vii)

Current educational practices, such as the U.S. K-12 Common Core State Standards, which specify what students should be able to do by the end of a course of study, lesson, or unit, are rooted in the rationale provided by Tyler's model (Gamson & Eckert, 2019). This pioneering work has also laid the foundation for subsequent curriculum models.

Taba's Model: Classroom Piloting

Another instrumental model to curriculum development, expanding on Tyler's (1949/2013), was proposed by Hilda Taba (1962) in her book *Curriculum Model: Theory and Practice*. Taba's (1962) model consists of the following seven steps (p. 12):

1. Diagnosis of needs
2. Formulation of objectives
3. Selection of content
4. Organization of content
5. Selection of learning experiences
6. Organization of learning experiences
7. Determination of what to evaluate and of the ways and means of doing it

Taba began her discussion by outlining key sources of data for determining the general aims of an educational institution, its specific curricular objectives, and the learning experiences it seeks to generate. These data sources include the analysis of the culture and society in which an institution operates (i.e., the macro context); the study of learners' needs, interests, and deficiencies; and the examination of subject matter to identify essential disciplinary knowledge and skills. This data helps form a holistic understanding of the nature and focus of the curriculum. The development of concrete curricular elements involves diagnosing learners' educational needs, assessing the classroom environment, and considering factors impacting the attainment of educational objectives.

Taba emphasized the importance of diagnosing needs as an essential and continuous step in all curriculum activities, including curriculum development and revision as well as the planning of instructional units and materials. She stated that "to keep the curriculum in tune with the needs of times and of students, and to help determine which objectives to stress, diagnosis should be a continuous part of ongoing curriculum and teaching" (p. 231). Taba suggested diagnostic tools such as classroom interviews, open-ended questions, recorded discussions, students' writing, and special assignments and tests.

Subsequent steps in Taba's model are similar to those in Tayler's (1949/2013), but Taba's model is distinct in its emphasis on creating and piloting curriculum units. These pilot units, developed by teachers and tested with actual students, allow for translating theoretical ideas into practical curricula and identifying issues before full implementation. This approach allows curriculum development to occur inductively, moving from specific units to a more general curriculum plan, with teachers playing a key role in the process. Taba (1962) noted that "in this sense, then, curriculum development should be an inductive process, beginning at the grass roots and with natural small units and proceeding into more general problems of over-all organization" (p. 345).

A major strength of Taba's model is its emphasis on testing conceptual and theoretical ideas as part of the curriculum development process before broader implementation, with teachers actively involved as curriculum developers. Taba argued that since teachers are most attuned to students' needs and are responsible for applying theoretical frameworks into practice, they should play a central role not only in curriculum implementation but also in its conceptualization and development. Although Taba's model is considered naturalistic, untraditional, and descriptive rather than prescriptive (Lunenburg, 2011), it has faced criticisms similar to Tyler's for relying on predefined objectives (Hunkins & Hammill, 1994). Nevertheless, Taba's model emphasized needs analysis as an essential and ongoing component of curriculum development, a procedure that remains integral to many contemporary practices.

Goodlad's Model: Values-Based

Building on Tyler's (1949/2013) model, John Goodlad, in Goodlad and Richter (1966), proposed a modified approach that, while sharing similar curricular elements, differs in its starting point. Unlike Tyler's model, which begins with identifying objectives, Goodlad's model starts with articulating *values*. Values are defined as beliefs about what "is good or bad, desirable or undesirable" (Goodlad & Richter, 1966, p. 16). Value statements may include aspirations like achieving world peace, increasing life expectancy, and promoting democracy. These values are derived from societal needs and serve as the foundation for setting educational goals aimed at helping individuals reach their potential and moving society forward. In contrast to Tyler's model, where values come later as a filtering measure for objectives, Goodlad posits that values should drive curriculum development from the outset.

The next phase in Goodlad's model involves specifying *educational aims*, which results in a "larger system of values that is to guide educational purposes" (Goodlad & Richter, 1966, p. 17). This is followed by formulating *educational objectives* that outline what students should know, do, or believe. Subsequently, *learning opportunities* (e.g., writing papers, reading plays, or conducting experiments) are identified. The final step involves *organizing centers for learning*, which specifies the learning opportunities (e.g., the use of a specific book or topic) to achieve educational aims. These last two elements are similar to what Tyler (1949/2013) referred to as learning experiences.

In addition to Goodlad's emphasis on using values as a primary source for deriving curricular elements, he also identified two additional data sources for refining educational aims and formulating objectives: *conventional wisdom* representing popular beliefs about education, and *funded knowledge* encompassing theoretical and empirical research on teaching and learning (Goodlad & Richter, 1966). Another key aspect of this model is that *evaluation* serves not only as a final step for assessing students' performance but also as an ongoing process to ensure that all curricular elements are kept in check and aligned with the established values. Evaluation, thus, functions as "reciprocal processes of derivation and evaluation" (Goodlad & Richter, 1966, p. 66) and involves a backward reevaluation to validate curricular elements and their relationships. Goodlad (1981) also advocated for teacher engagement in curriculum making, emphasizing that schools should allocate time and resources for teachers to engage in this process.

A major contribution of Goodlad's curriculum model is its emphasis on the influence of values and beliefs (i.e., philosophies) of stakeholders and society at large on curriculum making. Recognizing these values and beliefs as an essential first step is central to the entire process. While both the Goodlad and Tyler (1949/2013) models share similarities, Tyler's model, with its four basic questions and straightforward concepts, may come across as easier to implement. However, Goodlad's offers more than just a process for curriculum development; it presents a philosophy advocating for a humanistic curriculum rooted in human values, with the aim of nurturing each citizen's full potential and fostering a democratic society (Goodlad, 1967, 1968, 1994).

Nicholls and Nicholls' Model: A Cyclical Approach

Audrey Nicholls and Howard Nicholls (1972/2018) developed a cyclical model of curriculum, as presented in their book *Developing a Curriculum: A Practical Guide* (which was reissued in 2018). Their model views curriculum development as a dynamic and continuous process rather than a one-time activity. It consists of five stages arranged in a cyclical order:

1. Situation analysis
2. Selection of objectives
3. Selection and consideration of content
4. Selection and organization of methods
5. Evaluation

Stages two to five are consistent with the models discussed earlier. What distinguishes this model is its emphasis on situation analysis as a fundamental first step. Nicholls and Nicholls argued that curriculum planning should encompass a broader range of factors beyond merely diagnosing students' needs. They defined situation analysis as "an analysis of all the factors which make up the total situation followed by the use of knowledge and insights derived from this analysis in curriculum planning" (p. 21). While a deeper analysis is required when developing a fresh curriculum, this step can be less extensive when reevaluating an existing one. The cyclical nature of the model allows for insights gained from evaluation to inform further development or refinement of the curriculum.

Nicholls and Nicholls also advocated for teachers to play a major role in curriculum development. They noted involving teachers allows them to understand the rationale behind curricular choices and helps prevent the disconnect between theory and practice that often occurs in top-down decision-making processes. Furthermore, they viewed teacher participation as an opportunity for professional growth and ongoing education. This model expects teachers to conduct the situation analysis themselves. The authors justified this by stating that "the teacher is not only part of the whole situation but to some extent he [or she] is the controller of it, or at least some of it" (p. 24). Factors that make up a situation and should be analyzed in the planning stage include:

- The teacher: Self-analysis of personal capabilities and deficiencies
- The students: Identification of individual differences
- The students' environment: Considerations of family and peer group influences

- The school building: Evaluation of materials, equipment, and facilities
- The school climate: Examination of the values and philosophies of the school

Nicholls and Nicholls presented a systematic model of curriculum development as a process of continuous improvement that necessitates teacher involvement. However, the idea of teachers as curriculum developers is often a point of concern, as they need expertise, skills, time, and resources to fulfill this role effectively. These concerns, as clarified by Nicholls and Nicholls, can be addressed by integrating curriculum development into teacher education and training. Their participation in these activities should also be seen as venues for professional development.

Stenhouse's Model: Pedagogically Oriented

In *An Introduction to Curriculum Research and Development*, Lawrence Stenhouse (1975) critiqued curriculum models that emphasize the prespecification of educational objectives and the controlling role that these prescribed objectives play over the subsequent curricular elements. He argued that objective-based models confine education because the "prespecification of explicit goals prevents the teacher from taking advantage of instructional opportunities unexpectedly occurring in the classroom" (p. 73). Stenhouse was particularly concerned with the nature of objectives being exclusively behavioral, as such objectives focus on specifying the types of behaviors that demonstrate learning. Behavioral objectives were prevalent during that time. In fact, Tyler (1949/2013) believed that the purpose of education is "to bring about significant changes in the students' patterns of behavior" and, thus, "it becomes important to recognize that any statement of the objectives of the school should be statement of changes to take place in students" (p. 44). Stenhouse contended that specifying objectives in terms of behavior often overlooks or underemphasizes deep knowledge and understanding, as not all types of knowledge can be demonstrated through observable behaviors. Drawing on arguments from scholars who have similar concerns, Stenhouse (1975) explained:

> The translation of the deep structures of knowledge into behavioral objectives is one of the principal causes of the distortion of knowledge

> in schools. The filtering of knowledge through an analysis of objectives gives the school an authority and power over its students by setting arbitrary limits to speculation and by defining arbitrary solutions to unresolved problems of knowledge. (p. 86)

Instead of reducing objectives to behaviors, Stenhouse proposed that educational objectives or intentions should be articulated as principles, or what he termed "*principles of procedures*." His alternative curriculum model advocates for schools to establish principles for the following areas:

a. Curriculum planning: Creating principles for selecting content, developing teaching strategies, sequencing content, diagnosing individual student differences, and then differentiating curricular elements accordingly
b. Empirical study of the curriculum: Implementing principles for evaluating both students' and teachers' progress, assessing the feasibility of curriculum implementation in various educational situations (e.g., peer and group work), and gathering information on variations in learning and their causes
c. Justification of curriculum: Establishing principles for formulating curriculum intentions or aims that should be "accessible to critical scrutiny" (p. 5)

Unlike models that prescribe orderly steps for curriculum development—articulating objectives, arranging them into learning experiences, and evaluating them—Stenhouse's process model provides guidance through principles. This allows the curriculum to serve as an educational proposal that is tested and modified by the teacher in the classroom. In this sense, Stenhouse (1975) commented, "the process model is the evaluation of the implications of a proposal which has a high degree of flexibility within the limitations imposed by a broadly stated purpose" (p. 123). Additionally, unlike other curriculum models that incorporate the diagnosis of students' needs and interests as a major or subsidiary step, Stenhouse believed that teachers should choose content that they deem worthwhile and make it engaging. Teachers can also involve students in setting their own objectives to foster a range of relevant and meaningful activities. Since this curriculum model focuses on pedagogical procedures, Stenhouse greatly emphasized teacher engagement in the development process. To facilitate this, he advocated for incorporating sufficient time and opportunities for such work as part of teachers' professional development. He also called for teachers' participation in curriculum-related research activities, viewing "each classroom [as] a laboratory, [and] each teacher a member of the scientific community" (p. 142).

Stenhouse's critique of the objective-based models has faced its share of criticism. Crittenden (1979) raised several points against Stenhouse's rejection of objectives. While agreeing that focusing primarily on predetermined objectives can be restrictive, Crittenden argued that setting educational objectives or intended learning outcomes, especially in terms of behaviors, is unavoidable. He noted that Stenhouse condemned the interpretation of objectives based on narrowly defined behaviors, yet his "alternative for curriculum design cannot avoid reference to desired learning outcomes, and these cannot be recognized unless some range of behavior counts as evidence that they have been achieved" (Crittenden, 1979, p. 128). Crittenden also highlighted potential confusion surrounding the term ***behavioral objective***. He questioned whether it is used to describe learning as viewed by behaviorist theorists (i.e., an observable response to a stimulus representing a learning outcome) or as evidence that learning has occurred. When used as evidence, Crittenden (1979) argued that it necessitates the use of specific and accurate instruments to measure learning objectively. He further critiqued Stenhouse's principles of procedures, suggesting that these principles themselves should be accompanied by "criteria of achievement" (p. 171) to assess whether the teacher and learners are succeeding in their learning activities. Stenhouse responded to these criticisms in a 1980 article by differentiating between objectives and outcomes, acknowledging the importance of outcomes but maintaining his rejection of predesignated objectives (James, 2012). Despite these critiques, Stenhouse's work is believed to offer a fresh perspective on curriculum development and continues to influence pedagogy, curriculum development, and teacher research (Elliott & Norris, 2012).

Wiggins and McTighe's Curriculum Model: A Prioritizing Approach

In 1998, Grant Wiggins and Jay McTighe introduced a backward design model for curriculum development in their first edition of *Understanding by Design* (UbD). This approach emphasizes that the goal of education extends beyond merely helping students recall information; it aims to cultivate a deep understanding of "big ideas" that provide "meaning and connection to discrete facts and skills" (p. 5). The model also emphasizes the ability to transfer these big ideas across various subjects and settings. Examples of big ideas include important concepts, issues, processes, and themes. A deep understanding of big ideas is demonstrated through one's ability to explain, interpret, apply, share perspectives, empathize, and regulate one's own knowledge.

Approaching curriculum development backward allows teachers to sieve the essential big ideas that students need to understand by the end of a learning experience. Accordingly, the backward design to curriculum development starts by defining desired results and the evidence needed to demonstrate these results (outputs). This initial step helps prioritize what skills and knowledge to teach (inputs) and leads to the mindful selection and development of instructional materials, activities, and assessments. Wiggins and McTighe (2005) observed that teachers often begin planning with activities and materials rather than first considering the learning objectives they want to achieve. They argued that "lessons, units, and courses should be logically inferred from the results sought, not derived from the methods, books, and activities with which we are most comfortable" (p. 14). The three-stage backward design model proposed by McTighe and Wiggins (2012, pp. 2–6) includes:

1. Identifying desired results
    a. What should students know, understand, and be able to do?
    b. What is the ultimate transfer we seek as a result of this unit?
    c. What enduring understandings are desired?
    d. What essential questions will be explored in-depth and provide focus to all learning?
2. Determining assessment evidence
    a. How will we know if students have achieved the desired results?
    b. What will we accept as evidence of student understanding and their ability to use (transfer) their learning in new situations?
    c. How will we evaluate student performance in fair and consistent ways?

3. Developing a learning plan
   a. How will we support learners as they come to understand important ideas and processes?
   b. How will we prepare them to autonomously transfer their learning?
   c. What enabling knowledge and skills will students need to perform effectively and achieve desired results?
   d. What activities, sequence, and resources are best suited to accomplish our goals?

The first stage is guided by the overall curriculum goals, important subject knowledge, and standards. In the second stage, teachers determine assessment methods, such as traditional tests and quizzes, as well as performance tasks that are authentic and allow students to demonstrate their cumulative understanding at the end of a unit. The final stage involves selecting teaching strategies, activities, and materials that extend beyond simply presenting information or practicing basic skills. They should support meaning-making and the application of knowledge in different situations.

This model is intended primarily for teachers to help them develop curricular units, positioning them as both designers and assessors of learning. By following the three-stage process, teachers can plan instructional units based on a clear understanding of desired learning outcomes and how these outcomes will be demonstrated. Wiggins and McTighe (2005) noted that this approach shifts teachers' focus from merely covering extensive material to uncovering essential knowledge and skills. They argued that "teachers can never cover all of the facts and skills on a given topic, given time restrictions and content overload" (pp. 63–65).

Due to its technical nature and emphasis on pre-identifying outcomes to guide subsequent pedagogical and evaluative decisions, background design is often viewed as a recycled version of the Tyler 1949/2013 model (Cho & Allen, 2005; McCreary, 2022). Like Tyler's model, backward design has elicited varied reactions. Proponents appreciate its value in systematizing and rationalizing the curriculum while critics argue that it is overly prescriptive and restrictive to the teaching and learning process (Cho & Allen, 2005; McCreary, 2022). Furthermore, while this approach helps teachers identify, prioritize, and enhance understanding of important knowledge, it lacks specific guidance on how to effectively foster that understanding. The model's focus on prioritizing big ideas has also been challenged for its subjective nature; what is considered valuable knowledge can differ among teachers, students, and other stakeholders, potentially overlooking diverse sociocultural backgrounds and experiences (Cho & Allen, 2005).

Despite these limitations, the backward design model is widely used in curriculum development and improvement. Initially intended to enhance instructional practices at the micro level, the backward design model is now commonly applied at the meso and macro levels by many U.S. schools and districts to meet state standards (McTighe & Thomas, 2003). Beyond the U.S. and K-12 contexts, the model is also adopted in higher education and various ESL/EFL settings (e.g., Boozer & Carlson, 2015; Johnson et al., 2017; Llerena, 2020; Michael & Libarkin, 2016; Uluçınar, 2021).

Other Considerations for Curriculum Development

The curriculum development models discussed above focus on outlining systematic and purposeful processes for curriculum development. They do not specify the content or nature of curriculum elements but offer diverse perspectives on framing the overall process, emphasizing whether it should be linear, cyclical, backward, value-based, or grassroots. The generic nature of these models makes them applicable to a wide range of curriculum contexts. While these models emphasize the technical aspects of determining and organizing learning, it is also important to consult other frameworks that address factors such as diversity, accessibility, inclusion, and power sharing in curriculum development.

The Universal Design for Learning

The Universal Design for Learning (UDL) is a framework used by educators, curriculum developers, and researchers to "improve and optimize teaching and learning for all people based on scientific insights into how humans learn" (Center for Applied Special Technology [CAST], 2018). Table 4.1 presents UDL principles that can be consulted during the curriculum development process to ensure that the curriculum is accessible and inclusive. These principles provide guidance on implementing multiple opportunities for engagement, representation, as well as action and expression.

Table 4.1 CAST's Universal Design for Learning Framework

Principles	Guidelines	Checkpoints
Engagement	Provide options for recruiting interest	• Optimize individual choice and autonomy • Optimize relevance, value, and authenticity • Minimize threats and distractions
	Provide options for sustaining effort and persistence	• Heighten salience of goals and objectives • Vary demands and resources to optimize challenge • Foster collaboration and community • Increase mastery-oriented feedback
	Provide options for self-regulation	• Promote expectations and beliefs that optimize motivation • Facilitate personal coping skills and strategies • Develop self-assessment and reflection
Representation	Provide options for perception	• Offer ways of customizing the display of information • Offer alternatives for auditory information • Offer alternatives for visual information
	Provide options for language and symbols	• Clarify vocabulary and symbols • Clarify syntax and structure • Support decoding of text, mathematical notation, and symbols • Promote understanding across languages • Illustrate through multiple media
	Provide options for comprehension	• Activate or supply background knowledge • Highlight patterns, critical features, big ideas, and relationships • Guide information processing and visualization • Maximize transfer and generalization

Table 4.1 (*Continued*)

Principles	Guidelines	Checkpoints
Action and expression	Provide options for physical action	• Vary the methods for response and navigation • Optimize access to tools and assistive technologies
	Provide options for expression and communication	• Use multiple media for communication • Use multiple tools for construction and composition • Build fluencies with graduated levels of support for practice and performance
	Provide options for executive functions	• Guide appropriate goal-setting • Support planning and strategy development • Facilitate managing information and resources • Enhance capacity for monitoring progress

Utilizing UDL principles in curriculum planning and development can yield a curriculum with flexible and adaptable goals, instructional methods, materials, and assessments to accommodate diverse student needs (Hitchcock et al., 2002; Meo, 2008; Meyer & Rose, 2000; Rose et al., 2005; Wu, 2010).

UNESCO's Framework for a Quality Curriculum

UNESCO's International Bureau of Education offers a framework that outlines the features of effective curriculum development processes and quality curricula. To construct a quality curriculum (Table 4.2), the curriculum development process should be systematic, well-planned, cyclical, sustainable, and inclusive of various stakeholders (Stabback, 2016).

Many of these characteristics of a quality curriculum can be cultivated by adopting or adapting any of the models outlined earlier in this chapter as well as the procedures proposed in the subsequent chapters of this book.

Table 4.2 The UNESCO's Description of a Quality Curriculum (Stabback, 2016, p. 17)

- Values each [learner] and holds that every [learner] matters equally
- Is comprised of high quality "content" that is
  - Up-to-date and relevant
  - Suitably demanding
  - Appropriately sequenced and progressive
  - Balanced
  - Integrated
- Is well-organized and structured
  - Clearly documented
  - Comprises a number of inter-related components expressed in consistent and coherent documents
- Is underpinned by a set of theoretical and philosophical beliefs about how [students] learn

Curriculum Negotiation

While the models discussed above offer procedures to create curricula that are responsive to students' interests and needs, some scholars emphasize the importance of involving students in curriculum decision-making (Beane, 1997; Boomer et al., 1992; Bron et al., 2016). The co-construction approach to curriculum, often referred to as *curriculum negotiation* (Boomer, 1982; Boomer et al., 1992) or *curriculum integration* (Beane, 1997), promotes power sharing, democracy, and agency. Edwards (2011) defined curriculum negotiation as "a dynamic process in which what is taught and learned (the curriculum) is negotiated between teacher and students, rather than being solely pre-determined by the teacher" (p. 144). In this process, students, as primary stakeholders, are given a voice in making decisions about their learning. The extent and nature of student participation can be influenced by various factors at different contextual levels, including curriculum mandates such as standards, assessments, and prescribed materials, as well as students' age and language proficiency.

While students' perspectives on curriculum elements (e.g., themes and topics that they find interesting or skills that they wish to develop) can be gathered through surveys and interviews during the planning phase (Chapter 7), curriculum negotiation typically occurs at the micro level. In this context, the teacher and students work together to find common ground between the formal or planned curriculum and what students believe is worth learning. This negotiation is often facilitated through individual and group tasks as well as a whole-class discussion where the teacher leads the discussion and acts as the curriculum negotiator (Edwards, 2011; Hyun, 2006; van der Laan & Bron, 2018). During these activities, students have opportunities to formulate questions about the subject matter they wish to explore, propose themes and topics, and review any existing curriculum requirements. Laan and Bron (2018) identified several factors in their curriculum intentions model that influence the negotiation process, which, in turn, shapes the operational and attained curricula. These factors include external curriculum requirements, teachers' professional knowledge and experience, and students' prior learning experiences, sociocultural backgrounds, and goals and interests. This collaborative approach is used to set the overall focus of the curriculum, and it is also applied to establish classroom rules and policies, plan lessons and units, and determine projects and evaluation criteria.

In conclusion, creating a well-organized and structured curriculum with high-quality content, grounded in philosophical and theoretical principles of learning, can be accomplished by utilizing one or a combination of the curriculum development models discussed in this chapter. The curriculum development process should ensure that the curriculum is inclusive, allowing "all students, regardless of ability, ethnicity, cultural background, gender, socio-economic circumstances or geographical location, to reach their individual potential as learners, and to develop their capabilities to the full" (Stabback, 2016, p. 18). It should also support differentiation by enabling teachers to adapt the curriculum to meet the needs of their students. Inclusion in curriculum development can be facilitated by collecting data on the intended student population and the local context of the curriculum (see Chapter 7 for tools and methods). Differentiation can be achieved through flexible curriculum plans that allow teachers to adapt instruction to meet students where they are (discussed further in Chapter 8 and Chapter 9). Additionally, providing students with opportunities to shape the curriculum can make the learning experience more relevant and meaningful, foster a stronger partnership between teachers and students, and encourage shared responsibility for learning (Edwards, 2011).

Curriculum Development Approaches in ELT

Historical Trends and a Paradigm Shift

A plethora of curriculum models in education have been developed over the years to guide the *totality* of the teaching and learning experiences. Curriculum efforts in ELT did not parallel those in broader education until the mid-1980s, when the field began to move away from a narrow to a more comprehensive view of curriculum.

A Narrower View of Language Curricula

Earlier ELT curricular efforts focused on specific aspects such as teaching methods, syllabus design, testing, and needs analysis (Richards, 1984). Between the 1940s and the 1980s, the ELT field was preoccupied with developing specific teaching procedures, giving rise to a range of methods, such as the Audiolingual Method, the Reading Method, and Total Physical Response (Brown, 2002). These methods prescribed fixed sets of instructional procedures and techniques. While such efforts have undoubtedly enriched our current repertoire of teaching practices, no single method can accommodate all teaching styles, instructional contexts, and learning needs. As Nunan (1991) remarked, "there never was and probably never will be a method for all" (p. 228). Kumaravadivelu (1994) further criticized such methods as artificial, arguing that they do not reflect the complex realities that teachers face in the classroom. What should guide pedagogical practices in the post-method era, Kumaravadivelu (2006b, 2001) urged, are the principles of:

- Particularity: Taking into account the local context
- Practicality: Basing instructional decisions on reflection, experience, and intuition
- Possibility: Recognizing the experiences that both the teacher and students bring to the classroom, which are shaped by their social, political, and economic contexts

The focus on developing new teaching methods began to fade in the late 1980s. As inquiry in L2 teaching and learning increased, the teaching profession shifted from reliance on specific teaching methods to grounding instruction in teaching approaches (Brown, 2002). An approach, as discussed in Chapter 2 of this book, provides the theoretical basis and rationale for pedagogical practices.

In addition to the prolonged focus on methods, curriculum development efforts were heavily focused on syllabus design, particularly in the 1970s, leading to various types of language syllabi. Traditionally, as explained earlier in this book, the ELT syllabus design process focused primarily on content specification and sequencing. In 1984, the British Council published *Curriculum and Syllabus Design in ELT,* a report from a two-week residential seminar. The following excerpt from the report highlights the concerns of ELT teachers and administrators at that time (Toney, 1984, p. 5):

> The title of this year's seminar reflects the broader concerns of practitioners in the English Language Teaching profession. Teachers and academics alike are becoming increasingly interested in trying to grasp the teaching/learning situation as a whole. This means looking beyond the narrow confines of one approach or one method and trying to include the practice and content of language learning, as well as the evaluation of these, in one coherent whole.

In the same year, Richards (1984) published an article titled "Language Curriculum Development," in which he criticized language curriculum development for its narrow focus on syllabus design and its misalignment with advancements in education. He argued that "the lack of rigor and accountability in many language teaching programs" might stem from not viewing language curriculum development as a systematic, interrelated set of processes (Richards, 1984, p. 1). The push for accountability driven by government reforms, accrediting agencies, international and national standards, and competency testing has required language programs and practitioners to demonstrate learning outcomes through measurable objectives and assessments (Bärenfänger & Tschirner, 2008; Philips, 2003; Norris, 2016; Richards, 1984). These trends necessitated a more comprehensive approach to language curricula. As a result, rather than focusing solely on individual aspects of teaching and learning, several works in ELT began to present curriculum development as a holistic process comprised of interdependent elements.

A Comprehensive Look at Language Curricula

In the 1984 article referenced above, Richards offered one of the earlier frameworks to guide language curriculum development, which he described as "as a system of interrelated [. . .] activities" (p. 2) consisting of:

1. Needs analysis
2. Objectives

3. Content and methodology
4. Evaluation

These activities are similar to Taba's (1962) model of curriculum development. Richards (1984), in fact, made explicit comparisons between his framework and Taba's seven-step model. The first two steps in both models involve analyzing needs and then formulating objectives accordingly. The subsequent third and fourth steps in Taba's focus on selecting and organizing content, which, as Richards noted, have traditionally been the focus of ELT syllabus design. The fifth and sixth phases in Taba's model address the selection and organization of learning experiences, which, as Richards (1984) explained, generally correspond to what constitutes a method in ELT. In his framework, Richards simplified these stages by combining Taba's activities on selecting and organizing content and learning experiences into a single step encompassing content and methodology. Evaluation is the final procedure in both Richards' and Taba's frameworks.

Several notable works have further developed comprehensive approaches to ELT curriculum development. Brown's *The Elements of Language Curriculum: A Systematic Approach to Program Development* (1995) outlines six components essential for developing and maintaining language curricula:

1. Needs analysis
2. Goals and objectives
3. Testing
4. Materials
5. Teaching
6. Evaluation

In *Designing Language Courses: A Guide for Teachers*, Graves (2000) presents "a systems approach" to guide language teachers in the following areas:

1. Defining the context
2. Articulating beliefs
3. Assessing needs
4. Formulating goals and objectives

5. Developing materials
6. Designing an assessment plan
7. Organizing the course
8. Conceptualizing content

Richards published the first edition of *Curriculum Development in Language Teaching* in 2001 and a revised second edition in 2017. In these editions, he provides a comprehensive account of various processes involved in language curriculum development and implementation, including procedures for needs analysis, goals and outcomes, methods, materials, and evaluation.

Nation and Macalister contributed the first edition of *Language Curriculum Design* in 2010 and a second revised edition in 2020 (Macalister & Nation, 2020). In these works, they outline seven steps for language curriculum development, which are as follows:

1. Examining the environment
2. Assessing needs
3. Deciding on principles
4. Setting goals and arranging the sequence of content
5. Designing the lesson format
6. Determining assessment procedures
7. Evaluating the course

These proposed approaches to language curriculum development share analogous interrelated elements, though they vary slightly in the sequence of processes. While there is a consensus that needs analysis is a fundamental initial step preceding the formulation of objectives, some approaches also emphasize additional preliminary measures, such as exploring beliefs and context (Graves, 2000) or examining the actual environment and identifying guiding principles (Nation & Macalister, 2010).

Brown (1995) presented curriculum development as a linear process, with evaluation as an ongoing activity "to constantly improve each element of a curriculum on the basis of what is known about all of the other elements, separately as well as collectively" (p. 24). Graves (2000), on the other hand, depicted her framework as a flow chart, illustrating that the process can begin at any point depending on what is most relevant to the individuals involved. She intentionally positioned articulating beliefs and defining the context at "the bottom of the chart to serve as the foundation for the other processes" (p. 3).

Additionally, while defining the context and analyzing the environment are highlighted as the initial steps in Graves (2000) and Nation and Macalister (2010), other frameworks incorporate the study of context or situation as a subprocess within the needs analysis phase. The step concerning the identification of principles is presented as a separate process in Nation and Macalister (2010). However, in other ELT curriculum models, drawing on principles is discussed either explicitly or implicitly within various phases of the development process. Unlike other frameworks, Brown (1995) suggested that, following the specification of goals and objectives, the development of tests should occur next to "shape [. . .] the expectations of the students and their teachers" (p. 22). This focus on testing is particularly relevant in the context of language program development, where establishing clarity on aspects such as placement, proficiency, and diagnostic testing can inform subsequent planning for materials and instruction.

Language Curriculum Development Recap

The process of language curriculum development and the elements prioritized have evolved over the years, resulting in three major approaches identified by Richards (2013): forward design, central design, and backward design. *Forward design* represents traditional practices where curriculum development begins with planning the syllabus content and sequence (i.e., input). This is followed by selecting suitable instructional methods, activities, and materials (i.e., teaching process) and finally determining how learning outcomes will be assessed (i.e., output).

Central design focuses primarily on planning instructional methods, activities, and techniques first, with content and assessment addressed subsequently. This approach reflects the methods era in the ELT field but remains relevant today. Richards (2013) noted that "research on teachers' practices reveals that teachers often follow a central design approach when they develop their lessons by first considering the activities and teaching procedures they will use" (p. 14). This approach represents aspects of Stenhouse's (1975) process model, where the curriculum emerges from teaching situations. It also allows for incorporating elements of curriculum negotiation in which students are given a voice in shaping the curriculum, leading to what is known in ELT as the negotiated syllabus (Breen & Littlejohn, 2000; Azarnoosh & Kargozari, 2018) and participatory curriculum (Auerbach, 1992).

Backward Design, the current prevalent approach, begins with identifying learning objectives and defining desired outcomes before planning content and instructional methods. This approach is reflected in the curriculum development frameworks of Brown (1995), Richards (1984, 2001, 2017), Nation and Macalister (2010), and Macalister and Nation (2020). It is grounded in the traditions of Tyler (1949/2013) and Taba (1962) and aligns with the backward design model proposed by Wiggins and McTighe (2005). The backward design aims to enhance accountability and efficiency in teaching and learning practices.

Common Types of Language Curricula

Language curricula vary widely in their design and implementation, often incorporating elements from different approaches and methods. Because L2 teaching and learning have long been rooted in practice, it can be unclear whether a particular teaching approach refers to methodology (i.e., the instructional techniques and procedures used in the classroom), design (i.e., the specific learning objectives and outcomes, content and sequence, and assessment), or both (Ellis, 2003). For example, task-based language teaching might suggest that the curriculum is developed around a series of tasks (design), or it might refer to the pedagogical practices employed by the teacher (methodology) to meet the objectives of a content-based curriculum or a communicative curriculum. An integrated-skills approach can refer to the design of a curriculum that incorporates receptive (listening and reading) and productive (speaking and writing) skills, as well as grammar and pronunciation, all within the same course (design). Alternatively, the curriculum might be designed as a discrete-skill course focusing on a particular language skill, such as listening, but the teacher uses an integrated-skills approach (methodology).

Adopting one of the comprehensive approaches to curriculum development discussed above allows for tackling the totality of the curriculum, including what students will learn, how this learning will be facilitated, and how effective these learning experiences are in achieving the desired outcomes. This allows for providing some clarification to whether a certain approach refers to curriculum design, methodology, or both. The following subsections provide a brief overview of some common language curricula.

Communicative Curriculum

Globalization and other supra-contextual factors have driven many countries to reform national EFL curricula by implementing communicative language curricula (e.g., Kirkgöz, 2019a; Li, 2016; Rahman, Islam, et al., 2019). Nonetheless, the term *communicative* is often used in a general sense without clear specifications of what constitutes a communicative curriculum. Graves and Garton (2017) noted that when governments introduce such reforms, they "rarely define what they mean by 'communicative'" (p. 447).

Breen and Candlin (1980) defined a communicative curriculum as one that focuses on "learning how to communicate effectively as a member of a particular socio-cultural group" (p. 90). A communicative curriculum identifies the types and extent of communicative situations students are likely to encounter and the knowledge and skills they need to handle those situations. It creates meaningful opportunities tailored to the communicative needs of the students, aiming to develop both productive and receptive language skills. Since the ultimate goal is effective communication in the target language, a communicative curriculum emphasizes practical communication over the rote memorization of grammar rules and contextualizes the learning of linguistic structures. It also integrates authentic materials, tasks, and assessment methods (Brown & Lee, 2015; Graves & Garton, 2017).

Content-Based Curriculum

Content-Based Instruction (CBI), or Content and Language Integrated Learning (CLIL), refers to approaches "that make a dual, though not necessarily equal, commitment to language- and content-learning objectives" (Grabe & Stoller, 2011, p. 155). CBI may represent a teaching philosophy, methodology, program framework, or curriculum design (Stryker & Leaver, 1997). It falls within the paradigms of communicative language teaching and constructivism (Brown & Bradford, 2017; Leaver & Stryker, 1989; Wesche, 2010), as the integration of language and content fosters meaningful learning that is relevant to learners' needs and interests (Dueñas, 2003; Grabe & Stoller, 1997).

The extent and nature of the integration of content and language vary based on learner needs, context, and educational goals. Met (1999) placed CBI on a continuum ranging from *language-driven* to *content-driven* approaches. Content-driven CBI emphasizes content learning and assesses students based on their content knowledge. In contrast, language-driven CBI prioritizes language acquisition and evaluates students on their language proficiency and skills. Depending on the focus—whether on content or language learning—the content may center around subject matter knowledge or relevant, intellectually engaging topics and themes (Met, 1999).

Brinton and colleagues (1989) identified three models of CBI: theme-based instruction, sheltered instruction, and adjunct instruction. Theme-based instruction centers around specific themes relevant to students' goals and interests. This model is integral to language curriculum design and is discussed below as a separate sub-category. Sheltered instruction, commonly used in mainstream education (Brinton et al., 1989; Stryker & Leaver, 1997), places students whose L1 is not the mainstream into separate groups or classes where content-area instruction is made accessible through comprehensible input (Krashen & Terrell, 1983). This model not only focuses on the subject matter but also helps learners develop academic and language skills specific to the subject, such as the language needed for mathematics. The adjunct instruction model of CBI, typically found in higher education, involves students taking both a subject course and a language course simultaneously (Brinton et al., 1989; Snow & Brinton, 1988). The language course is designed to support and reinforce the learning of the subject course through coordinated objectives, materials, and assignments tailored to students' linguistic and academic needs.

Although CBI has been around since the 1980s, it remains a prevalent approach to curriculum and instruction in various educational settings, including ESL and EFL contexts (Grabe & Stoller, 1997; Met, 1999; Snow, 2001). The approach supports global initiatives such as EMI and study abroad programs. For instance, in Japan, CBI is employed by university EAP programs to prepare students for overseas education (Miller et al., 2021) and is also utilized to support EMI initiatives aimed at internationalizing higher education (Brooks, 2014; Shimauchi, 2018).

Theme-Based Curriculum

To create a meaningful teaching and learning environment, a theme-based approach to curriculum and instruction contextualizes language use through organizing the curriculum around thematic units. Themes are selected based on the curriculum purpose, context, and the target student population's goals, interests, and English proficiency.

Theme-based curricula are used across various contexts—including EGP, EAP, and ESP. Themes in EGP courses may range from personal (e.g., family or the community) to global (e.g., environmental ethics or human rights), depending on the factors listed above. Themes are typically selected and developed by programs and/or teachers, ideally with input from students to align with their interests. Teachers may incorporate authentic materials, such as novels, published articles (for non-pedagogical purposes), and popular media, into a theme-based curriculum. Commercial theme-based textbooks are also frequently used to support this approach.

Furthermore, theme-based CBI is extensively used in ESP and EAP courses (Snow, 2001). In ESP, themes and topics are tailored to students' disciplinary or professional goals, catering to a specific and homogeneous student population (e.g., English for Business). EAP courses, on the other hand, may serve a homogeneous or heterogeneous student population. A homogeneous demographic allows for themes directly related to the students' academic major (e.g., STEM topics for STEM majors), whereas an EAP course with a heterogeneous group may feature varied themes with an academic focus.

Task-Based Language-Teaching Curriculum

Task-based language teaching (TBLT) focuses on using meaningful tasks to achieve specific learning objectives in language curriculum and instruction. The use and extent of tasks depend on whether TBLT is implemented as a teaching methodology or as the basis for the entire curriculum. Ellis (2003) distinguishes these as "task-supported language teaching" when tasks are supplementary and "task-based language teaching" when tasks are central to the curriculum (p. 27). TBLT aims to foster communication and build fluency but can also include tasks that target accuracy in language use (Ellis, 2019; Willis, 1996).

Beyond developing communicative competence, TBLT can also enhance problem-solving skills and logical thinking. In discussing TBLT's implementation in India, Prabhu (1987), emphasized the cognitive processes involved in task completion. He defined a task as an activity that requires "learners to arrive at an outcome from given information through some process of thought" (p. 24), with the teacher regulating this process and offering guidance as needed. Additionally, tasks can be structured to improve metacognitive skills by prompting students to assess, regulate, and be aware of the task demands (Ellis & Sinclair,

1989). TBLT can also support humanistic language teaching by designing tasks that target the learner's needs, feelings, and other affective factors (Ellis, 2003).

Several scholars have outlined frameworks for structuring TBLT (Prabhu, 1987; Willis, 1996). Prabhu's (1987) framework includes three phases: a *pre-task* phase, where task criteria and expectations are clarified and negotiated; the actual *task* phase, where students complete the task individually or collaboratively (e.g., creating a menu or a train map); and a *post-task* phase, where students assess their outcomes and the teacher collects feedback on the challenges faced. Willis' (1996) framework also consists of a pre-task phase but divides the actual task into three stages: *task* (students complete the task), *planning* (students prepare to report on their process and the outcome), and *report* (students present their findings to the whole class). Following these stages, students engage in language-focused activities to analyze and practice language forms.

To balance communicative tasks with formal instruction on linguistic structures, R. Ellis (2019) proposed a modular approach to structure a TBLT curriculum. A TBLT modular curriculum consists of task-based modules complemented by additional modules dedicated to explicit teaching and practice of the linguistic structures necessary for effective task performance. This explicit focus on structure, achieved through consciousness-raising tasks, allows learners "to make use of the knowledge they gain from the structural component of the curriculum in their own way and in their own time when they engage in activities derived from the task-based component" (R. Ellis, 2019, p. 463).

To conclude, it is important to note that while a language curriculum may adhere to one of the types described above, it is also possible to design a curriculum that combines several types or incorporates other innovations to enhance teaching and learning. For instance, to offer students authentic learning and interactions, a communicative or task-based curriculum (or technically any type of curriculum) might utilize the local community for place-based or community-engaged learning. In this case, the development process would involve structuring the "curriculum around authentic investigations [of local questions] that bring students out into the community [. . .] and provide the context for content acquisition, engaged learning, and meaningful community service" (Demarest, 2015, p. 1). In brief, the choice of curriculum design and methodologies should be based on a clear understanding of the curricular context, including the purpose of the teaching and learning experience, the goals and needs of the learners, and the philosophies and values of the various stakeholders. Considering factors at the nano, micro, meso, macro, and supra levels is also essential for identifying the curriculum type that best suits its context.

After you read, consider the following questions:

1. Compare the curriculum development models discussed in the chapter. What common elements do they share? What distinguishes each model from the others? Which model do you find most logical and why?
2. Reflecting on your own educational context, which curriculum development model would be most suitable? Explain your choice and how it aligns with your specific needs and circumstances.
3. Create a visual representation of the three main approaches to language curriculum development: forward design, central design, and backward design. Analyze the strengths and weaknesses of each approach from your own perspective.
4. You have been tasked with developing a language curriculum for your school. Considering your school's content, objectives, and student population, which type of language curriculum would be most suitable? Describe its key features and specify the curriculum development model (or combination of models) you would employ. Provide a rationale for your choices.
5. Preview and then choose one of the following documents related to curriculum projects. After you read your selected text, respond to the questions below:
    - *The Taba Curriculum Development Project in Social Studies* https://files.eric.ed.gov/fulltext/ED040106.pdf
    - *Man: A Course of Study. Evaluation Strategies* (a handbook discussing assessment strategies for the Man: A Course of Study curriculum) https://archive.org/details/ERIC_ED064185/page/n9/mode/2up

- *English Curriculum Development Projects: A Representative Collection* https://archive.org/details/ERIC_ED028187/page/n33/mode/2up
    a. What is the context in which this curriculum project was developed?
    b. What are the key elements of the curriculum and how do they interconnect?
    c. What are the foundational philosophies and theories behind the curriculum project?
    d. How is the curriculum organized? Are there specific pedagogical techniques offered to characterize the teaching and learning experiences? If so, please specify.

6. In the article "Backward Design as a Mobile Application Development Strategy" (available at https://link.springer.com/article/10.1007/s11423-019-09662-7), the researchers discuss their implementation of the backward design model to develop an educational mobile application. Read the article and then answer these questions:

    a. What were the desired learning outcomes? How did the developers prioritize these outcomes, and why?
    b. What types of assessments were used to determine whether the desired results were achieved?
    c. How did the developers plan the learning process? What instructional activities were designed to support and evaluate learning?
    d. What similarities can you identify between curriculum development and mobile application design?

Part II

Curriculum Systemization in Practice

Chapter 5

A Framework to Curriculum

Before you read, reflect on the following questions:

1. When planning a lesson, activity, or even a presentation, what steps do you take to achieve your desired outcome?
2. When you use this lesson, activity, or presentation at a future time, how do you approach it? Do you use it as is or read through it and make updates? If you make updates, what are they typically based on and why?
3. In your opinion, what are the key phases of curriculum development?
4. What are some best practices to ensure curriculum coherence and effectiveness at the curriculum's nano, micro, and meso levels?

This chapter provides an overview of the CPDIE (conceptualizing, planning, developing, implementing, evaluating) framework designed to guide and enhance curriculum practices. It introduces the components of the framework and offers suggestions for developing the infrastructure needed to enhance curriculum effectiveness. Each of the subsequent chapters in Part II will focus on one of the framework's components.

The CPDIE Curriculum Framework Overview

As teachers, when approaching any curricular task—whether a unit, lesson, or activity—we start by figuring out what we are doing, why, and what we would like to accomplish. After forming and rationalizing our ideas, we begin planning, which may involve researching and gathering information and material. We then proceed to develop our plan, and, finally, we put what we planned and developed into action in the classroom. When reusing a unit, lesson, or activity in the future, we are likely to make tweaks, additions, or revisions based on self-assessment of how things went and how students responded to the material or activity and try to make improvements accordingly. This natural, continuous, and cyclical process of curriculum development can be captured in five phases, abbreviated as CPDIE:

1. Conceptualizing
2. Planning
3. Developing
4. Implementing
5. Evaluating

Each chapter in Part II focuses on one of the CPDIE phases (Figure 5.1). It is important to note that the CPDIE framework does not prescribe specific curriculum content or impose a particular educational philosophy, curriculum development model, or instructional approach. Instead, it is intended to be generic and flexible, making it adaptable to any educational context. The framework provides practical suggestions in the form of guidelines, measures, processes, and tools that can be adopted or adapted by programs (meso level) as well as individual teachers (nano/micro level) as suitable to their teaching context and circumstances. It is important to stress that the relationship of curriculum development at the meso and micro level is reciprocal. What emerges from each level complements and feeds the other. The aim of the CPDIE framework is

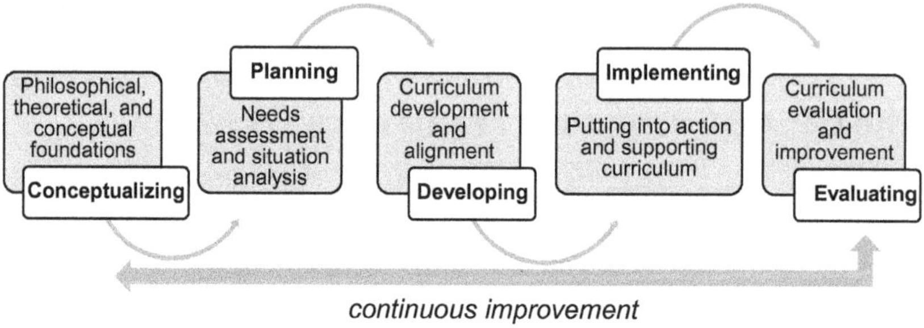

Figure 5.1. An Overview of the CPDIE Curriculum Framework

to systemize, improve, and enrich practices to ensure curriculum coherence, clarity, and consistency, thereby maximizing effectiveness at both the meso and micro levels.

Brief Definitions of the CPDIE Phases

The CPDIE framework consists of five key phases, which can be defined as follows:

- Conceptualizing: This phase involves recognizing the philosophical, theoretical, and conceptual bases that frame practice. It is about consciously exploring and reflecting on our own thinking, assumptions, and beliefs regarding teaching and learning.
- Planning: This phase sets the stage for curriculum development by investigating the specific context of the curriculum and the needs of the targeted student population.
- Developing: This phase focuses on addressing specific curricular objectives and learning outcomes, organizing the sequence of these objectives, determining course topics and themes, and establishing means for formative and summative assessment.
- Implementing: This phase is concerned with putting the curriculum into practice through measures at the micro and meso levels that support effective implementation and nurture a community of practice.
- Evaluating: This phase involves procedures for periodic evaluation, review, and revision of the curriculum to facilitate continuous improvement, enhance quality, and ensure responsiveness to any changes within its context.

The Role of the Meso Context in Supporting Curriculum CPDIE

To ensure the interconnectedness of the CPDIE processes and that each phase informs and supports the subsequent one, this curriculum framework emphasizes systematic planning, open communication among different stakeholders (including students), collaboration among teachers, and continuous improvement and innovation. These principles are crucial for minimizing the disconnect that may occur between the planned and implemented curriculum and ensuring curriculum coherence and fidelity.

The meso context (e.g., program, department, or institute) in which the curriculum operates plays a critical role in instilling these principles and bridging different levels of context. This can be achieved by creating an environment that supports teachers' involvement in curriculum making. Collaborative work among teachers is essential for producing an optimal curriculum and fostering professional growth and teaching effectiveness. Nicholls and Nicholls (1972/2018) emphasized this point by saying, "when curriculum development is carried out on a group basis[,] it can provide a means of continuing teacher education" (p. 24).

Even if the curriculum is outsourced, textbook dependent, or governed by external standards, programs must implement measures that enable teachers to collaborate in making sense of what is required and how it can be best implemented or adapted to fit the actual context, the program's goals, their philosophical beliefs, and student needs. Such measures facilitate a systematic and consistent translation of curriculum into the classroom. Given that curriculum decisions are influenced by various factors and conceptions, Figure 5.2 illustrates decision-making on a top-down/bottom-up continuum to show the important role of the

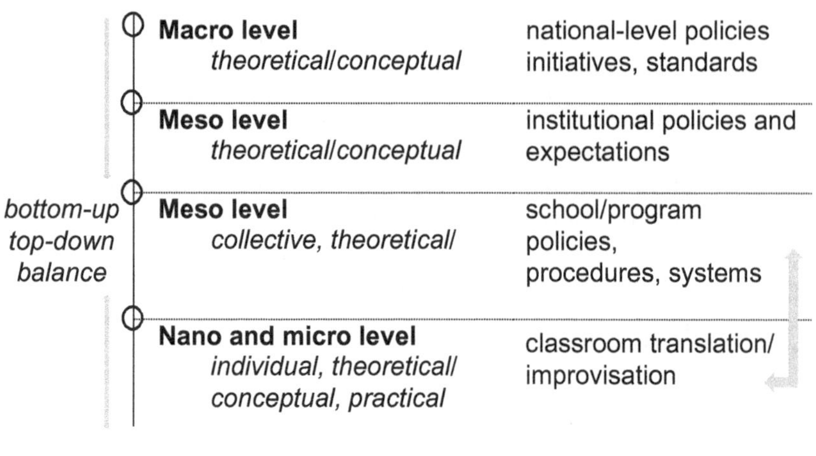

Figure 5.2. Decision-Making and the Important Role of the Meso Level

program as a mediator at the meso level. This balance is particularly significant when the program is embedded within several hierarchical layers of the meso context (e.g., an ESL/EFL program within a larger school and school district) and regulated by external factors at the macro level (e.g., standards, policies, or national curricula or exams). Achieving this balance involves creating opportunities for teachers to understand, negotiate, and translate conceptual and theoretical ideas into practical plans.

Infrastructure for the CPDIE Framework

The following suggestions can help build the infrastructure for curriculum practices at the meso level and facilitate the principles of systematic planning, open communication, and collaboration:

1. Creating a curriculum resource
2. Identifying curriculum personnel
3. Establishing a digital space for curriculum-related materials

Creating a Curriculum Resource

It is essential that there is a written framework in place that defines goals, sets parameters, and provides a roadmap for curriculum practices. Being clearly documented is one of the characteristics of UNESCO's quality curriculum (Stabback, 2016). This framework should provide clarity and guidance, functioning as "a system of light houses at sea. It does not tell where to go or restrict movement, but it is necessary to guide movement and warn of the danger spots" (Emans, 1966, p. 327). It can be a standalone document or part of a faculty manual or handbook covering the following:

- the program's purpose, goals, mission, philosophy of instruction, student population, organization of courses and levels, student services, facilities, equipment, and policies, among other information
- instructors and staffing, including roles and responsibilities, teaching requirements, instructor coordination, professional development, and faculty evaluation

- curriculum development processes outlining what informs the process, who is involved, and how it is facilitated
- curriculum-related information for each course, such as descriptions, goals, objectives, outcomes, themes, assessments, and skill progression
- a clear plan for curriculum review and revision, including the frequency, process, data and resources used, and the individuals involved

This document can be a valuable tool for organizing and communicating information and a resource for current and new teachers to consult and draw information from when planning syllabi and other curricular tasks. It can also function as the primary document to be updated during program reviews and curriculum revisions. Consolidating all information in one place ensures consistency and eliminates information discrepancies and chaos.

Identifying Curriculum Personnel

The CPDIE framework emphasizes the critical role of teacher involvement and collaboration in curriculum activities. In addition to their knowledge of the actual teaching and learning situation, Nicholls and Nicholls (1972/2018) highlighted several benefits of teachers working together on curriculum matters:

> There is the benefit of their joint knowledge and experience, the benefit of their complementary skills and expertise, the benefit of the ideas that are developed through interaction with each other as well as the benefit of a wider application of the results of their work. [Lastly,] there will be a consistency in the curriculum they plan. (p. 19)

Depending on the program's structure, size, and available roles, a designated individual, group, or committee should be responsible for facilitating curriculum-related matters. This could include the program director, assistant director, manager, curriculum coordinator, or a standing curriculum committee consisting of instructors and possibly administrators. Curriculum responsibilities may involve arranging review sessions, forming ad hoc committees (if a standing committee does not exist), preparing materials for reviews, and updating the master curriculum document.

Establishing a "Digital" Space for Curriculum-Related Materials

Establishing a digital space for sharing and storing materials is crucial for fostering a community of practice, documenting innovations, and building a resource inventory. While physical spaces like faculty libraries are valuable for housing textbook collections (e.g., purchased books, desk copies, and exam copies), a digital space becomes essential due to our growing reliance on online resources and the variety of instructional modes available. This space can also facilitate collaboration among instructors on material development and provide access to instructional resources created by faculty, such as lessons, exams, and activities. It can be established through shared folders on an institution's network, through cloud storage services (e.g., Microsoft OneDrive, Dropbox, Google Drive, or Box), or through learning management systems (e.g., Blackboard or Canvas). It is important that this space is organized in a meaningful way and that a system is in place to maintain its organization for ease of navigation and usability.

In summary, the CPDIE framework introduced in this chapter aims to bring attention to the different phases a curriculum should undergo and how to ensure their interconnectedness. It provides a flexible framework that can be adapted at the nano, micro, and meso levels to enhance curriculum practices. Subsequent chapters will highlight each component of the framework.

After you read, consider the following questions:

1. Based on the definitions provided for each phase of the CPDIE framework, what processes and tools can be used to navigate these phases effectively?
2. This chapter highlights the crucial role of the meso context in supporting curriculum conceptualization, planning, development, and review. What are some effective ways to provide such support? How can the connection between the

micro and meso levels of the curriculum be strengthened? What strategies can facilitate systematic planning, open communication, and collaboration?

3. Respond to the following questions based on your own teaching context. If you do not have direct teaching experience, you may speak with another teacher and base your responses on their context: Is there a curriculum guide or framework in your/their teaching context? What does it consist of? Who is responsible for managing curriculum-related matters (an administrator, teachers, or a standing committee)? What role do teachers play in curriculum activities? How are curriculum-related materials and innovations shared among instructors? Is there a designated space for storing and sharing these materials?

Chapter 6

Curriculum Conceptualization

Before you read, reflect on the following questions:

1. In what ways do educators' personal views and beliefs shape the development and implementation of a curriculum?
2. Why is it crucial for educators and educational programs to clearly express their teaching and learning philosophies? What strategies can be used to communicate these beliefs effectively?
3. How do educational theories inform and influence the design and structure of a curriculum?

Chapter 6 sheds light on the conceptualization phase of the CPDIE framework. It discusses the rationale for curriculum conceptualization and provides specific guidelines for navigating this phase.

CPDIE: The Curriculum Conceptualization Phase

Conceptualization is generally defined as formulating, grasping, and interpreting ideas and then working out a plan accordingly. Before the actual planning and development of the curriculum, the conceptualization phase of the CPDIE framework involves reflecting on one's own beliefs about teaching and learning, understanding the beliefs of other stakeholders, and familiarizing oneself with the theoretical and conceptual knowledge that guides practice. This phase allows for identifying the philosophical perspectives and theoretical knowledge underlying actions, developing an understanding of the whole, and fencing practices. It provides clarity and guides subsequent phases. Developing a conscious awareness of our beliefs, assumptions, and values concerning teaching and learning enables us to contribute to, make sense of, and negotiate decisions and practices related to curricula and instruction.

This form of reflective thinking can enhance pedagogical practices (Farrell, 2007) and improve the learning environment (Kearns & Sullivan, 2011). Dewey (1910) defined reflective thinking as an "active, persistent, and careful consideration of any belief or supposed form of knowledge in light of the grounds that support it and the further consequences to which it leads" (p. 6). Farrell (2015) proposed five levels of reflective practices for ELT teachers: philosophy, principles, theory, practice, and beyond practice.

The conceptualization phase focuses on engaging in reflective thinking at the first three levels (i.e., philosophy, principles, and theory) to inform curriculum planning, development, and, ultimately, its implementation. Knowledge from various areas of study, such as TESOL, applied linguistics, linguistics, cognitive linguistics, education, psychology, and neuroscience, helps us understand and rationalize the complex process of learning. This knowledge, combined with an understanding of our own philosophies and those of other stakeholders, assists in building the theoretical basis for rational practices. The conceptualization phase consists of:

1. Formulating a philosophy
2. Identifying the theoretical knowledge that underpins practice
3. Building a curriculum theory

Table 6.1 provides an overview of the types of knowledge and resources that can direct the conceptualization phase.

Articulation of Philosophy

It is crucial for educational programs and practitioners alike to explore and articulate their educational philosophy (or philosophy of teaching) to provide a rationale for practice. There is a consensus, whether in mainstream education (Ornstein, 1990) or ELT (Farrell, 2015; Farrell & Kennedy, 2019; Richards et al., 2001), that philosophy directs curriculum development and instruction. It shapes all elements of the curriculum and "is crucial to nearly all decisions regarding teaching and learning" (Ornstein & Hunkins, 2018, p. 47). A philosophy reflects one's educational beliefs and core values. A quality curriculum, as described by UNESCO (Chapter 4), is grounded in a set of philosophical and

Table 6.1 What Informs the Conceptualization Phase

Bases of the Conceptualization Phase	Examples of Knowledge and Resources
Philosophy	• Personal philosophies on teaching and learning • Principles of contemporary versus traditional philosophies (e.g., *progressivism* or *reconstructionism* vs. *essentialism*) • E.g., *Teacher-centered, subject-centered,* vs. *student-centered* design [refer to Chapter 2]
Conceptual, theoretical, and empirical research	• Theories of learning [refer to Chapter 2] • Vygotsky's zone of proximal development and scaffolding • Piaget's theory of cognitive development (e.g., schema) • Freire's critical pedagogy • Kumaravadivelu's post-method pedagogy • Basic Interpersonal Communicative Skills (BICS) and Cognitive Academic Language Proficiency (CALP) (Cummins, 2008) • Culturally sustaining pedagogies (Paris & Alim, 2017) • Critical language awareness pedagogy (Shapiro, 2022) • United Nations Sustainable Development Goals • Universal Design for Learning • Communicative competence • Inductive versus deductive learning • Explicit versus implicit grammar teaching • Language transfer
Teaching approaches and methods	• Communicative language teaching • Task-based language teaching • Content-based instruction • Community-based learning
Principles	• TESOL International Association's *6 Principles for the Exemplary Teaching of English Learners* • American Council on the Teaching of Foreign Languages (ACTFL) *Guiding Principles for Language Learning* • International Academy of Education's *Guiding Principles for Learning in the Twenty-First Century*

(*Continued*)

Table 6.1 (*Continued*)

Bases of the Conceptualization Phase	Examples of Knowledge and Resources
Standards	• National, state, and/or local language standards (e.g., The U.S. Common Core State Standards for English Language Arts and British Columbia's English Language Learners Standards) • International language standards (e.g., Common European Framework of Reference for Languages (CEFR)) • Accreditation standards (e.g., Commission on English Language Program Accreditation (CEA) and Accreditation UK) • Other non-language focused standards (e.g., The Social Justice Standards)

theoretical beliefs about learning (Stabback, 2016). For instance, a curriculum rooted in the social reconstructionist philosophy will reflect the principles of this orientation (see Figure 6.1).

Radical differences in philosophical orientations or lack of clarity in philosophical views driving curriculum conception and implementation can have serious ramifications on curriculum coherence, fidelity, and effectiveness. Therefore, it is essential that a philosophy is conceptualized and articulated at both the individual and program levels. Being aware of one's personal philosophy is crucial, as expressing and communicating these philosophical standpoints is an inherent part of the teaching profession. This often occurs formally through written statements, in job interviews, or informally during discussions with colleagues and other stakeholders. Farrell (2018) emphasized the importance of providing opportunities for language teachers "to articulate their beliefs and what they mean to them and ask if they still remain valid in light of present-day research in teaching and learning before being encouraged to make any changes" (p. 5). Establishing a program-level framework that clearly outlines its philosophy and approach to L2 teaching helps teachers examine and reflect on how their personal beliefs align with the program's philosophy. This can be supported through workshops, collaborative discussions, and feedback sessions. It is also important that a program's philosophy is periodically reviewed and refined to ensure that philosophical ideals align with practical realities.

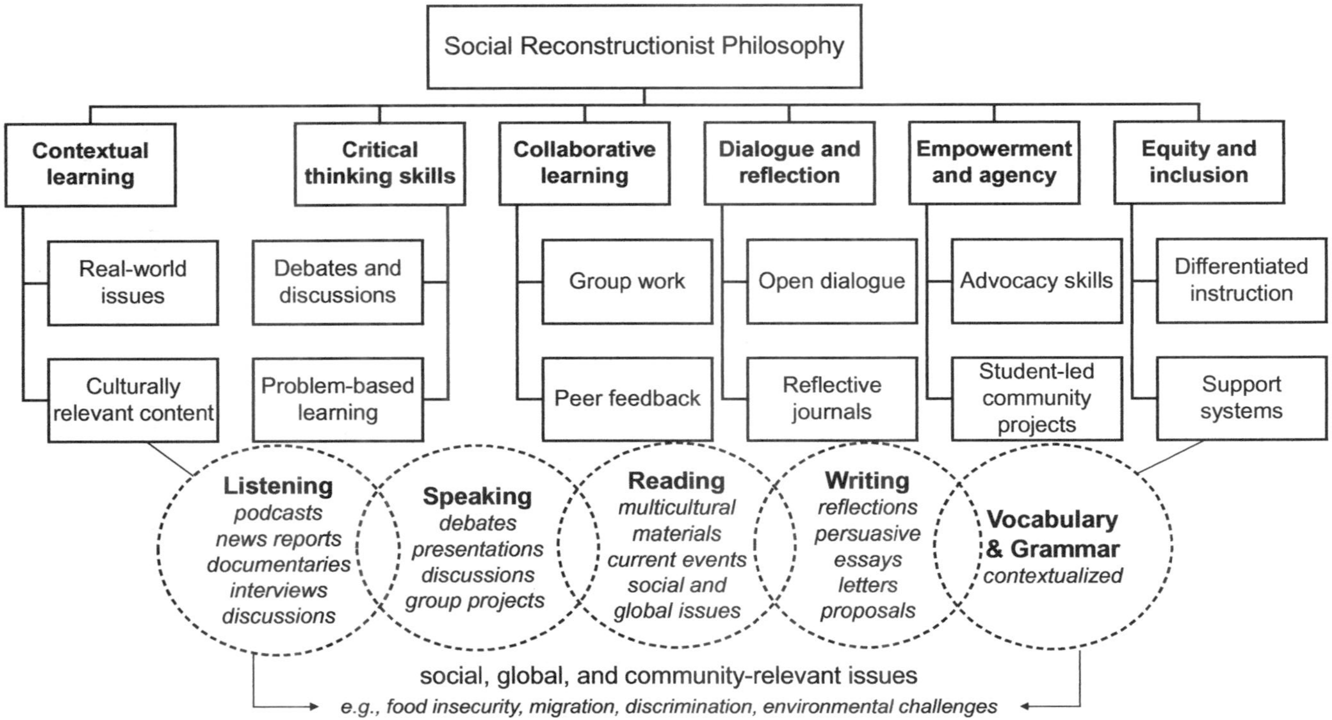

Figure 6.1. Sample Features of a Curriculum from a Social Reconstructionist Lens

Articulating a program philosophy in writing facilitates a shared understanding of the educational program's philosophical assumptions. It clarifies the philosophical bases of the curriculum and can function as a compass for guiding curriculum development and review. A philosophy statement defines the values and beliefs of the educational program regarding teaching and learning in relation to its context, scope, mission, and goals. Below is a summary of the philosophy of teaching and learning of the English Language Program (ELP) at the University of Pennsylvania (n.d.) (a complete philosophy statement is available online).

> We believe that students learn language best when they feel comfortable in their classes and are given as many opportunities as possible to participate. Our teachers provide students with meaningful content in all of our classes and encourage students to use that content to interact (talk and listen) with their classmates and teachers. Students in the ELP receive frequent and detailed feedback from their teachers on their reading, writing, listening, and speaking. This helps students discover their individual strengths and the weaknesses that they need to work on to improve their language. We believe that our students should be accountable for their own learning and will be most motivated when they have some choice in what and how they learn.

This sample statement captures the program's beliefs on effective language learning and teaching, including its approach, the value of feedback, and its emphasis on student autonomy. Based on these philosophical principles, we can infer that curriculum and instruction are communicative, student-centered, content-based, and task-based. They also adapt to students' needs and learning styles, integrate the four language skills, and provide ongoing opportunities for formative assessments.

Identification of Theoretical Underpinnings and Core Principles

Developing a clear understanding of the theoretical knowledge and principles that shape practice is crucial for systematically planning and developing curriculum and instruction. Before discussing the role of theory in the conceptualization phase, it is important to highlight a significant early call for integrating theory to guide ELT practices. This call predates the formal establishment of SLA as a distinct field, which began to take shape in the 1960s (Ellis, 2021; Selinker & Gass, 2008). In 1941, Charles C. Fries (1945), as the founder and director of the first university-based intensive English language program at the University of Michigan, advocated for developing an ESL theory. This theory was envisioned as a framework outlining the principles and processes that guide pedagogical decision-making for L2 teaching and the creation of an effective learning environment. Due to his pioneering work in ESL theory, Morley and colleagues (1984) described Fries as "one of the most important figures of the century, [for] it sometimes seems that everything that has come after Fries and much of what we do today is, in some important way, either following Fries or reacting to him" (p. 182). They further characterized Fries' comprehensive approach as "a careful tying together of diverse threads—theoretical factors, material-related factors, teacher-related factors, learner-related factors—into what clearly seems to have been a coherent and harmonious whole" (p. 202). Fries called for the development of an ESL theory based on three elements (Morley et al., 1984, p. 196):

1. theoretical perspectives,
2. perspectives of those engaged to organize and carry out the teaching,
3. perspectives of those involved in the learning, that is, the students.

Since philosophy and theory intersect to a large degree, examining the complete philosophy statement of the English Language Program at the University of Pennsylvania (available through https://www.elp.upenn.edu/about/mission-and-philosophy) reveals that the statement incorporates knowledge from SLA and learning theories. For instance, to foster students' communicative competence, the program emphasizes that input should be meaningful, authentic, varied, and "at and above the student's current level of competence," aligning with Krashen's i + 1 input hypothesis and Vygotsky's concept of the zone of proximal development. An ESL theory at the program level considers established theoretical assumptions about teaching and learning as well as the perspectives of practitioners. As an example, Fries' curricular and pedagogical choices in developing the intensive ESL program back then were grounded in his oral approach, which served as a theoretical framework. The oral approach, discussed in Chapter 2 and elaborated on in his 1945 book *Teaching and Learning English as a*

Foreign Language, focuses on building learners' inventory of L2 linguistic structures and sound system, particularly in the early stages of language learning, to facilitate oral production (see sample lessons in Lado & Fries, 1958). Fries (1945) offered an articulation of the theoretical aspects that underline methodologies while also accounting for the humanistic aspects of learning. Influenced by his work, Morley and colleagues (1984) emphasized the importance for ELT professionals "to develop an awareness of and appreciation for the complex network of factors which connect the carrying out of learning/teaching to the various theories and beliefs held about learning and teaching second language" (p. 201).

Knowledge from the field of education can guide the formulation of measurable objectives and student learning outcomes (SLOs), while theories and research from SLA and ELT fields help explain how second languages are learned or acquired. This knowledge points out relationships among variables and provides insights into best practices in L2 teaching and learning. Additionally, exploring the perspectives of teachers and students on teaching and learning is crucial for maximizing the effectiveness and completeness of learning experiences. This can be achieved by involving teachers in curriculum planning and development and by accounting for students' views and preferences through needs analyses when designing, implementing, and improving learning experiences. An ESL theory helps create a coherent and harmonious teaching and learning environment by intentionally considering and explicitly understanding its theoretical foundations and then articulating guiding principles accordingly.

Guiding Questions for Formulating a Philosophy and ESL Theory

The following guiding questions are intended to help formulate a philosophy, recognize theoretical bases of practice, and create principles to direct curriculum and instruction. These questions should be addressed by drawing on resources like those presented in Table 6.1 and considering the perspectives of various stakeholders. This conceptualization can be outlined in the program's curriculum guide or manual and reviewed as part of the curriculum review cycle. Answering these questions should also serve as the starting point of any curriculum development event. Table 6.2 presents fundamental questions and related sub-questions that need to be answered considering the specific educational *context*, the *purpose* or the overarching *goals* of the educational program, and the target *student* population. The next chapter discusses ways to explore the curriculum context and the target student population.

Table 6.2 Guiding Questions for the Conceptualization Phase

Essential Questions	I. What is the purpose of curriculum and instruction? II. How can this purpose be realized?
Sample Sub-Questions	• How is an L2 best learned? • What theories and research support this positionality on L2 learning? • What teaching approaches and methods can best foster L2 learning and support the needs and learning styles of the target student population? • What is the role of the teacher? • What is the role of the student? • What does effective teaching look like? • What does effective learning look like?

Building a Curriculum Theory

Although there is no single unified definition for curriculum theory—similar to the varied interpretations of curriculum and related concepts—there is general agreement that it focuses on identifying and defining curricular constructs and their relationships (Beauchamp, 1972, 1982). While an ESL theory provides theoretical perspectives that rationalize L2 teaching and learning, a curriculum theory aims to clarify the curriculum and its components. Since curriculum is defined differently across contexts, establishing a curriculum theory within an educational program helps clarify and reach a consensus on what curriculum is, its ingredients, and how these ingredients work together.

Curriculum theory, in a sense, complements philosophy. It is interpreted by Cheung and Wong (2002) "as a collective set of beliefs about curriculum elements such as curriculum intent (aims, goals and objectives), content, teaching strategies and instructional assessment" (p. 226). Newton (1970) described curriculum theory as a midpoint between philosophy and the act of teaching. That is, it is not fully the former nor exclusively the latter; it is a bridge of guiding principles that provides clarity and direction to practice. MacDonald (1971) offered a broader view of curriculum theory as "the study of how to have a learning environment" (p. 199). In curriculum studies, curriculum theory does not imply an already established theory that seeks to theorize a specific phenomenon, like a learning theory or an SLA theory. Instead, curriculum theory is context dependent, formulated within an educational setting to explain or reconstruct vague terms and notions (Kliebard, 1982).

Why establish a curriculum theory? As Ornstein and Hunkins (2018) put it, "anyone charged with developing and delivering curriculum has a conception or conceptions of curriculum and its components" (p. 176). It is crucial to articulate, explore, and clarify these conceptions. Curriculum, as we know, is a complex phenomenon with various constructs, and its definition and operation vary across contexts and stakeholders. Curriculum theory provides a foundation for identifying constructs, establishing relationships among variables, and predicting and describing curricular actions concerning objectives, learning experiences, content, and evaluation (Endeley & Zama, 2021). It is crucial for teachers, who are by default involved in developing and implementing daily curricular elements, to have a clear conception of the curriculum to make informed day-to-day decisions when realizing curriculum plans (Zmuda et al., 2004). As Glatthorn and colleagues (2019) asserted, a curriculum theory offers "a set of conceptual tools for analyzing curriculum proposals, for illuminating practice, and for guiding reform" (p. 120). When preparing for a specific curriculum development task within an educational program, it is essential to establish a mutual understanding for identifying, defining, and interpreting curricular elements.

Curriculum Theory-Building Tasks

Beauchamp (1964, 1975) suggested engaging in curriculum theory-building tasks to fence an educational program by identifying and then defining essential terms to ensure clarity and consistency of use. The outcomes of these tasks can yield a general framework, chart, or map of curricular elements and their relationships (McCutcheon, 1982). Curriculum theory-building tasks in the conceptualization phase may involve the following:

1. Identifying curricular constructs (e.g., *curriculum, teaching, goals, objectives, outcomes, assessment, vertical and horizontal alignment, syllabus*)
2. Formulating definitions
3. Determining the relationship between the identified curricular constructs

These measures help prepare the groundwork and set parameters for the curriculum planning and development phases. They promote a shared vision of curricular elements, their meanings, and their interactions within a given educational context. Engaging in these tasks at the program level can be valuable for logically interpreting how curricular elements interact, building consensus, and establishing a well-grounded curriculum. Table 6.3 provides an overview of basic

Table 6.3 An Example of the Outcome of a Curriculum-Building Task

- ***Goals, Objectives, and Outcomes:*** These statements define the intended knowledge, skills, and attitudes to be acquired from teaching and learning experiences. Although often used interchangeably, they have distinct differences (CEA, 2022; Elturki, 2022):
    - Goals: Broad statements describing the overall long-term aims of a curriculum
    - Objectives: Teaching-oriented statements detailing specific knowledge and skills to be taught
    - Outcomes: Learning-oriented statements defining achieved learning
- ***Content:*** Curriculum content concerns what is taught and in what order, including topics, themes, materials, and resources used to achieve course goals, objectives, and outcomes. Instructional materials are selected, planned, and developed to align with student needs and support the overarching goals of the curriculum, including course objectives and outcomes.
- ***Learning Experiences:*** These refer to how the planned curriculum (e.g., objectives, topics, and instructional materials) unfolds in the classroom. Learning experiences involve the teacher's approach, methods, and strategies for scaffolding learning, providing feedback, forming groups, maintaining student engagement, and fostering respect and inclusion. They emerge from the interactions between teachers and students, among students, between students and material, and between students and their broader environment (including outside the classroom).
- ***Evaluation:*** While curriculum *objectives* define the intended learning, *content* serves as the means to realize the intentions, and *learning experiences* represent the practical realization of both. *Evaluation* allows for monitoring progress and determining if learning has been realized and to what extent. It allows us to go back to the curriculum objectives and measure the extent to which all the things in between have produced the intended outcomes. Assessment tools and events are used to gauge existing knowledge and skills (diagnostic assessment), support learning and inform teaching (formative assessment), and measure the extent of learning (summative assessment).

curricular elements and their definitions to illustrate the outcomes of a curriculum-building task.

To conclude, this chapter highlighted the conceptualization phase, which aims to help teachers and programs consider their practice's philosophical and theoretical underpinnings. Understanding of this knowledge aids in rationalizing and making informed decisions during the subsequent phases of curriculum planning and development. Given the complex nature of the curriculum, these phases may be navigated in a linear or non-linear manner. The curriculum planning, development, implementation, or review phases might reveal theoretical or conceptual knowledge that was initially overlooked, necessitating going back to the conceptualization phase to address and integrate this new understanding.

After you read, consider the following questions:

1. Reflect on your own thinking, assumptions, and beliefs of teaching and learning using the "Guiding Questions for the Conceptualization Phase" presented in Table 6.2. Write a statement of teaching philosophy based on this reflection.
2. Outline the theoretical, conceptual, and/or empirical knowledge that grounds your teaching practices. Explain how this knowledge informs and rationalizes your pedagogical decision-making.
3. If you were to develop a curriculum theory for your teaching context, what would its key components be? Describe how these components interact and work together.
4. You are tasked with developing an ESL/EFL curriculum that emphasizes the social aspects of learning. Identify the curriculum type, its purpose, the targeted student population, and the context. Using brainstorming methods (e.g., mind mapping, freestorming, bubbles, round robin if working in a group), identify the theories, concepts, and research that would underpin a language curriculum with a social orientation. What is your philosophical standpoint on such a curriculum?

5. Examine the theoretical foundations of the WIDA (World-Class Instructional Design and Assessment) English Language Development Standards Framework, available through this link https://wida.wisc.edu/sites/default/files/resource/WIDA-Standards-Framework-and-its-Theoretical-Foundations.pdf. Identify the philosophy and theoretical assumptions that ground this framework and the principles it promotes.

Chapter 7

Curriculum Planning

Before you read, reflect on the following questions:

1. What factors should be considered before starting curriculum development? Why are these important?
2. What types of information should be gathered during the curriculum planning phase to prepare effectively for curriculum development?
3. Based on previous chapters and your own understanding, what constitutes the curriculum context? What tools can be used to identify factors at different levels (e.g., student, classroom, program, community) that influence curriculum planning?

In the previous chapter, we explored the conceptualization phase, which helps explore and frame the philosophical and theoretical foundations of the curriculum. Building on that foundation, the curriculum planning phase of the CPDIE framework focuses on gathering concrete information to guide curriculum development. Chapter 7 will cover specific procedures and tools to aid in curriculum planning and inform its development.

CPDIE: The Curriculum Planning Phase

Before proceeding with the actual development of curriculum events, the planning phase involves closely examining the targeted student population and considering any potential situational factors that could impact curriculum effectiveness. This step is crucial for making informed decisions about the type of learning experiences that will be meaningful and appropriate for the specific curriculum context. Depending on the nature and scale of the curriculum development activity, programs and individual teachers can conduct a needs analysis and situational analysis to gather information about the student population and the context in which the curriculum will be implemented. This information aids in formulating objectives that address students' specific needs. Additionally, it facilitates the selection of topics, themes, and materials of interest to students and teachers to ensure relevance to the sociocultural context. It also helps identify effective means for nurturing and monitoring learning.

Needs analysis and situation analysis are standard procedures for collecting data to inform curriculum development. Various terms are used in the literature to describe these processes for assessing learners' needs, such as ***needs analysis***, ***needs assessment***, or ***diagnosis of needs***. Terms such as ***situation(al) analysis***, ***environment(al) analysis***, or ***context analysis*** refer to the evaluation of the context in which the curriculum will be implemented. These processes are sometimes combined, with student needs assessed as part of the situation analysis. Alternatively, needs analysis procedures may also inspect the curriculum context in addition to student needs. This chapter discusses needs analysis and situation analysis as two separate procedures.

Needs Analysis

Brief Background on Needs Analysis

Since the early works of Bobbit (1918, 1924), Tyler (1949/2013), Taba (1962), and other curricularists, diagnosing student needs to define the knowledge and abilities required to nurture individuals and better societies has been considered an integral step in curriculum planning and development. Tyler (1949/2013) was one of the early scholars to define ***need*** in the context of curriculum development, describing it as the gap between "the present condition of the learner and the acceptable norm" (p. 6) or, more simply, "the gap between what is and what should be" (p. 8). These needs or gaps are identified through ***studies of the learner*** (a term used by Tyler that aligns with today's notion of needs assessment or analysis). According to Tyler, studying the learner involves gathering information on the learner's life experiences, interests, and attitudes, among other factors. This is achieved by drawing on relevant research on cognitive and psychological development and methods such as teacher observations, student and parent interviews, questionnaires, tests, and examination of school records. Examining such data and comparing it to standards or norms provides insights into potential needs that school programs could address and forms the basis for selecting relevant, focused, and purposeful curricular objectives (Tyler, 1949/2013). Needs analysis is therefore seen as a tool for assessing student needs to create a "responsive and responsible curriculum" (English & Kaufman, 1975, p. 52).

In the ELT field, the shift to more comprehensive and systematic approaches to language curriculum necessitated a focus on student needs rather than on the development of courses solely based on linguistic analysis of language items (Long, 2005; Richards, 1984). This shift was partly driven by increased accountability from legislation and accreditation requirements, which demanded evidence of educational effectiveness. Additionally, the communicative teaching approach shifted the emphasis to identifying the specific language skills necessary for learners to function effectively in L2 communicative situations instead of focusing primarily on the mastery of grammatical items (Nunan, 1988b). In the 1970s, needs analysis became increasingly popular for designing ESP courses tailored to various student groups' specific academic or occupational needs (Hutchinson & Waters, 1987) and remains crucial in ESP/EAP curriculum development (Flowerdew, 2013). Contemporary approaches to language curriculum development, as outlined by scholars such as Brown (1995), Graves (2000), Richards (2001/2017), and Macalister and Nation (2020), have established needs analyses as a standard procedure. These procedures ensure that curriculum and pedagogy provide learners with the language, skills, texts, and tasks necessary for effective communication, whether those learners are students, tourists, immigrants, or refugees navigating academic, professional, vocational, or everyday contexts.

Needs Analysis Definition and Purpose

Needs analysis is a systematic and continuous process that uses different methods and sources of data to identify and understand learners' needs. As previously mentioned, it has become integral to contemporary language curriculum approaches, whether the course is designed for specific or general purposes (Kitzman, 2009; Richards, 1990; Seedhouse, 1995; West, 1994), as there is always a discernible need (Hutchinson & Waters, 1987). Long (2005) further emphasized that rather than adopting a uniform approach, each course should be considered as serving distinct purposes and tailored to its specific students' needs. Much of the current information on needs analysis comes from the literature on

Table 7.1 Application of Needs Analysis (NA) in an EGP Context

- **Study:** Seedhouse, 1995
- **Context and population:** EFL, EGP, Barcelona, 29 young learners aged 14–18
- **NA purpose:** To assess learners' engagement with course materials and inform the design of instructional resources accordingly
- **Method:** Questionnaire
- **Major highlights**:
    - The current coursebook was misaligned with students' needs; it did not cater to their age group, and the topics were irrelevant to their target speech community.
    - Students expressed interest in travel and socializing with foreigners, which was not reflected in the course materials.
    - Social and psychological factors emerged as primary motivators for learning English, particularly interests in travel, social connections with peers from other countries, the significance of English for global communication, and improved employment opportunities.
    - Supplementary materials were developed, featuring activities related to international travel and conversations that aligned with the learners' target speech community.
    - Tasks were designed based on preferred learning methods, including computer simulations, video-based activities, conversations, and group work.

ESP and EAP. However, studies like Seedhouse's (1995), captured in Table 7.1, highlight the importance of understanding learners' needs in EGP contexts, which challenge the "belief that it is not possible to specify the needs of general English learners" (p. 59).

In addition to its relevance for all types of teaching and learning contexts, needs analysis can serve as a preliminary, ongoing, and evaluative procedure (Figure 7.1) to inform curriculum development, implementation, and refinement (Belcher, 2006; Bocanegra-Valle, 2016; Dudley-Evans & St. John, 1998; Jordan, 1997). Hyland (2006) provided a thorough definition of needs analysis, emphasizing its various benefits:

> *Needs analysis* refers to the techniques for collecting and assessing information relevant to course design: it is the means of establishing the *how* and *what* of a course. It is a continuous process, since we modify our teaching as we come to learn more about our students, and in this way it actually shades into *evaluation*—the means of establishing the effectiveness of a course. *Needs* is actually an umbrella

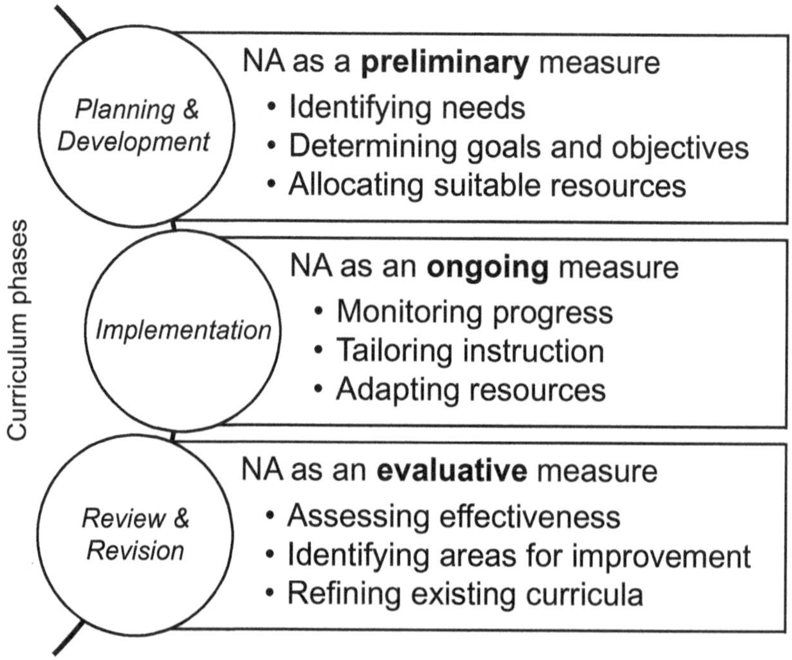

Figure 7.1. Needs Analysis (NA) as a Preliminary, Ongoing, and Evaluative Measure

> term that embraces many aspects, incorporating learners' goals and backgrounds, their language proficiencies, their reasons for taking the course, their teaching and learning preferences, and the situations they will need to communicate in. Needs can involve what learners know, don't know or want to know, and can be collected and analysed in a variety of ways. (pp. 73–74)

Using needs analysis as a preliminary measure is essential for guiding curriculum planning and decision-making. It defines objectives and outcomes while ensuring that the curriculum is meaningful for learners. Incorporating ongoing needs analysis during implementation allows for responsive pedagogical decisions, which helps maintain a balanced approach between curriculum as a product and as a process. This ongoing evaluation ensures the curriculum matches real learning experiences, improving coherence, fidelity, and effectiveness while guiding necessary adaptations and revisions.

Considerations for Planning Needs Analysis

The planning and design of needs analysis depends on several factors, including its purpose and specific objectives; the context, scale, and nature of the curriculum project; and the timeframe and available means for data collection and analysis.

The considerations outlined in Table 7.2 serve as a guide for effective planning, design, and execution of a needs analysis. Defining and determining the purpose, objectives, scale, and context of the needs analysis is a prerequisite for effectively addressing data collection and logistical planning. A needs analysis designed to inform a curriculum element on a smaller scale will require different considerations regarding time, budget, personnel, resource management, and procedures compared to a curriculum project at larger scales, such as the meso or macro levels. The

Table 7.2 Considerations for Planning Needs Analysis (NA)

Factor	Considerations
Purpose and Objectives	1. What is the primary purpose of the NA? • Establish a new program or course • Revise an existing program or course • Develop instructional units, lessons, or tasks • Select or develop new materials, themes, or topics • Introduce a curriculum innovation (e.g., a new technology, delivery mode, pedagogy, assessment) • Understand and improve learning conditions (e.g., motivation, engagement, collaboration, inclusion) 2. What are the specific objectives based on the selected purpose from the list above? How will the NA deliverables inform its intended purpose?
Context and Scale	3. What are the breadth and depth of the curriculum project? What are the context and scale of the NA? • Is the assessment intended for a national, school district, institutional, program, or classroom level? • What is the size of the target student population? • Who is the targeted student population, including their proficiency levels (if available), L1, age, and location? • What are the most effective methods for reaching and engaging the target population?

(Continued)

Table 7.2 (*Continued*)

Factor	Considerations
Data and Logistics	4. What type of data needs to be generated? What are the logistical considerations of the NA? • What are the data sources? • What is an ideal and feasible sample size? • What methods and instruments will be used to collect the data? How will they be validated? • What are the procedures for data collection? How can the reliability and validity of the results be ensured? • How will the data be analyzed? • How extensive will the data collection and analysis be? What level of expertise is required? • Who will be conducting the analysis? What are their roles and responsibilities? What training is needed? • What measures will be taken to ensure the confidentiality and privacy of the data collected? • What resources are available, including financial, technological, and human resources? • What is the budget for the NA? How will it be allocated? • What is the timeline for the assessment, including key phases and deadlines? • Are there any potential logistical challenges or other contextual factors or constraints that could affect the NA (e.g., access to participants, data collection tools, resource limitations, political climate)? How will they be addressed? • How will the results of the NA be communicated and used to inform decision-making? • How will the success and effectiveness of the NA process be measured? How will feedback to refine the NA be gathered and incorporated?

following brief examples illustrate how a curriculum project's purpose, scope, and scale influence the complexity of needs analysis.

- Suppose that a teacher is planning a needs analysis at the micro level to provide students with the opportunity to negotiate curriculum elements such as objectives, topics, and assessments. They might use surveys to gauge student interests and preferences and/or engage students in discussions and activities. In this case, the data collection methods, procedures, analyses, and deliverables are relatively straightforward and manageable due to the smaller scope and more focused objectives.

- Conversely, consider a school district conducting a needs analysis to improve its curriculum for English Language Learners (ELLs) across multiple schools (meso level). The goal is to ensure that the curriculum effectively supports ELLs' language development and academic achievement. At this scale, the needs analysis becomes more complex. It involves gathering and analyzing data from a diverse student population with varying levels of English proficiency and cultural backgrounds. Data collection methods might include district-wide surveys to understand ELL students' experiences and challenges, focus groups with ELL teachers to identify instructional gaps, and classroom observations to assess current teaching practices. The analysis must account for the diverse needs of students across different schools, and the results must inform curriculum adjustments that cater to varying proficiency levels and support language acquisition.
- At the macro level, such as a national initiative to redesign ELL programs, the complexity increases significantly. The needs analysis would require engaging with policymakers, educational authorities, and educators across the country to address national standards for ELL education. It would involve extensive data collection through large-scale surveys, national assessments, and longitudinal studies to understand trends and gaps in ELL education. The analysis would need to synthesize data from diverse regions, accounting for different linguistic, cultural, and educational contexts to develop a comprehensive national framework that ensures equitable and effective support for ELLs across the country.

In brief, as the scale and context of the needs assessment expand from micro to meso to macro levels, the complexity of managing data collection, analysis, and logistics grows proportionally. Each level requires tailored approaches to ensure the needs analysis effectively informs curriculum development and improvement, reflecting the scale's demands and the broader impact on the educational system. Hence the purpose and the context of the curriculum project necessitate different considerations in planning needs analysis. As the scale and context of the project expand, the complexity of managing data collection, analysis, and logistics increases proportionally.

Needs and Approaches

Various terms in the literature define or characterize needs (Figure 7.2), leading to different approaches to needs analysis. Traditional methods, as outlined in Jordan (1997) and West (1994), focused on identifying the language skills learners needed to acquire by the end of a course for success in the target context through ***target-situation analysis*** (Munby, 1978). For example, this could involve analyzing the language requirements of a specific job role to design targeted training or focused courses. Data may be collected through interviews with employers, questionnaires, or by reviewing documents that outline job descriptions. Other approaches, such as ***present-situation analysis*** (Richterich, 1972; Richterich & Chancerel, 1978), assessed learners' current abilities at the beginning of a course. This might involve evaluating existing language skills

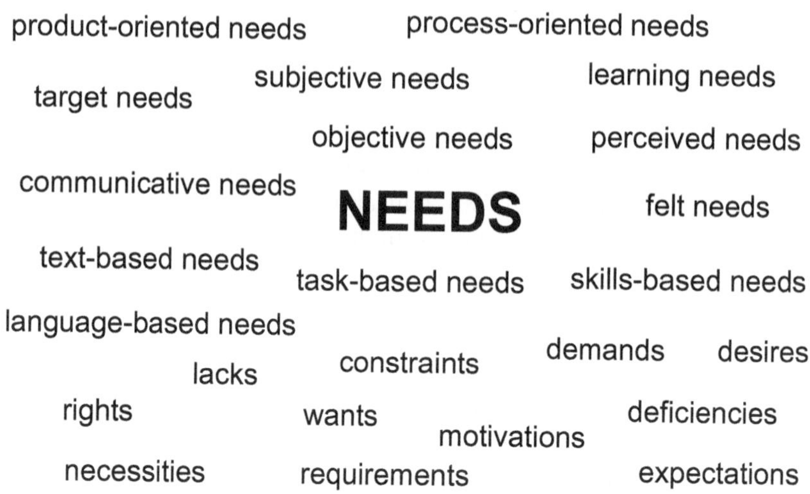

Figure 7.2. Dimensions and Characteristics of Needs

through tests or other assessment methods. Such data provided insights that shaped syllabus content, addressing the "what" of the curriculum. Later approaches shifted focus to teaching methodologies and learning strategies that addressed the "how" of the curriculum through *strategy analysis*. This may involve identifying effective teaching and assessment methods tailored to learners' needs, as well as understanding their preferred learning styles, strategies, and feedback mechanisms.

Instead of isolating the target, present, and learning needs, Hutchinson and Waters (1987) proposed a *learning-centered approach* to needs analysis that emphasized collaboration among learners and stakeholders to comprehensively shape the teaching and learning experience. This approach considers the "entirety" of the curriculum. That is, in addition to gathering information on why, how, and where the language is needed (target-situation-oriented questions), it seeks to understand who the learners are, their motivations for taking the course, their preferred learning methods, appealing teaching strategies, and the available resources to support effective teaching and learning (Hutchinson & Waters, 1987). Current needs analysis practices integrate these approaches to assess different dimensions of needs (Bocanegra-Valle, 2016).

Key concepts in needs analysis that stem from earlier works include *target* needs, *learning* needs, *objective* needs, and *subjective* needs (Brindley, 1989; Hutchinson & Waters, 1987; Munby, 1978; Nunan, 1988b; Richterich, 1972; Richterich & Chancerel, 1978). These concepts can be succinctly defined as follows, with illustrative examples presented in Table 7.3:

- Target needs: The knowledge and skills required for learners to perform effectively in their intended L2 settings, further categorized into (Hutchinson & Waters, 1987):
    - Necessities: The communicative skills and linguistic knowledge demanded by the target situation
    - Lacks: The disparity between learners' current proficiency and the proficiency required for the target situation
    - Wants: Learners' perceived necessities, lacks, and desires regarding their learning objectives
- Learning needs: The conditions, skills, and resources necessary for learners to achieve effective learning and address their target needs

Table 7.3 Illustrative Example of Common Types of Needs Identified during Curriculum Planning

By conducting questionnaires, interviews with the target student population in their L1s, and diagnostic testing, a needs analysis can provide valuable insights as a preliminary step in planning a curriculum for high-beginner adult English language learners who are recent refugees in an English-speaking country. This analysis may uncover immediate *target needs,* such as the language skills required to understand public transportation, access healthcare services, and communicate with schools or daycare facilities about their children. It may also identify the following lacks, wants, and necessities:

Necessities (objective needs):

- Communicative skills: Ability to ask for directions and understand public transportation schedules, express health concerns, and communicate effectively regarding their children's schooling needs
- Sociolinguistic knowledge: Using vocabulary and phrases related to healthcare (e.g., common medical terms and symptoms), transportation, and everyday interactions; understanding sentence structure for various types, including questions and affirmative statements; differentiating between present and past tenses; and recognizing cultural nuances that influence communication in these contexts (e.g., appropriate greetings, gestures, and expectations in different social interactions)
- Practical skills: Basic conversational skills for interacting with others in learners' specific day-to-day settings

Lacks (objective needs):

- Current proficiency: Limited understanding of everyday vocabulary and phrases needed for public transport and healthcare settings
- Grammar skills: Insufficient knowledge of basic sentence structures to form questions and convey information effectively
- Cultural knowledge: Lack of familiarity with local customs and practices related to education and healthcare

Wants (subjective needs):

- Learning objectives: A desire to focus on practical language skills that will help them navigate daily life
- Preferred teaching methods: An interest in interactive and scenario-based learning that reflects real-life situations they will encounter
- Support resources: A wish for access to bilingual materials and community services that can assist them in practicing language skills in a safe environment

Table 7.3 (*Continued*)

To help learners navigate their new environment effectively and build confidence and practical skills, ***learning needs*** may involve: • Daily practice of vocabulary and sentence formation: Engage in daily practice of functional vocabulary and sentence formation through contextualized and interactive in-class activities, such as role-playing exercises that simulate real-life scenarios, as well as independent methods like flashcards and mobile apps to reinforce learning outside the classroom • Complete real-life tasks: Undertake specific assignments that involve real-life tasks, such as filling out forms or making phone calls to practice applying their language skills in context • Collaborate with peers: Work in small groups or pairs to practice conversational skills, providing mutual support and opportunities for peer feedback Employing ongoing needs analyses throughout the course—through formative assessments, observations, and discussions with students—can help identify more specific learning needs, including individual learning preferences, allowing instruction to be tailored accordingly.

- Objective needs: Needs based on factual or normative data, such as a learners' personal information, educational background, current proficiency level, and present or anticipated studies or employment
- Subjective needs: Needs related to cognitive and affective factors, including learning preferences, abilities, desires, goals, attitude, and personality traits, as expressed by learners themselves or observed by others

While traditional approaches to needs analysis focus primarily on linguistic units—such as words, grammatical structures, and language functions—within the target situation or discourse to determine what learners need for effective communication, scholars like Long (2005, 2014) advocated for using tasks as the primary units of analysis. A ***task-based learner needs analysis*** aims to identify the specific real-world tasks that learners need to perform using the target language (e.g., booking a flight, scheduling a doctor's appointment, or ordering food online). Data collected during this analysis is classified into broader task types (e.g., making bookings), which serve as the foundation for curriculum development.

From these task types, pedagogical tasks are derived, sequenced, and implemented in the classroom (Long, 2014). Long (2005) noted that task-based needs analysis can be applied to various types of curricula, not just those specifically designed for TBLT. By focusing on tasks, this approach tailors curriculum and instruction to provide students with relevant, practical, and context-driven language learning experiences. Table 7.4 highlights the application of a task-based needs analysis for planning a business English course, as reported by Huh (2006).

Beyond the technical assessment of skills and tasks needed for effective performance in the target language, *critical* approaches to needs analysis seek to address deeper issues that can impact learning experiences and outcomes, including the cultural, social, political, and institutional contexts in which learning occurs (Benesch, 1996). Such approaches reject a deficit-based perspective that focuses on learners' lacks and deficiencies (Helmer, 2013), challenge the reliance on conventional expertise and native norms in determining language needs (Belcher, 2006), and prioritize learner voices and empowerment

Table 7.4 Application of Task-Based Needs Analysis in an ESP Context

- **Study:** Huh, 2006
- **Context:** Intensive English language program in Hawai'i, U.S.
- **Curriculum project and needs analysis:**
  - Aimed to develop a business communication course for international students, primarily from Korea, who plan to conduct business in their home countries or the United States.
  - Employed task-based needs analysis to identify target tasks for Korean business professionals (a business and language expert was recruited to assist with curriculum development for the U.S. context), as well as their attitudes and goals regarding business English courses, by utilizing:
    - Literature review of business English
    - Semi-structured interviews with five Korean business professionals
    - Questionnaire administered to 73 Korean business professionals (developed from interview data)
  - Analyzed data by identifying target tasks (e.g., giving presentations, writing resumes and cover letters, conducting job interviews) and classifying them into abstract target task types (e.g., getting a job)
  - The findings provided a foundation for the curriculum development phase, informing the selection and design of relevant tasks aligned with learners' specific needs and goals in business communication
  - *Refer to pages 59–64 in Huh for the task-based needs analysis instruments used in the study.*

(Benesch, 1996). Moreover, scholars such as Benesch (1996, 1999a, 2001) and Helmer (2013) argued that needs analysis should incorporate ***rights analysis*** to uncover issues of power within the teaching and learning context as well as in curriculum and instruction. A critical needs analysis, or rights analysis, may examine issues such as classroom power relations, institutional hierarchies, institutional demands, curriculum requirements, fairness of assessment, inclusion, and representation and sensitivity in course materials. Tables 7.5 and 7.6 provide examples of employing critical needs analysis to inform the curriculum development of EAP courses situated within the multiple levels of institutional hierarchies typical of such programs.

Data Collection and Analysis

Selecting the appropriate data sources, methods, and procedures for a needs analysis depends on the curriculum project's nature, scale, objectives, and context. More specifically, is the needs analysis intended as an initial step in curriculum development? Is it employed as an ongoing procedure to inform teaching and respond to student needs? Is it used as an evaluative tool to improve an existing curriculum and instructional practices? Is the needs analysis aimed at a curriculum project at the micro, meso, or macro level? Is the needs analysis used to determine students' occupational, academic, or general/survival needs?

Data Sources

While data from learners are crucial, drawing from multiple sources is highly recommended for an effective needs analysis (Bocanegra-Valle, 2016; Long, 2005; Serafini et al., 2015; West, 1994), especially for new course design. Utilizing a variety of data sources ensures a more comprehensive understanding and supports well-informed decision-making. In the context of ESP, Long (2005) identified five sources for needs analysis:

- Published and unpublished literature: Research studies, job descriptions, and other relevant documents
- Learners: Data collected directly from students
- Teachers and applied linguists: Insights from educators and language specialists

Table 7.5 Application I of Critical Needs Analysis in an EAP Context

- **Study:** Benesch, 1996
- **Context:** EAP, paired ESL/psychology university course (adjunct instruction), United States
- **Curriculum project and critical needs analysis:**
  - Aimed to develop an EAP curriculum for the paired ESL/psychology course that helps students navigate various institutional demands while empowering them to challenge these requirements and identify opportunities for change
  - Conducted a critical needs analysis to uncover hierarchical academic requirements affecting student learning in a large, lecture-based psychology course by utilizing interviews with psychology faculty and students, pre-course and post-course student questionnaires, and observations of psychology lectures
  - Identified conflicting requirements students faced in the target situation:
    - University level: Passing a writing assessment test (an argumentative essay)
    - College level: Attending large lectures without recitation sections, limiting additional instructional support
    - Psychology department level: Reading extensive material without opportunities for meaningful discussion, leading to challenges in applying knowledge in real-life settings (a course requirement) and focusing on memorization due to multiple-choice testing
    - English department level: Expectations to assist students in passing the university's written exam while linking ESL writing to course content to enhance student engagement
- Incorporated three types of activities into the EAP curriculum to address the issues uncovered through the needs analysis:
  - Aligned activities: Supporting students in navigating the limitations of the target situation through note comparisons, oral presentations on textbook topics, and peer-generated multiple-choice questions for test preparation
  - Challenging activities: Encouraging students to challenge the requirements by having them generate questions for the psychology professor during lectures and hosting the professor in the ESL class for more interactive and personal discussions
  - Transcendent activities: Promoting critical thinking and moving beyond institutional constraints through research assignments on social issues like anorexia and encouraging involvement in political advocacy related to education funding, raising awareness of the impacts of governmental decisions on students' educational opportunities

Table 7.6 Application II of Critical Needs Analysis in an EAP Context

- **Study:** Chowdhury and Kamal, 2014
- **Context:** First-year compulsory EAP course for undergraduate students, Dhaka University, Bangladesh
- **Curriculum project and critical needs analysis:**
  - Aimed to identify gaps in the existing ENG101 curriculum while accounting for broader social and institutional factors that influence student learning
  - Conducted a critical needs analysis involving reviewing and modifying curriculum artifacts by including current and former students in the process (e.g., encouraging them to categorize textbook units and provide feedback to voice their needs and preferences) and interviewing instructors on the course's effectiveness and areas for improvement
  - Identified issues and solutions, including:
    - Skill development: Both students and instructors highlighted the neglect of speaking and listening skills, leading to modifications in the assessment structure to incorporate these essential components.
    - Tailored approaches: The analysis indicated that a standardized course was insufficient for the diverse student population, advocating for customized approaches that better address individual learning needs.
    - Engaging learning environment: A strong demand was for more interactive and practical activities, reflecting students' desire for a dynamic and engaging learning experience.

- Domain experts: Individuals with specialized knowledge in relevant fields
- Triangulated sources: Combining multiple data sources for a comprehensive analysis

When conducting task-based needs analysis to assess students' needs within specialized contexts, Serafini et al. (2015) emphasized the importance of consulting both insider and outsider sources:

- Insider sources: Comprising domain experts who can provide insights into the specific tasks and requirements of the domain
- Outsider sources: Encompassing language teachers, administrators, and applied linguists, who are crucial for identifying the language skills necessary for learners to operate effectively within their context

Within the EAP context, three main sources of data are outlined in Bocanegra-Valle (2016):

- Primary stakeholders: Current and former students and EAP teachers
- Secondary stakeholders: Subject-matter teachers and tutors, administrators, language and domain experts, and policymakers
- Tertiary stakeholders: Employers, company representatives, sponsors, and the broader society

In addition to the learners and the different stakeholders listed above, the following sources of data can further inform a needs analysis:

- Curriculum-related materials: Existing curricula or prospective ones (especially in the case of EAP), syllabi, instructional resources, competencies, and standards
- Institutional reports and data: Student records, student achievement data, standardized testing data, and course and program evaluations
- Other texts and artifacts: Student writing, samples of target genres and texts, and corpora

Sampling

Along with determining data sources, careful consideration of the selection process for target population members is crucial for the needs analysis (Long, 2005; Serafini et al., 2015). Possible sampling options include (Alvi, 2016):

- Convenience sampling: Recruiting participants who are readily accessible and available (e.g., Huang & Yu, 2023; Serafini et al., 2015). This method is often practical but may not always provide a representative sample and, thus, limits the generalizability of findings.
- Purposive sampling: Selecting participants based on specific criteria relevant to the needs analysis (e.g., Nateghian, 2024).

This approach is useful for obtaining targeted insights from particular groups.

- Stratified random sampling: Dividing a heterogeneous population into distinct subgroups based on certain characteristics and randomly selecting participants from each subgroup (Kim et al., 2018). This method ensures broad representation and generalizability across different regions, demographics, and educational settings.

While convenience sampling is often practical and commonly used in many ELT needs analysis studies, the sampling technique should align with the purpose and scale of the needs analysis. For instance, convenience or purposive sampling may be suitable for obtaining targeted insights in micro- or meso-level needs analyses, such as those within a single classroom, school, or language program. Conversely, stratified random sampling might be used for larger meso- or macro-level needs analyses to collect data across multiple institutions or nationwide curriculum initiatives. This approach ensures broad representation and generalizability across diverse regions, student demographics, and educational settings.

Methods, Techniques, and Instruments

Data on student needs can be collected using various quantitative or qualitative methods and analyzed either inductively or deductively (Brown, 2009; Long, 2005; Serafini et al., 2015; West, 1994). Qualitative methods, such as observations or unstructured interviews, typically employ an inductive approach to uncover needs-related patterns and themes. For example, classroom observations or informal interactions with students or other stakeholders can reveal insights that inform curriculum development. In contrast, quantitative methods, such as questionnaires or structured interviews, facilitate a deductive approach to needs analysis. This process begins with established hypotheses or specific questions about student needs. For instance, respondents can be asked to rate a series of statements related to their goals or learning requirements. The results are then quantified, enabling generalizations to be drawn.

Using both qualitative and quantitative methods offers a more thorough understanding of needs and can improve the effectiveness of needs analysis procedures. Serafini et al. (2015) suggested employing both inductive and deductive processes by integrating these two approaches. For instance, starting with a qualitative method like informal interviews can uncover previously unconsidered needs (i.e., an inductive approach). This initial exploration helps generate insights and identify emerging patterns, which can then inform and improve subsequent deductive methods, such as structured interviews or questionnaires, for broader implementation with larger samples. The following list outlines common methods and techniques for data collection found in the needs analysis literature (Brown, 1995, 2009; Jordan, 1997; Long, 2005; West, 1994), and Table 7.7 presents examples of studies that have utilized some of these methods:

- Interviews: Gathering insights from stakeholders in *structured* (e.g., predetermined questions), *semi-structured* (e.g., guiding questions with flexibility), or *unstructured* (e.g., open-ended and conversational) formats
- Surveys and questionnaires: Collecting data (e.g., biodata, opinions, self-ratings, and judgmental ratings) from participants to quantify needs on a broader scale
- Focus groups: Moderating discussions with a small group of stakeholders to gather diverse perspectives on needs
- Journals and logs: Providing detailed records of experiences and needs over time, particularly useful in longitudinal studies
- Role plays and simulations: Understanding how individuals might respond to or handle specific situations related to their needs
- Discourse analysis: Examining how language is structured and expressed within specific contexts
- Register/rhetorical analysis: Understanding the specific language, styles, and conventions used in particular situations
- Corpus analysis: Analyzing language patterns (e.g., collocations and lexicogrammatical sequences) in large collections of texts using a concordance tool or program
- Genre analysis: Understanding the conventions and structures of specific genres of texts or communications relevant to the needs of a group

- Content/document analysis: Examining materials such as existing curricula, textbooks, syllabi, or other documents to identify gaps and/or align with learners' needs
- Record analysis: Examining existing records, such as academic transcripts and performance data, to identify trends, gaps, or needs based on historical information
- Literature review: Reviewing existing research to gain insights into previously identified needs and inform current analysis
- Feedback forms: Collecting structured feedback from participants after specific activities or courses to gauge their needs and perceptions
- Tests: Measuring learners' language abilities through *language proficiency tests* (norm-referenced tests), *placement tests*, and *diagnostic tests*
- Assessments: Measuring progress and learning outcomes in relation to the curriculum through *formative* (ongoing checks of understanding) and *summative* assessments (including achievement tests)
- Case studies: Providing an in-depth understanding of specific instances, useful for identifying needs in particular contexts
- Ethnographic methods: Gaining a comprehensive understanding of needs through immersive observation and participation
- Triangulated methods: Combing two or more methods to provide a robust and comprehensive understanding of needs

As shown in Table 7.7 and highlighted in the literature (Bocanegra-Valle, 2016; Long, 2005; Serafini et al., 2015), the most prevalent instruments for needs analysis include questionnaires and interviews, often complemented by other methods such as document analysis and observations. These instruments typically incorporate a mix of closed-ended and open-ended questions. Closed-ended questions offer specific response options, often in the form of multiple-choice, yes/no, or rating scales. For example, a question might ask, "*Which skills do you feel are most important to focus on in the ESL curriculum*? (1- Speaking, 2- Listening, 3- Reading, 4- Writing)." In contrast, open-ended questions invite

Table 7.7 Sample Studies Employing Different Needs Analysis Methods and Techniques

Study and Focus	Methods/Technique
Huang and Yu (2023) • Communication skills of preservice nurses in clinical settings, ESP nursing courses, China	• Video-recorded observation of simulated role plays • Ethnographic discourse analysis
Arias-Contreras and Moore (2022) • Target needs of agricultural technicians, vocational education and training, Chile	• Semi-structured interviews • Document analysis
Smith et al. (2022) • Task-based, academic oral communication needs, EAP listening and speaking curriculum, University of Hawai'i at Mānoa, U.S.	• Triangulated methods • Document analysis (course syllabi and published/unpublished NA reports) • Semi-structured interviews • Observations • Questionnaire • Follow-up document analysis, interviews, and observations
Nateghian (2024) • Perceptions on English language needs of civil engineers, ESP curriculum for civil engineering, Iran	• Observations • Interviews • Focus group
Thi and Cheng (2024) • Linguistic needs and problems of Food and Beverage (F&B) staff at a five-star resort, ESP training for F&B employees, Vietnam	• Case study • Questionnaires • Semi-structured interviews • Content analysis (Tripadvisor reviews)
MacPherson (2019) • Communicative needs, General English course for Japanese university students, Nagasaki Junshin Catholic University, Japan	• Survey • Diagnostic tests (speaking, grammar and vocabulary, reading and listening)
Galante & Piccardo (2022) • Pronunciation needs, speaking and pronunciation course for adult multilingual ESL students, Canada	• Assessment (completion of audio-recorded speaking tasks using VoiceThread)

respondents to express their thoughts in their own words. For example, a question might ask, "*What aspects of learning English do you find most challenging?*" (for sample questionnaire and interview instruments, see the appendices in Thi and Cheng, 2024, pp. 87–104). Closed-ended questions yield quantitative data that can be analyzed statistically while open-ended questions generate qualitative data that can be examined for themes and patterns. Diagnostic tests and other assessment forms, like those used in MacPherson's (2019) and Galante and Piccardo's (2022) studies, are vital for assessing students' needs and tailoring the curriculum. For further sample instruments, including practical information on conducting needs analysis as an initial and ongoing measure for adult English language learners, see the Center for Applied Linguistics' needs assessment toolkit (https://www.cal.org/caela/scb/III_A_AssessingLearnerNeeds.pdf).

Analyzing the Data and Using the Results

Once data has been collected, the next critical step is analyzing it to draw meaningful conclusions. The analysis can be approached in several ways, depending on the nature of the data (qualitative or quantitative) and the objectives of the needs analysis. Quantitative data analysis may include summarizing descriptive statistics, identifying frequency distributions, analyzing relationships between different variables through cross-tabulation, and/or determining statistical significance by conducting tests such as t-tests (to compare means) or chi-square tests (to examine associations between categorical variables). In contrast, qualitative data analysis may involve coding and identifying themes in open-ended survey responses, interview transcripts, or observational notes. Cross-checking and validating the data is essential to ensure accuracy and reliability if results are derived from multiple methods.

Finally, summarizing the findings in relation to the initial goals or questions is crucial for generating actionable insights and drawing conclusions about how the data can inform curriculum discussions. For instance, in the study by MacPherson (2019), highlighted in Table 7.7, the analysis of the needs analysis survey and diagnostic tests guided the development of a communicative General English course specifically tailored to the target population's needs. MacPherson identified important curriculum priorities, including a focus on in-class skills to enhance listening and speaking, reading and writing practice that aligns with learners' interests, along with strategies to "expand lexical knowledge through exposure to authentic, needs-based texts" (p. 147). These priorities were then used to formulate goals and establish curriculum objectives. Additionally, the needs analysis results contributed to shaping instructional approaches, selecting materials, sequencing topics, and determining methods for formative and summative assessments.

Reliability and Validity of Needs Analysis

To ensure that a needs analysis accurately reflects the needs of the target student population, it is essential that data is gathered from multiple sources and validated through various instruments. The following procedures are recommended for conducting a systematic, credible, and reliable needs analysis (Bocanegra-Valle, 2016; Brown, 2009; Flowerdew, 2013; Hyland, 2006; Serafini et al., 2015):

- Multiple sources: Collecting input from diverse stakeholders and sources (e.g., learners, teachers, experts, records, artifacts) provides a comprehensive view of needs from various perspectives and enhances the depth and accuracy of the analysis.
- Data sampling: Choosing a sampling technique (e.g., convenience, purposive, or stratified random sampling) that is appropriate to the needs analysis purpose and scale can significantly affect the generalizability and applicability of research findings.
- Multiple methods: Combining different data collection methods (e.g., qualitative methods such as interviews with quantitative methods such as surveys) helps mitigate the limitations of a single approach.
- Triangulation: Verifying findings by utilizing various sources, methods, and analysts ensures the accuracy and consistency of conclusions.
- Piloting: Testing instruments such as questionnaires or interviews with a sample of participants allows for refining and improving questions and procedures.
- Debriefing: Reviewing and verifying analyses by discussing them with participants ensures that interpretations of needs are relevant and accurate.

- Prolonged engagement: Spending sufficient time observing participants in their social setting, particularly when using observational or ethnographic methods, allows for an accurate understanding of needs in a contextualized manner.

Table 7.8 illustrates the methodological procedures designed to improve the reliability and validity of task-based needs analysis research carried out by Serafini and colleagues (2015).

Table 7.8 Example of Methodological Practices for Improving Needs Analysis Validity and Reliability

- **Study:** Serafini et al., 2015
- **Purpose:** To assess the communicative language needs of trainees and inform the design of ESP TBLT courses
- **Population and context:** International post-docs, visiting fellows, research fellows, and clinical fellows working in a U.S. scientific research institution
- **Data sources:** Triangulated sources, including NS (native speakers) and NNS (non-native speakers) of English, using convenience sampling:
  - Insiders: In-service trainees (the learners) and domain experts (supervising Principal Investigators, PIs) from various scientific fields
  - Outsiders: Applied Linguistics graduate students and faculty from a TBLT seminar
- **Methods:** Triangulated methods, including quantitative and qualitative, using inductive and deductive approaches:
  - Interviews: Tape-recoded semi-structured interviews with 25 international post-docs and 6 PIs. Questions varied between groups but focused on communicative tasks and issues.
  - Questionnaires: Three online questionnaires were completed by 860 NS and NNS trainees and 278 PIs. Data from the interviews informed the creation of the questionnaires.
  - Additional follow-up methods: Non-participant observation and recorded language-use samples from lab meetings
- **Methodological procedures for NA validity and reliability:**
  - Multiple sources and methods were employed to collect consistent and comprehensive data.
  - Instruments were piloted to refine questions and improve data quality.
  - Interviews with NS trainees helped determine whether communication challenges stemmed from linguistic and cultural differences or other non-language-related factors.
  - Data triangulation validated preliminary findings across multiple sources and methods, providing a nuanced understanding of communicative needs and identifying the most frequent, important, and difficult target tasks.

Steps for Conducting Needs Analysis (NA)

The process of conducting a needs analysis for the purpose of curriculum planning and development can be outlined as follows (see Table 7.9 for an illustrative example):

- Step 1: Define the scope, purpose, and goals (or questions) of the needs analysis.
- Step 2: Identify data sources, select or develop appropriate instruments, and specify data collection procedures, including the timeline.
- Step 3: Implement the data collection procedures.
- Step 4: Analyze the data, identify trends, make comparisons, validate findings, and draw conclusions that address the goals or questions formulated in Step 1.
- Step 5: Use the conclusions to guide curricular decision-making.
- Step 6: Evaluate the effectiveness of the needs analysis and use the feedback to improve future needs analysis activities.

Table 7.9 Example of a Needs Analysis Activity

Context overview: A university-based intensive English language program (IEP) in the United States is conducting a needs analysis for developing an EAP reading and writing curriculum for international graduate pathway students. These students will be taking this EAP course alongside major-specific courses in their respective colleges. The needs assessment process, managed by the Curriculum and Assessment Committee, will take place over two semesters before the course is offered in the fall semester. The committee includes teachers with expertise in advanced academic writing and those with administrative roles related to curriculum, assessment, and material selection. Committee members will work collaboratively, with each responsible for specific procedures listed under Steps 2–4. Findings and next steps will be discussed collectively.

Table 7.9 (*Continued*)

<table>
<tr><th colspan="2">Needs assessment process overview:</th></tr>
<tr><td>Step 1</td><td>Scope, purpose, goals, and questions:

The needs analysis aims to identify curricular elements for the EAP reading and writing curriculum as a preliminary step in curriculum development. The goals include:

I. Understanding the targeted student population:
1. Who is the targeted student population (demographic data)?
2. What are their intended majors? What colleges will they attend?
3. What are the students' levels of English language proficiency?
4. What are students' existing knowledge and skills (linguistic and academic), experiences, abilities, priorities, and attitudes?
II. Understanding the target situation:
5. What academic reading and writing skills are essential for graduate studies?
6. What are the specific reading and writing requirements within the targeted disciplines?</td></tr>
<tr><td>Steps 2 and 3</td><td>Data sources and data collection procedures:

• Compile <u>student admission data</u>, including <u>proficiency scores</u> [Questions 1, 2, and 3 from Step 1]
• Collect syllabi, assignments, and writing samples from colleges within the pathway program for <u>content analysis</u> [Questions 5 and 6 from Step 1]
• Conduct <u>non-participant observations</u> of five to eight courses in the targeted disciplines [Questions 5 and 6 from Step 1]
• Perform individual <u>semi-structured interviews</u> with five to eight college instructors [Questions 5 and 6 from Step 1] (interview questions will be based on data from the previous methods and existing literature on international pathways students' language and academic needs.)
• Design and administer an online comprehensive <u>student survey</u> using Qualtrics [Questions 1, 2, and 4 from Step 1] (e.g., covering questions about students' goals, perceived reading and writing skills, knowledge of disciplinary vocabulary, past writing and research experiences, learning preferences, and attitudes toward specific instructional techniques and academic demands)</td></tr>
</table>

(*Continued*)

Table 7.9 (*Continued*)

Step 4	***Data analysis procedures and summary of findings:*** I. The targeted student population • Tabulation of demographic and proficiency information from admission and survey data. *A summary of findings may include the total number of admitted students and then quantitative and qualitative data with demographic information, undergraduate degree major and GPA, intended college and program, years learning English, and TOEFL or International English Language Testing System (IELTS) scores (e.g., findings may reveal that the targeted student population is predominantly from China (85%) followed by India (15%) with 80% of students applying for programs in the College of Engineering (55% computer science, 25% electrical engineering, and 20% mechanical engineering) and 20% of the students applied for the College of Education).* • Extraction of information on students' learning experiences from survey results, including perceived linguistic and academic abilities, difficulties, priorities, expectations, goals, and attitudes. *Recurrent themes can be highlighted when reporting findings (e.g., "notetaking" as difficulty or "using sources" as a goal).* II. The targeted learning situation • Identification of common writing assignments within disciplines, including genres, rhetorical modes, papers' average length, and general requirements. *Findings can be reported by highlighting similarities and differences across the disciplines in terms of the nature of reading and writing (e.g., lab reports and exercises unique to engineering, summaries and critiques more common in education, research/ course projects were present across the disciplines).* • Prioritization of reading and writing knowledge and skills required for graduate students based on the content analysis and data from interviews and observations *(e.g., critical reading skills are essential across all majors; interpreting and reporting data from graphs and tables are required for engineering students; locating reliable and credible sources is important for all majors; Institute of Electrical and Electronics Engineers [IEEE] as a documentation style is required for engineering and American Psychological Association [APA] for education).*

Table 7.9 (*Continued*)

Step 5	***Overall recommendations for curricular implications*** *Example*: Based on input from students, college instructors, and content analysis, the EAP curriculum should emphasize research skills, critical reading, documentation using APA and IEEE styles, the composition of well-supported papers, academic integrity, and writing proposals, academic essays, and lab reports. Course objectives, student learning outcomes, corresponding assignments, and instructional resources will be developed to reflect these priorities.
Step 6	***Evaluation of the needs analysis process*** Individuals involved in data collection should document any necessary revisions to the needs analysis process instruments and procedures (e.g., unclear questions). The Curriculum and Assessment Committee should utilize the feedback on the effectiveness of the needs analysis to improve future assessments.

Situation Analysis

Brief Background on Situation Analysis

While needs analysis focuses on assessing various aspects of student needs—including current and target language skills, learning preferences, goals, and rights—situation analysis (or environment analysis) examines factors at different levels of the curriculum context (nano, micro, meso, macro, and supra) that can impact curriculum effectiveness and usability. This process investigates the specific context in which a curriculum is developed and/or implemented to offer more targeted learning, determine curriculum project feasibility, and assess the potential impact of internal and external factors on its success. This aspect of curriculum planning gained popularity in education in the 1970s, particularly with the emergence of cyclical models of curriculum development (Print, 1993). One such model is Nicholls and Nicholls' (1972/2018), discussed in Chapter 4, which approaches curriculum in a cyclical manner and employs situation analysis to assess factors related to the teacher, students, and the school environment. Situation analysis can also tackle external factors, as Skilbeck (1984) suggested, such as culture, society, ideology, community expectations, employer requirements, and relevant policies.

In the ELT context, conducting a situation analysis is crucial for aligning a language curriculum with the local context and ensuring its effectiveness and compatibility. Situation analysis, in this sense, aligns with aspects of means analysis (Holliday & Cooke, 1982), as discussed in Dudley-Evans and St. John (1998) and Jordan (1997). Dudley-Evans and St. John stated that means analysis, "an adjunct to needs analysis," recognizes that "what works well in one situation may not work in another" (p. 124). By examining the environment in which a course will be implemented, it can be ensured that it will "grow healthily and survive" (Dudley-Evans & St. John, 1998, p. 124). Jordan described this curriculum planning procedure as "an environmentally-sensitive teaching approach" that can help avoid "the imposition of alien models (of teaching, methodology, learning, etc.)" (p. 28).

Contemporary language curriculum frameworks, as proposed by researchers such as Graves (2000), Richards (2001), and Macalister and Nation (2020), stress the importance of defining the curriculum context and considering factors that can influence decisions regarding curriculum objectives, topics, materials, and activities. Graves (2000) and Macalister and Nation (2020) identified factors related to students—including demographics, educational backgrounds, and reasons for enrollment—as well as those pertaining to teachers, such as English proficiency, training levels, and teaching experience. They also emphasized examining factors that can impact the teaching situation, like classroom conditions and available resources. In addition to these, Richards (2001) expanded the scope of situation analysis by incorporating societal factors such as teaching policies, cultural traditions, and public attitudes. He further proposed considering curriculum project–related elements like team expertise, responsibilities, resource availability, progress monitoring, and timelines. Additionally, Richards highlighted adoption factors such as curriculum clarity, practicality, and perceived benefits to ensure compatibility with existing practices and acceptance among teachers. In a nutshell, conducting a situation analysis is important for the success of a curriculum project to enhance its effectiveness and relevance.

How Can Situation Analysis Support Curriculum Planning?

As discussed in Chapter 3, curricula are complex because their effectiveness can be affected by various factors at different levels of context: nano (student- and teacher-related factors), micro (classroom factors), meso (institutional factors), macro (national and sociocultural factors), and supra (global factors). As a curriculum planning procedure, situation analysis considers these factors to allow for rational and informed decision-making during the curriculum development phase. Table 7.10 offers a holistic overview of factors across various levels of curriculum context that can influence curriculum development. It outlines a comprehensive list of considerations and potential data collection methods for each level. This information can be tailored by selecting factors relevant to a specific curriculum project and customized to fit an educational setting or regional characteristics.

The following situations, drawn from the author's experience or reported in the literature, illustrate the importance of adopting a holistic approach to curriculum planning to identify factors that can influence the success and usability of a course.

The Case of the Pathway EAP Engineering Elective Course

Developing a new curriculum at the micro or meso levels requires defining key factors related to students, teachers, and the overall teaching and learning environment that can impact its effectiveness. While there is recognition of the importance of assessing learners' needs to devise a tailored curriculum, other important factors—such as teachers' backgrounds, training, and confidence in facilitating the teaching of certain objectives—are often overlooked. These elements can significantly influence the effectiveness of the course, as demonstrated by the following example.

In a university-based intensive English language program offering pathway programs for international students, engineering pathway students were observed to struggle with their coursework. In response, an elective course titled "English for Engineering" was developed to support these students. The development process involved a comprehensive review of relevant literature, analysis of syllabi and assignments from engineering courses, discussions with the students, observation of engineering classes, and consultation with engineering faculty. This thorough approach helped identify specific curriculum objectives and the writing skills students needed to master. However, challenges arose during the course's implementation. The teachers assigned to the course did not have a background in engineering and had not received training in teaching engineering concepts. A critical area that students needed support in was writing lab reports, but the teachers struggled to effectively

Table 7.10 Factors to Consider at Various Levels of Curriculum Context in Situation Analysis

Levels of Curriculum Context	Major Question	Sample Considerations for Analysis	Sample Data Collection Means
NANO	What are the characteristics and needs of the target *student* population?	• Demographics • Language proficiency levels • Linguistic and cultural backgrounds • Socio-economic status and access to resources • Composition of the student body (homogeneous vs. heterogeneous) • Learning goals • Student attitudes toward language learning • Learning preferences	• Interviews • Surveys • Student records • Testing (proficiency, placement, diagnostic)
	What qualifications, experiences, and teaching philosophies do the *teachers* bring to the program?	• Academic and professional credentials • Relevant teaching experiences • Employment status (full-time, part-time, etc.) • English language proficiency • Teaching styles and methodologies • Personal teaching philosophies and motivations • Engagement with ongoing professional development	• Program teaching requirements • CVs • Teaching philosophy statements • Course evaluations • Teaching observations

Table 7.10 (*Continued*)

Levels of Curriculum Context	Major Question	Sample Considerations for Analysis	Sample Data Collection Means
MICRO	How do the physical conditions of the *classroom* support or hinder effective learning?	• Physical space dimensions and flexibility for activities • Classroom layout • Environmental factors (lighting, noise levels, temperature) • Availability of teaching tools (whiteboards, projectors) • Access to reliable Internet and technology	• Inventory of classroom tools and equipment • Physical assessments • Observations • Surveys • Interviews
	How well do the available *materials* and *resources* support teaching and learning?	• Textbooks (quality and relevance) • Supplemental materials • Topics and themes • Handouts/course packets • Multimedia tools • Electronic devices • Learning management systems • Computer labs • Teaching aids (e.g., posters, realia, flashcards) • Accessibility of materials for all students	• Inventory of materials • Facility assessments • Material evaluations • Surveys • Interviews • Course evaluations • Program evaluations • Classroom observations

(*Continued*)

Table 7.10 (*Continued*)

Levels of Curriculum Context	Major Question	Sample Considerations for Analysis	Sample Data Collection Means
	How does *instruction* align with the curriculum objectives, foster effective learning, and meet student needs?	• Lesson planning • Instructional approach • Methods and techniques • Classroom dynamics • Assessment procedures • Inclusive teaching and differentiated instruction	• Lesson plans • Classroom observations • Course evaluations • Interviews • Surveys • Student achievement data • Published literature
MESO	What is the purpose of the language *program*, and how does it address the needs of its intended *audience*?	• Program's purpose, mission and goals • Student population	• Program documents (e.g., mission statement) • Stakeholder interviews • Surveys
	What are the *organizational* and *operational structures* that facilitate the program's goals?	• Available positions and duties • Budget and finances • Teaching loads • Courses and levels (and the connection between each) • Facilities and supplies • Leadership style • Policies and expectations • Philosophy and values • Student services • Professional development	• Program handbook • Stakeholder interviews • Accreditation documents • Standards and policy statements

Table 7.10 *(Continued)*

Levels of Curriculum Context	Major Question	Sample Considerations for Analysis	Sample Data Collection Means
	What processes are involved in *curriculum development*, and how is stakeholder input integrated?	• Top-down vs. bottom-up approach • Curriculum type (national, school-based, imported, textbook-based) • Teacher involvement in decision-making	• Curriculum guide • Program handbook • Meeting minutes • Interviews • Surveys
MACRO	How does the *geographical context* influence the language program's implementation and effectiveness?	• EFL vs. ESL contexts • Rural vs. urban settings • Role of the English language • Existing language programs • Employment demands	• Descriptive data (e.g., location, languages spoken, demographics) • Policy statements • Local program analysis • Job market analysis
	How do *local beliefs, norms,* and *values* shape the community's language learning expectations? How do a *country's present conditions* impact learning?	• Expectations of parents or sponsors • Community and employer perspectives • Current local or national circumstances	• Surveys • Interviews • Observations • Ethnographic methods • Assessment of current conditions

(Continued)

Table 7.10 (*Continued*)

Levels of Curriculum Context	Major Question	Sample Considerations for Analysis	Sample Data Collection Means
SUPRA	What are the key *global* and *local factors* influencing government policies on English teaching, and how do they affect program implementation?	• Global trends (e.g., globalization, economic developments, technological advancements) • Governmental policies	• Policy documents • Legislations • Assessment of current conditions/ trends

teach this genre, defaulting to generic five-paragraph essays instead. Throughout the course, teachers expressed concerns to the administration regarding their ability to meet the needs of engineering students and attempted to request assistance. Meanwhile, students felt the course was similar to a standard academic writing class and did not adequately address their specific challenges in engineering.

Despite thorough research during the curriculum planning and development phases to identify the needs of engineering students, a vital element was overlooked: teachers' knowledge and training requirements necessary to achieve the desired learning outcomes. This oversight caused significant stress for teachers, leading to feelings of incompetence, while students felt that their time and money were wasted. Ultimately, the curriculum project failed to achieve its goals.

How can situation analysis identify and address these issues in the curriculum planning phase? A situation analysis could have identified the expertise and background needed for effective implementation. For instance, it could have pinpointed teachers with experience in teaching technical writing or ESP tailored to engineering. If no ELT instructors possessed this expertise, the program could have arranged training prior to launching the curriculum. Alternatively, depending on budget constraints, collaboration with a faculty member from the engineering department or the hiring of a teaching assistant to support the ELT teachers could have been considered.

The Case of Macro-Level Initiatives

As was demonstrated in Chapter 3, curriculum decisions stemming from factors at the macro level—often shaped by supra-level factors—sometimes do not translate as envisioned into the micro context. Existing literature indicates that curriculum reform initiatives in some EFL contexts aimed at replacing grammar-based curricula with communicative or task-based language teaching approaches (e.g., Alharbi, 2022; Ali & Walker, 2014; Butler, 2011; Rahman, Islam, et al., 2019; Rahman, Johan, et al., 2019; Littlewood, 2007) or implementing the EMI model (e.g., Mustafawi & Shaaban, 2019) often encounter challenges in execution. Reported reasons for these shortcomings include:

- Misconceptions or insufficient knowledge of the adopted approach to curriculum development
- Conflicts with local values and cultural norms
- Lack of proper classroom equipment
- Overcrowded classrooms
- Grammar-focused examination systems
- Inadequate teacher training
- Preference for traditional teaching styles
- Low teacher confidence and gaps in English language skills
- Passive learning environment
- Lack of interest and motivation in learning the target language

How can situation analysis identify and address these issues in the curriculum planning phase? A comprehensive situation analysis is essential for assessing the compatibility and suitability of macro-level curriculum initiatives within the local context. By conducting a thorough situation analysis, stakeholders can uncover specific challenges that may hinder effective implementation. This analysis can provide valuable insights into the appropriateness of various curricular elements—such as teaching approaches, technological tools, or instructional materials—in the given context. It can further inform targeted strategies to mitigate potential issues, such as pilot programs or gradual implementation phases to test new curricula and address any challenges before full rollout. It can also highlight the need for targeted training and professional development opportunities for teachers to ensure effective delivery. Additionally, situation analysis can guide budget allocations to create an appropriate classroom environment and supply the necessary pedagogical means for successful curriculum implementation. In brief, rigorous situation analysis is crucial for macro-level curriculum initiatives to inform curriculum development and enhance the likelihood of its success by proactively addressing contextual challenges.

The Case of Imported Instructional Materials

The impact of imported textbooks on effective teaching and learning is a significant concern, documented in the ELT literature, as these materials often fail to align with the local sociocultural context. In her analysis of popular textbook series from major ELT publishers aimed at adult learners globally, Hilliard (2014) found that these textbooks typically cover a narrow range of topics, feature a limited variety of accents, underrepresent minority groups, and provide superficial cultural information. Further studies evaluating the alignment of imported textbooks with local beliefs, norms, traditions, and values across various EFL contexts (e.g., Abdollahzadeh & Baniasad, 2010; Ahmed, 2011; Köksal & Ulum, 2021; Kim, 2011; Lee, 2009; Seidi et al., 2016) have echoed these concerns. Common issues include minimal representation of local culture, the promotion of Western ideologies and practices, linguistic imperialism, and the perpetuation of cultural stereotypes. Such textbooks often face resistance from both teachers and learners due to their perceived relevance or insensitivity. However, as noted by Forman (2014), some teachers, while expressing discomfort with these issues, may not actively oppose the use of such materials. In situations where the textbook effectively serves as the curriculum, they might refrain from questioning its authority or challenging its content.

How can situation analysis identify and address these issues in the curriculum planning phase? Incorporating situation analysis into the curriculum planning phase can effectively identify and address issues related to instructional materials. By considering these materials as part of the analysis, stakeholders can ensure that the selected resources are accessible and affordable for the student population, effective in supporting curriculum objectives, and appropriate to the sociocultural context. Language textbooks should be regarded as social and cultural artifacts rather than merely neutral technical tools (Xiong, 2012). Therefore, dedicating time during the curriculum planning process to evaluate textbooks against clear criteria for effectiveness and relevance is essential. This evaluation should encompass aspects such as cultural representation, alignment with local values, and inclusivity. Involving teachers in the review process and gathering periodic feedback from students on materials can enhance this evaluation. Additionally, a systematic situation analysis can help identify gaps in existing materials, allowing for the recommendation of supplementary resources or alternative texts that better align with student needs. This proactive evaluation can lead to more effective curriculum implementation, minimizing resistance and enhancing the overall learning experience.

The Case of the Asynchronous TEFL Course

Two ESL teachers from Libya, Layla and Dina (pseudonyms), who reside in the United States, initiated a collaborative project to develop free online courses for current and prospective EFL teachers in Libya. Through informal communications with fellow teachers in Libya, they identified a strong interest in such offerings. The project involved navigating various logistics, including identifying overarching goals, outlining courses and their objectives, designing and building a website to communicate project details, and exploring platforms for course delivery. The project also involved designing a needs analysis survey to gather information about the students, including their experiences and goals for the course. Following best practices in asynchronous course design, Layla and Dina co-developed the first course in the series, "Introduction to Teaching English as a Foreign Language (TEFL)," consisting of five modules: (1) Principles of Language Teaching and Learning, (2) Teaching Grammar, (3) Teaching Reading and Writing, (4) Teaching Listening and Speaking, and (5) Teaching Vocabulary. Each module was structured consistently and included videos recorded by Layla and Dina, readings, supplemental resources, and formative and summative assessments accompanied by rubrics. For example, each unit featured a mini multiple-choice quiz to reinforce learning, a discussion board question for personal reflections and community building, and an end-of-unit task that provided students with the opportunity to apply their knowledge in meaningful ways. The course was launched using the learning management system (LMS) CourseSites by Blackboard, which provided free course delivery. Layla and Dina also created short video tutorials and written guidelines to facilitate student navigation of the course site and completion of assignments. The course was piloted with a small cohort of students.

Despite their diligent curriculum planning, the project overlooked critical meso-level factors that hindered student engagement. Ongoing unrest and post-war challenges in Libya created significant obstacles, such as frequent power outages and unreliable Internet connectivity. These issues severely limited students' access to the LMS platform, preventing them from viewing recorded content and completing assignments. One student recounted her struggle to connect, stating she would wake up in the middle of the night hoping for a stable Internet connection but often found that "even when there is Internet, it would be very slow, and pages take forever to open." Due to the course being unusable, Dina and Layla did not proceed with fully developing the other courses in the series that they wished to create as part of the project.

How can situation analysis identify and address these issues in the curriculum planning phase? A situation analysis could have highlighted the significance of these macro-level challenges posed by the unrest and infrastructural issues in Libya. Rather than focusing solely on demographic information, professional backgrounds, and preferences for course topics and skills, the needs analysis survey could have included questions about the students' local context to better understand their specific challenges related to technology and Internet access. This insight would have guided course design to align with students' realities. Understanding these challenges during the curriculum planning phase would have enabled the developers to consider alternative formats for course delivery, such as downloadable content or offline resources that could be shared through accessible applications like WhatsApp, allowing students to engage without needing to log in to an LMS. Piloting the course with a smaller group of students—as was done in this scenario—could have helped identify those specific issues, which indeed emerged during the pilot. However, due to the time and effort invested in developing the full course discussed here, the piloting phase may have only involved working on and testing a single module.

General Guidelines for Conducting Situation Analysis

Situation analysis is a process that investigates the circumstances of the actual curriculum context to determine what is feasible, appropriate, and necessary for effective learning. This process utilizes the same guidelines for planning needs analysis and the methods and procedures for data collection and analysis discussed in this chapter. It is important to note that while there is extensive research on the use of needs analysis in ELT, studies focusing on situation analysis are comparatively rare. This is likely because needs analysis findings can often be generalized across different student populations, whereas situation analysis is more context specific as it aims to understand localized curriculum contexts. It could also be due to the fact that some curriculum developers may be confident in their intuition about the local context, leading them to disregard this important procedure, as argued by Print (1993):

> Some curriculum developers may argue that they don't need a situational analysis to understand the context of their curriculum. After all, they have an intuitive understanding of student needs and necessary curricula to meet those needs! However, we should question curriculum developers as to where this intuitive response comes from and to what degree is it valid. Amongst other things, a situational analysis provides a clearer vision of the curriculum context as well as a systematically devised database, both of which provide a more reliable and valid source for later curriculum decisions. (p. 114)

Given the impracticality of examining every potential factor that could influence a curriculum initiative, it is advisable to identify and prioritize key factors that may significantly affect curriculum fidelity and effectiveness if overlooked (Print, 1993). The specific factors will depend on the nature of the curriculum project. The curriculum development team should collectively brainstorm potential factors that could impact the project and then rank them based on importance. The following are general steps for conducting a situation analysis:

1. Define the curriculum project: Clearly articulate the project's scope and objectives.
2. Identify relevant factors: List and rank situational factors that could significantly influence the project's success, considering both internal and external elements.
3. Determine data collection and analysis methods: Outline methods, responsibilities, and timelines for data collection and analysis.

4. Collect data and document findings: Implement the data collection plan and document findings.
5. Interpret data: Analyze the findings in relation to the curriculum project's objectives and identify actionable insights.

To illustrate the steps for planning a situation analysis, consider an elementary school in California that has witnessed an increase in its Hispanic student population, leading to requests from parents in the immigrant community to preserve their children's native language. In response, the school is piloting a bilingual curriculum for 3rd-grade students aimed at enhancing both English and Spanish language proficiency, improving academic performance, and promoting cultural awareness. Table 7.11 outlines an approach to conducting a situation analysis for the proposed bilingual curriculum.

Table 7.11 Example of a Situation Analysis Process

- **The curriculum project:** Designing a bilingual English-Spanish curriculum for 3rd-grade students to promote language proficiency in English and Spanish, enhance student academic performance, and foster cultural awareness of student heritage.
- **Situational factors that can influence or inform the project:**
  - Nano-level student factors: Assessing current students' language skills in both English and Spanish, understanding the cultural diversity of students, and exploring their attitudes toward bilingual education and motivation levels
  - Nano-level teacher factors: Evaluating the language proficiency, training, and beliefs of teachers regarding bilingual education
  - Meso-level program factors: Assessing resource availability, such as bilingual textbooks and online tools and applications for building students' language proficiency and supporting content area knowledge, as well as examining the school culture and existing curriculum structures
  - Macro-level community factors: Investigating parental involvement, the availability of community resources (e.g., public libraries), and local organizations that support bilingual education and cultural events
  - Macro-level policy factors: Reviewing state and district standards for bilingual education, as well as understanding federal policies and funding opportunities that might impact the program

Table 7.11 (*Continued*)

- **Data collection and analysis methods and steps:**
  - The methods will incorporate both qualitative and quantitative approaches:
    - Surveys of students and parents: To gather insights into preferences for teaching methods, perceptions of bilingual education, and any concerns regarding the program
    - Interviews with teachers and administrators: To explore challenges they foresee with the implementation of the new curriculum and their insights on effective practices
    - Classroom observations: To evaluate teaching practices and student engagement using specific observation frameworks or criteria
    - Analysis of student performance data: To identify trends and areas for improvement in both languages
    - Review of literature on bilingual education: To gather information on best practices, challenges, and success stories in similar contexts
    - Examination of educational standards and existing curricula
    - Community asset mapping (see Feuerherm & Oshio, 2020; Ordoñez-Jasis & Myck-Wayne, 2012): To ensure alignment with state and district requirements
  - A curriculum development committee consisting of teachers, administrators, and parents will collaborate to design or adapt instruments and collect data. Responsibilities and tasks will be assigned as follows:
    - Design and distribute surveys (Weeks 1–3)
    - Prepare interview questions and conduct semi-structured interviews with teachers and administrators (Weeks 4–5)
    - Collect observational data in classrooms (Weeks 3–4)
    - Gather existing student performance data (Week 5)
    - Summarize findings from bilingual education literature (Weeks 5–6)
    - Identify and compile educational standards (Week 6)
    - Analyze collected data (Weeks 7–9)
    - Compile findings and prepare a report (Weeks 10–11)
    - Review findings with stakeholders and make recommendations (Week 12)

The findings from this situation analysis can identify specific objectives to guide curriculum development, outline the necessary instructional materials, and highlight effective teaching approaches to support bilingual education. Since this is a large project that involves various factors and dimensions, the synthesis of findings and assessment of the situational context can benefit from a SWOT analysis (Strengths, Weaknesses, Opportunities, Threats) (see Pardo & Díaz, 2020; Praveen,

2020; Santoso, 2021). This analysis may reveal the need for the school to hire more bilingual teachers proficient in both English and Spanish, pursue professional development opportunities in bilingual education, and invest in instructional materials and technology to enhance the curriculum. As a curriculum planning procedure, situation analysis considers these factors and thus allows for rational and informed decision-making during the curriculum development phase. More specifically, it can provide thoughtful insights that help in setting realistic and achievable curriculum objectives, selecting or developing materials appropriate to the local context, and identifying the resources or training needed to implement a curriculum innovation.

To conclude this chapter, the curriculum planning phase focuses on gathering information to enable effective curriculum development. Both needs analysis and situation analysis are essential in this process. Needs analysis allows for assessing the present and target language needs of students as well as other information such as their learning preferences, goals, and rights. These insights not only enhance the relevance of the curriculum but also allow for the creation of tailored courses that meet student needs. Meanwhile, situation analysis provides a contextual lens for examining the individual, institutional, sociocultural, and global factors that can impact curriculum effectiveness. By integrating these two analyses, a responsive and inclusive curriculum can be created that authentically reflects learners' needs and aligns with the local context, ultimately fostering a more meaningful and impactful language learning experience.

After you read, consider the following questions:

1. Identify a specific course you hope to teach, and respond to the following:
    a. What is the context and purpose of the course? Who will it be designed for?
    b. What information do you think is important to collect about the target student population? What specific questions do you have regarding the students? How do you plan to gather answers to these questions?
    c. What key local contextual factors could impact decision-making and should be investigated before developing the curriculum (rank these factors in order of importance)? How will you investigate these factors?

2. Read the following scenarios and then determine what sources of data and methods can best support the curriculum planning for each scenario. Start by generating a list of factors that can impact the effectiveness of the teaching and learning experience. Then, decide which tools or procedures to use and describe the data they will yield:

    a. An after-school language institute in Korea is planning a thematic listening and speaking curriculum for EFL middle and high school students. The overall goal of the curriculum is to develop the learners' communicative skills, including their pronunciation and vocabulary. The curriculum is envisioned to be largely task-based.

    b. An adult education community program in Australia is launching an ESL night school for adult English language learners. The program will offer classes ranging from beginning to high intermediate levels. The curriculum is going to be integrated with an emphasis on reading and opportunities for digital literacy.

    c. A public school for elementary education in Kenya is piloting a curriculum for the English language subject based on the United Nations Sustainable Development Goals. The curriculum aims at integrating both local and global issues. Situating learning in the students' environment, raising consciousness of social and environmental issues, as well as connecting students to their communities are among the ideas that were articulated during the conceptualization phase of the curriculum.

    d. An EAP program at a Canadian university is establishing a content-based instruction (CBI) course for an undergraduate history class (HIS 101) to support international students. Input from previous history instructors indicated a lack of participation and engagement of international students in group discussions in comparison to their Canadian classmates.

    e. As an initiative at the macro level, the Ministry of Education in Egypt, in collaboration with the British

Council, is working on replacing grammar-translation curricula in rural secondary schools with communicative language curricula. Currently, the team that is working on this initiative is considering several textbook series by international ELT publishers.

3. Read the following texts discussing constraints impacting language curriculum initiatives in various contexts, then respond to these questions: What factors have influenced curriculum development and implementation in each context? How can these influences be addressed?

    a. Zhang, E. Y. (2007). TBLT—Innovation in primary school English language teaching in mainland China. In K. Van den Branden, K. Van Gorp, & M. Verhelst (Eds.), *Tasks in action: Task-based language education from a classroom-based perspective* (pp. 68–91). Cambridge Scholars. https://repository.nie.edu.sg/handle/10497/20463

    b. Huang, S. H. (2016). Communicative language teaching: Practical difficulties in the rural EFL classrooms in Taiwan. *Journal of Education and Practice*, *7*(24), 186–202. https://eric.ed.gov/?id=EJ1112915

    c. Tarlanialiabadi, H. (2022). Communicative language teaching implementation in Iran: The case of junior high school Iranian state English teachers. *Journal of English Language and Literature Teaching*, *1*(2), 81–98. https://elt.cfu.ac.ir/article_2172.html

Chapter 8

Curriculum Development

Before you read, reflect on the following questions:

1. What is the difference between curriculum conceptualization, planning, and development, and how can they inform one another?
2. What does curriculum development involve?
3. To what extent do you think the curriculum development activity at the meso level should specify the different components of the curriculum? Why?

This chapter outlines the key elements involved in curriculum development and provides guidelines for formulating objectives and outcomes, identifying means of assessment, and determining content and learning experiences.

CPDIE: The Curriculum Development Phase

In a holistic sense, the conceptualization phase in the CPDIE framework establishes the philosophical, conceptual, and theoretical foundations that ground practice, while the planning phase fences the practice by identifying specific information to support the curriculum development activity. Think of these phases as a plot of land. Before proceeding with actual construction, a bird's-eye view is crucial to determining borders, size, terrain, possibilities, and constraints, among other factors. After forming a rationale and setting parameters, a more focused approach is needed to specify curriculum components and ensure their interconnectedness. Guided by the information gathered during the conceptualization and planning phases regarding the underlying philosophical and theoretical foundations, the target student population, the educational context, and the specifics of the curriculum development task at hand (e.g., scope, goals, timeframe, and involved individuals), the curriculum development phase addresses the following questions:

- What will students learn? (*aims of the curriculum*)
- How will this learning be monitored, observed, and measured? (*formative and summative assessments*)
- What content, instructional methods, and learning experiences are needed to facilitate effective, consistent, and inclusive learning? (*content and learning experiences*)

In the following subsections, this chapter will first illustrate how the curriculum planning phase informs the curriculum development process, and then it will shed light on each of the curriculum elements addressed in the three questions listed above. It will conclude by providing a detailed example of a curriculum development project to illustrate its resulting components.

How Curriculum Planning Informs Curriculum Development

As an overview of how data collected during the planning phase informs decision-making in curriculum development, Tables 8.1 and 8.2 capture the overall curriculum development process for an ESP and EGP course as reported in the literature (Edwards, 2000; MacPherson, 2019). These examples demonstrate the link between curriculum planning and development and highlight how information gathered during the planning phase informs key elements of the curriculum development process.

The examples in Tables 8.1 and 8.2 illustrate how data collected during the curriculum planning phase facilitates effective curriculum development. In the ESP context, Edwards' (2000) study demonstrates how needs analysis can lead to a tailored curriculum that addresses specific skills required by learners in their professional environments. The emphasis on learner input and flexible curriculum design underscores the importance of adaptability in meeting diverse learner needs. Similarly, MacPherson's (2019) study in the EGP context illustrates the significance of both objective and subjective data (testing and learner survey data) in

Table 8.1 Using Curriculum Planning Data to Inform Curriculum Development: An ESP Example

- **Study:** Edwards, 2000
- **Context:** ESP for business, a course designed for senior bankers, facilitated at their workplace in Germany
- **Curriculum planning:**
  - Needs analysis methods: (1) Employer interview and (2) learner survey conducted on the first day of class focusing on students' past experiences and goals
  - Learners' needs: Increased speaking confidence, participation in business meetings, negotiation skills, presentation delivery, report writing, comprehension of spoken and written material, vocabulary development
  - Student input: Collected feedback on curriculum objectives at the beginning of the course and additional input on content and course direction during the session
- **Curriculum development:**
  - Goals and objectives: Enhance students' overall confidence in business communications to be able to:
    - Participate in business meetings and negotiations.
    - Give presentations using various types of charts and graphs.
    - Write effective reports.
    - Read and comprehend banking-related texts.
    - Understand spoken language used by native speakers.
    - Employ general and specialist vocabulary confidently.
  - Syllabus design: Flexible, allowing for the supplementation of materials and topics as needed
  - Instructional materials:
    - Core texts: Three primary texts focusing on meetings, international business, and business vocabulary
    - Supplementary texts: Authentic materials including articles and transcripts from various media sources such as *The Economist*, *The Guardian*, *The Times*, *Time*, *Spotlight,* and BBC's *World Business Report*
  - Instructional techniques and learning experiences:
    - Top-down, student-centered approach emphasizing meaning and context by drawing on learners' background knowledge with brief deductive presentations to review grammatical structures. Learning activities include:
      - Information-gap and opinion-gap exercises to complete financial statements and reports
      - Jumbled texts for recognizing the structure of business letters and reports
      - Jumbled sentences to familiarize students with discourse patterns in meetings, negotiations, and small talk

(*Continued*)

Table 8.1 (*Continued*)

- Short articles on economics and banking for analyzing discourse markers, skimming, and detailed reading comprehension
- Role plays using authentic interview transcripts
- Vocabulary exercises, including cloze tests, matching, crossword puzzles, and sentence completion

- Assessments and feedback:
  - Vocabulary quizzes: Oral quizzes administered at the beginning of each class
  - Error correction: Instructor notes errors during class discussions and summarizes them for self-correction or peer feedback, as requested by the students
  - Self-assessment: Self-evaluation of recorded role plays and class discussions simulating meetings or negotiations

Table 8.2 Using Curriculum Planning Data to Inform Curriculum Development: An EGP Example

- **Study:** MacPherson, 2019
- **Context:** General English course for Japanese university students at Nagasaki Junshin Catholic University in Japan
- **Curriculum planning:**
  - Needs analysis methods:
    - Learner survey: Collected both objective data (e.g., years studying English, use outside class, past examinations) and subjective data (e.g., motivations, goals, perceived abilities, topics of interest) to identify learners' wants and interests
    - Diagnostic tests: Assessed learners' speaking, grammar, vocabulary, reading, and listening abilities to determine necessities and lacks
  - Needs analysis survey findings:
    - Desire to enhance English for travel and daily communication
    - Need for more speaking opportunities and pair/group work
    - Lack of opportunities to use English outside of class
    - Limited interest in reading and writing
  - Diagnostic testing findings:
    - Speaking (pair interviews): Identified frequent grammatical errors, restricted vocabulary, and reliance on L1
    - Vocabulary and grammar: Highlighted a need to focus on negative forms, modals, imperatives, infinitives, conditionals, and phrasal verbs
    - Listening and reading: Indicated a need for more exposure to authentic texts and practice in inference and synonym recognition

Table 8.2 (*Continued*)

- **Curriculum development:**
  - Goals and objectives: The curriculum development process involved identifying course priorities based on the survey and diagnostic testing data, extracting course goals from these priorities, and then formulating a statement of objectives outlining what students should be able to do to achieve the course goals (see MacPherson, 2019, pp. 147–148).
  - Curriculum organized based on relevance to learners and course goals, progressing from more familiar to less familiar topics
  - Instructional materials: A mix of existing coursebooks, original activities, and authentic texts, with materials created or adapted as necessary to meet learner needs and align with course goals
  - Instructional techniques and learning experiences: Inductive learning, error correction, PPP (Presentation, Practice, Production), TTT (Test-Teach-Test), varied interaction patterns (pair, group, and independent activities), collaborative learning (peer teaching/learning), homework for additional practice
  - Assessments and feedback:
    - Ongoing informal and formal assessments: Concept check questions, monitoring and recording output/utterances, mini systems tests, recording freer practice/communicative tasks
    - Formal summative assessments at the end of the course: Written test and pair communicative task

informing curriculum choices. These two examples highlight the interconnectedness of planning and development to provide students with learning experiences that address their needs.

Key Element of the Curriculum Development Process

While curriculum *aims* (*goals*, *objectives*, and/or *outcomes*) express the intended learning, *content* serves as the means to realize these intentions. *Learning experiences* represent the realization of the first two elements. *Assessment* allows for monitoring learning and determining if student learning *outcomes* have been achieved and to what extent (Figure 8.1). The following subsections shed light on each of these curriculum elements.

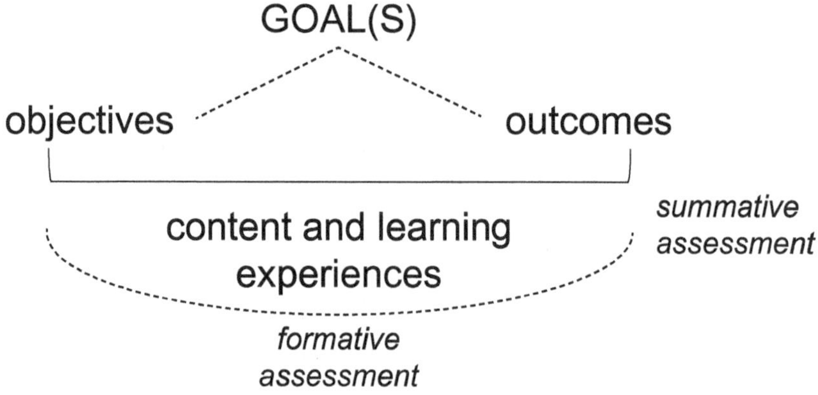

Figure 8.1. The Relationship among Curricular Elements

Aims of the Curriculum

A Product or Process Model for the ELT Curriculum?

The initial needs analysis and examination of the curriculum context serve as a solid foundation for developing a curriculum that addresses student needs and aligns with the educational environment. As noted in Chapter 4, while many curriculum development models emphasize the importance of clearly defined objectives from the outset, some argue that this early specification can constrain teaching and learning. These perspectives can be balanced by employing needs analysis as an initial, ongoing, and evaluative procedure to facilitate the development of a curriculum that is both focused and adaptable to the needs of learners.

The articulation of goals, objectives, and outcomes provides a framework, purpose, and direction for the teaching and learning situation. Developing a clear sense of what needs to be accomplished is a natural starting point for any task in our day-to-day life (whether it is as simple as cleaning around the house or running an errand). However, we often adjust our goals as we engage in the task due to factors such as time constraints, task difficulty, or exhaustion. Similarly, regardless of whether the curriculum development model is product or process oriented, the aims of curriculum and instruction must be conceptualized.

However, it is crucial that this conceptualization is neither too narrow nor confining to actual teaching and learning experiences.

Predefined objectives in the curriculum development process should be written in a way that ensures flexibility in addressing knowledge and skills that may arise through ongoing needs assessment or teacher-student negotiations. This flexibility is particularly possible in ESL/EFL courses in comparison to mainstream subjects. To explain, the nature of content in subjects like chemistry or mathematics requires specifying precise knowledge—such as mastering algebraic equations or understanding scientific principles—that curriculum and instruction are expected to instill at a certain grade level. In contrast, language learning is largely concerned with developing the linguistic and communicative abilities necessary for recognizing, comprehending, and producing an L2 suitable for the learner's proficiency level. This allows for flexibility in formulating less rigid objective statements. Language learning is also a gradual process that evolves over time. Therefore, defining the specific needs and existing language abilities of students is vital for identifying curriculum objectives that are purposeful, meaningful, and appropriately leveled. Gathering data through needs analysis—including diagnostic, placement, and language proficiency testing—is typically a prerequisite in language curriculum development.

Another way to balance the product and process approaches to curriculum development is by distinguishing between two levels of objectives: educational (or learning) objectives and instructional objectives (Anderson et al., 2001). Educational objectives are identified during the curriculum development process to pinpoint the type of knowledge and abilities the curriculum aims to achieve, and they serve as benchmarks. These objectives justify the existence of a course and specify the knowledge, skills, and abilities students are expected to acquire. Establishing this framework ensures transparency, uniformity, and consistency in what students gain from the curriculum, regardless of the instructor. Teachers then use this general framework to guide their lesson planning, from which they can extract and formulate specific instructional objectives "that fit their particular students' needs and readiness" (Anderson et al., 2001, p. 20). Instructional objectives will be discussed further in the following chapter, "Curriculum Implementation" (Chapter 9). This chapter focuses primarily on the learning or educational objectives that determine the focus of a given curriculum.

Goals, Objectives, and Outcomes

Guided by the information gathered in the curriculum planning phase, the answer to the first question in the curriculum development process: "What will students learn?" may yield a statement of course goals, objectives, and/or outcomes. Which of these curricular elements should be included—and the differences between them—should be clarified in the curriculum theory established during the conceptualization phase (Chapter 6). As discussed before, this allows for reaching a mutual understanding of what each entails within a particular educational context.

Goals tend to be abstract and long-term as they describe the broad intents of the curriculum and may be part of the course description statement (e.g., "In this course, students will develop comprehension and production of basic spoken English at the beginner level"). Objectives and outcomes are often used interchangeably to communicate observable and measurable learning. Some programs might have one or both in place. Curriculum standards set forth by CEA (2022) require English language programs and institutions to have course goals, objectives, and outcomes in writing (p. 13):

> Written curricular materials must include carefully developed course goals (the overall intended outcome or target for the course), course objectives (what will be taught), and student learning outcomes (what the student knows or can do as a result of the course of instruction), a process for teaching and learning, and suggested methods of assessment. The curriculum must be implemented using appropriate methodologies and materials.

Because of their importance in serving as a roadmap for curricular targets and a compass for instruction, objective and outcome statements at the meso level should be "collaboratively authored and collectively accepted" (Maki, 2004, p. 60). If the curriculum development process seeks to formulate objectives and outcomes as two separate statements, it is important to understand the nature of these two. First of all, both objectives and outcomes are specific, achievable, and assessable. The difference is that objectives tend to focus on instruction and are often more detailed while outcomes are oriented toward the learning that results from completing a learning experience and are often written more succinctly. Additionally, one outcome may sum up several objectives.

It is also important to note that rather than describing a specific activity (e.g., "Use the Oxford Picture Dictionary to look up the meaning of unknown words"), a student learning outcome (SLO) should articulate the skill, knowledge, or ability that students will acquire at the end of a unit or course and can apply in various contexts. For example, an effective SLO might be: "Students will be able to utilize online resources and digital tools (such as thesaurus and dictionaries) to independently determine the meanings of unfamiliar vocabulary within readings." This emphasis on broader competencies ensures that outcomes are relevant beyond a single task.

Examples of Curriculum Goals, Objectives, and Outcomes

To illustrate the relationship between goals, objectives, and outcomes, we will build on two examples that were provided in Chapter 7. The first example is the EAP pathway reading and writing course for graduate students (Table 7.9). The insights gained from the needs analysis findings identified the development of reading strategies, among other needs, as one of the key skills students need to navigate their graduate courses. Table 8.3 highlights the broad goal of the curriculum and outlines three sample reading objectives that culminate in one student learning

Table 8.3 Example I Illustrating the Differences between Goals, Objectives, and Outcomes

Course Goal
In this course, students will develop critical reading and inquiry skills to process texts and construct papers at the graduate level.
Course Objectives
In this course, students will learn to: 1. Annotate texts to identify main ideas, supporting details, relationship between ideas, and organizational patterns. 2. Use critical reading strategies to identify text purpose, author's tone, biases, hidden assumptions, and logical fallacies. 3. Interpret data from charts, graphs, and tables and report the information in writing.
Student Learning Outcomes
Upon successful completion of this course, students will be able to: 1. Apply active and critical reading strategies to read and analyze academic texts and data.

outcome. The three provided objectives specify discrete skills that serve as foundational building blocks for achieving the outcome.

To further illustrate the relationship between goals, objectives, and outcomes, let us refer back to the example presented in Table 7.3 from Chapter 7. This example demonstrates how needs analysis procedures were employed to identify the needs of high-beginner adult English language learners who were recent refugees in an English-speaking country. The needs analysis data uncovered several priority needs that the curriculum must address:

- Communicative skills: Develop the ability to ask for and give directions, express health concerns in healthcare settings, and communicate effectively with school personnel regarding their children's needs.
- Sociolinguistic knowledge: Enhance language proficiency and cultural understanding to communicate the aforementioned points effectively.
- Practical skills: Build the skills necessary to navigate real-life tasks.

Based on the identified needs, the curriculum development process for this high-beginner adult integrated-skills English language course involved establishing a broad goal and subsequently extracting specific objectives and outcomes. A sample course goal and objective and outcome statements from this curriculum development activity are presented in Table 8.4.

The provided goal articulates the overarching aim of the curriculum. The sample objectives are specific, measurable, and actionable, clearly outlining what students are expected to learn. Additionally, the objectives are designed to be flexible, allowing for adjustments based on ongoing needs analysis. The SLOs encapsulate these objectives, reflecting the broader competencies that students will acquire by the end of the course. This alignment ensures that the curriculum remains relevant and responsive to student needs.

Domains of Knowledge and Objectives/Outcomes

Concrete action verbs (Table 8.5) are typically used to avoid vague, general, or unattainable objectives and outcomes. Bloom's Taxonomy

Table 8.4 Example II Illustrating the Differences between Goals, Objectives, and Outcomes

Course Goal

In this course, students will develop practical English language skills at the beginner level necessary for navigating daily life effectively.

Course Objectives

In this course, students will learn to:

1. Utilize key vocabulary and phrases related to healthcare, transportation, and daily interactions in spoken and written contexts.
2. Construct and identify oral and written affirmative and negative statements and wh-questions (*who, what, when, where, why,* and *how*)—and yes/no questions in the present, past, and future tenses.
3. Ask for and understand directions using phrases like "Where is . . . ?" and "How do I get to . . . ?"
4. Read and interpret public transportation schedules and related materials.
5. Listen to and interpret spoken information (e.g., instructions and announcements) in various contexts.
6. Recognize and apply cultural norms in communication, such as greetings, etiquette, and body language.
7. Use basic digital tools and resources to assist in language learning and daily communication.

Student Learning Outcomes

Upon successful completion of this course, students will be able to:

1. Use and understand vocabulary and phrases in daily interactions.
2. Produce basic sentences including affirmative and negative statements and questions.
3. Express present, past, future events accurately by utilizing appropriate verb tenses and sentence structure.
4. Comprehend spoken English in everyday contexts.
5. Apply knowledge of cultural norms to navigate social interactions effectively.
6. Utilize digital resources for language support and communication.

(Bloom et al.,1956; Anderson et al., 2001) is a widely used framework for devising objectives and outcomes. Bloom and colleagues grouped educational objectives into six domains of cognition representing a continuum of lower-order (less complex) to higher-order (increasingly complex) cognitive demands, as illustrated in Table 8.5.

Table 8.5 Bloom's Taxonomy Domains and Corresponding Verbs for Objectives and Outcomes

Cognitive Complexity	Cognitive Dimension	Sample Concrete Verbs
Higher-order thinking skills	Creating	compose, construct, create, synthesize, design, develop, integrate, make, modify, prepare, formulate, reconstruct
	Evaluating	assess, critique, decide, determine, defend, test, judge, justify, measure, predict, prove, estimate, validate
	Analyzing	analyze, categorize, compare, contrast, deconstruct, differentiate, examine, infer, diagram
Lower-order thinking skills	Applying	apply, carry out, choose, illustrate, employ, show, solve, use
	Understanding	describe, summarize, discuss, locate, distinguish, clarify, classify, explain, identify, relate, report, restate
	Remembering	define, list, underline, describe, identify, label, list, match, name, order, recall, recognize

The types of skills and abilities that objectives target can be further classified into psychomotor, affective, and cognitive (Bloom et al.,1956). While most of the objectives listed in the table above draw on cognitive abilities, some also require psychomotor skills involving physical movement and coordination (Simpson, 1966). An objective such as "Use a word processor to compose well-supported, structured, and formatted essays using cause-effect, compare-contrast, and argumentation as rhetorical modes" entails that the students need cognitive knowledge not only to construct coherent, cohesive, and well-supported essays but also psychomotor abilities to be able to use and navigate a computer effectively.

Affective objectives aim to stimulate students' interests, attitudes, desires, and motivation (Eissm & Harbeck, 1969; Holt & Hannon, 2006). For example, a course that focuses on extensive reading seeks to enhance L2 reading fluency by encouraging students to read enjoyable and interesting books. To promote reading for pleasure, the course may also include affective objectives that aim to boost learners' reading confidence and foster positive attitudes and appreciation for reading. Affective objectives are often neglected in curriculum and instruction due to the difficulty in measuring them compared to cognitive and psychomotor objectives. It is important to note that these three types of objectives may overlap. Psychomotor and affective objectives, however, are typically secondary, while cognitive objectives are the dominant type in curriculum and instruction (Bemis & Schroeder, 1969) simply because learning is largely a cognitive activity.

Curriculum Type and Objectives/Outcomes

In addition to the aims of the educational program (why it exists) and the needs of the target student population, another important aspect that shapes the objectives of language learning is the type of curriculum (or curricula) a program has in place. For instance, is the curriculum established as communicative, task-based, content-based, or genre-based, and to what degree? Or do these refer to approaches that ground the instructional methodologies? Or perhaps both? These factors can influence the formulation of curriculum objectives and need to be addressed in the conceptualization and planning phases.

For example, an objective for a high-beginner or pre-intermediate grammar or integrated-skills course may include an objective that focuses on students' ability to "Identify and use the simple present tense in affirmative, negative, and interrogative sentences." Instructional methods to facilitate the learning of this objective could include communicative, task-based, or content-based activities. In contrast, objectives of a curriculum grounded in task-based learning principles should emphasize performing tasks, such as "Students will be able to describe their daily routines using appropriate vocabulary and present simple tense during role plays." This objective reflects a focus on language use in context, rather than isolated grammatical forms.

For a content-based instruction curriculum, the derivation of objectives depends largely on the implemented version of CBI. That is, is the curriculum language or content driven (Met, 1999)? As we discussed in Chapter 4, the sheltered model of CBI is an example of a content-driven curriculum in which the focus is the learning of the subject matter (Brinton et al., 1989). This situation might require two types of objectives: content objectives and language objectives. For example, in a content-driven curriculum focusing on environmental science, a content objective might state, "Students will explain the water cycle," while a corresponding language objective could be, "Students will be able to

Table 8.6 Considerations for the Articulation of Aims during the Curriculum Development Phase

1. Goals are broad statements that summarize the overall intended purpose of the curriculum.
2. Objectives and outcomes may be used interchangeably to refer to the specific knowledge and skills students will acquire by completing a given course.
3. If incorporating both objectives and outcomes as part of the curriculum, it is important to define what each entails in the curriculum theory formulated during the conceptualization phase.
4. Objectives/outcomes are derived from student needs.
5. Objectives/outcomes need to be measurable, observable, and attainable.
6. Objective/outcome statements should guide and systemize the teaching and learning process, but there should be flexibility in their formulation to ensure responsive teaching to student needs.
7. Instructional objectives (discussed in Chapter 9) can promote teacher autonomy and a richer learning experience that is adaptable and responsive to student needs. They can also support further learning needs that emerge from the teaching and learning situation or are identified through ongoing needs analyses.
8. The type of language curriculum can shape how objectives/outcomes are formulated, and this should be clarified as part of the ESL theory established during the conceptualization phase.

describe the water cycle using key vocabulary such as evaporation, condensation, and precipitation." Language objectives are often derived as part of instructional objectives in lesson planning to support the type of language needed to learn and understand specific concepts and facts.

To sum up this subsection, Table 8.6 highlights important points concerning curriculum goals, objectives, and outcomes.

Evaluation and Feedback

Formative vs. Summative Assessments

Assessment is a process that allows us to gather data on students' progress and performance and use it to inform educational decision-making (Salvia & Ysseldyke, 2007). Assessments can be categorized into formative assessment and summative assessment. Formative assessments are ongoing informal and formal ways of assessment used to monitor, assist, and inform teaching and learning. As the name suggests, this type of assessment helps teachers gauge or *form* an idea about students' progress toward specific learning objectives (e.g., What is their progress?) as well as the effectiveness of the instructional activities and materials used (e.g., Are they working? Do I need to adjust or supplement?). This ongoing nature allows formative assessments to function as a continuous needs analysis, enabling teachers to identify and respond to students' evolving needs. Examples of formative assessments include quizzes, classroom discussions, and peer reviews. Because feedback is an important aspect of formative assessment, it also helps students monitor their own learning and progress. Formative assessment is a valuable facet of curriculum and instruction that can be enriching to the teaching and learning experience.

Summative assessments, on the other hand, *sum up* the learning experience. These assessments allow teachers to observe and measure the extent of learning, typically occurring at the end of a curriculum milestone (e.g., a unit or course). They are often higher stakes than formative assessments and include assessments such as final exams, standardized tests, and end-of-term projects. The primary purpose of summative assessments is to evaluate student learning at a specific point in time to measure overall achievement against curriculum objectives, SLOs, standards, or benchmarks. Thus, data gathered from summative assessments provides insights into the effectiveness of curriculum and instruction in accomplishing the intended outcomes and can inform future planning and instructional practices.

Both formative and summative assessments are crucial components of a comprehensive assessment strategy. Formative assessments can prepare students for summative assessments by providing practice and feedback, while summative assessments inform broader educational decisions such as curriculum effectiveness and student placement or progression to the next course or level.

Tackling Assessment in Curriculum Development

One of the principles of the Universal Design for Learning framework is aligning assessments to learning objectives (CAST, n.d.) to ensure fair and meaningful evaluations that reflect the knowledge and skills taught and learned. Thus, following the backward design model (Wiggins & McTighe, 2005), an important procedure in the curriculum development phase is identifying the forms of evidence that can demonstrate learning. This step early in the process allows for (a) checking the assessability of the identified objectives and outcomes and adjusting them accordingly,

(b) envisioning what students will be able to do once they have acquired the identified knowledge and skills, and (c) determining the means and experiences that will best facilitate learning and lead to the achievement of the outcomes.

The extent to which assessment events are specified during curriculum development depends on the level of coordination and uniformity within an educational program. To ensure that students receive comparable learning, summative assessments need to be consistent to maintain horizontal alignment across multiple sections of the same course. Since formative assessments support learning, there should be flexibility in the assessment tools teachers select for this purpose. The curriculum development task can focus on mapping the objectives and outcomes to summative assessments to ensure their alignment and logical connections (Elturki, 2020). Tables 8.7 and 8.8 illustrate the procedures for mapping

Table 8.7 Sample Assessment Mapping for the EAP Pathway Course

Objectives Number	SLOs Number	Summative Assessment	Suggested Ways for Formative Assessment
1, 2, 3	1	• Reading assignments and exams • Summary/ critique essays	• Deconstructing articles • Article discussions • Summarizing and responding to readings • Data commentary tasks

Table 8.8 Sample Assessment Mapping for the Adult High-Beginner ESL Course

Objectives Number	SLOs Number	Summative Assessment	Suggested Ways for Formative Assessment
1, 2	1, 2	• Writing test: writing dialogues based on role-play scenario	• Peer review of dialogues • Writing drafts with feedback • Vocabulary quizzes
1, 2, 3, 5	1, 2	• Speaking test: real-life scenario role plays in pairs	• Group and pair speaking activities • Observation checklists

objectives, outcomes, and assessments in curriculum development using the examples provided in Tables 8.3 and 8.4.

Utilizing a similar mapping chart during the curriculum development process provides an opportunity to closely examine curriculum objectives and outcomes while identifying forms of assessment that demonstrate learning and support student progress. This procedure helps ensure curriculum coherence.

Factors Influencing Assessment

It is important to note that the nature and success of assessment can be influenced by various factors at the nano, micro, meso, macro, and/or supra levels. These factors may include stakeholders' philosophical beliefs and values regarding assessment and feedback, the educational program's purpose, the learners' characteristics and goals, available resources, and the theoretical frameworks guiding practice. For instance, in an ESP vocational training program for healthcare professionals, assessment strategies may be shaped by the goal of ensuring students can use English to perform practical skills in real-life situations, grounded in the principles of task-based learning. This focus could lead to the use of practical assessments and simulations (e.g., virtual reality (VR) simulations mirroring real-life healthcare scenarios) instead of traditional written exams. However, implementing such assessments requires careful consideration of their feasibility and the availability of resources. Therefore, these factors should be incorporated into curriculum planning as part of a situational analysis to inform decision-making during curriculum development.

At the meso level, clear expectations for assessment practices are established in the conceptualization phase based on theory and research. This determines the answers to the following questions:

1. Will data on student achievement of intended outcomes be collected through formal final exams, portfolios, or an alternative form of assessment (e.g., service-learning projects)?
2. Who constructs summative assessments? How are they constructed and graded, and what grading scheme is used?
3. How will feedback be provided to students, and what mechanisms will be in place for students to reflect on their learning?

4. What procedures are in place to ensure the assessment events are reliable, valid, authentic, practical, and impactful? Below are brief definitions of each concept (Bachman & Palmer, 1996; Elturki, 2020):
    a. Reliable: The assessment can yield consistent results if repeated under similar circumstances.
        - Example: *A reading comprehension test should produce similar scores for the same student if taken multiple times.*
    b. Valid: The assessment measures what it intends to measure.
        - Example: *Testing pronunciation should involve actual pronunciation tasks rather than merely answering questions about proper pronunciation on paper.*
    c. Authentic: Assessment tasks incorporate real language use and align with students' communicative needs.
        - Example: *Students could complete a written report relevant to their field, requiring them to use discipline-specific terminology, and present their findings in a format typical of professional practice.*
    d. Practical: The assessment can be constructed, administered, evaluated, and interpreted within a reasonable time, effort, and resources.
        - Example: *A first-year composition instructor teaching three sections of the same writing course for international students might use a simple rubric to grade students' essays efficiently and effectively.*
    e. Impactful: The data generated informs teaching, learning, and curriculum evaluation.
        - Example: *Assessment results can be used to guide revisions to instructional materials to better meet student needs.*
5. Are there specific accommodations or considerations for diverse learners in the assessment process?

Establishing clear assessment expectations at the meso level informs the curriculum development phase and ensures fair and consistent assessment practices. Data on student achievement is also valuable for guiding curriculum review and revision as it provides insights into the attainment of intended learning outcomes and supports informed decision-making.

Content and Learning Experiences

Content and learning experiences in curriculum development focus on identifying materials, themes, topics, and the types of teaching and learning environments that best facilitate learning. This part of curriculum development at the meso level should be descriptive rather than prescriptive by providing guidelines, principles, best practices, sample materials, and resources that teachers can draw on to support their teaching. Prescribing exactly what happens in the classroom is neither practical nor beneficial for teachers or students, as each teacher has a unique style and every classroom presents its own dynamics. Provided with support and opportunities for collaboration and professional development, teachers should have autonomy to steer learning and adapt their teaching in order to be able to respond to actual student needs in the classroom.

Many of the curriculum elements discussed below can emerge from curriculum implementation when documented or shared in a systematic manner. One of the most important ways to optimize curricular coherence and establish curriculum plans that stem from actual practice, according to Green (2021), is when instructors take "responsibility for providing transparent and navigable curriculum" (p. 103). Earlier in Chapter 5, we talked about the importance of establishing an inventory of resources at the meso level to which teachers contribute instructional materials, activities, and assessment tools. This nurtures a community of practice and can serve as a resource for future curriculum development activities.

Selection of Materials, Themes, and Topics

Materials. The selection of curricular elements depends on the systems and resources available at the meso level. Since this chapter is not directly concerned with program development, it assumes that there is an established inventory of textbooks and/or teacher-made course packets. It also assumes that new textbooks are evaluated before full adoption to assess their candidacy (e.g., methodology and content scope and breadth) and suitability for the target context and audience through situation analysis. During the development of a curriculum for a specific course, the curriculum development team can review several candidate texts that have already gone through a vetting process that determines their appropriateness to the educational context and target student population. Using a chart similar to the one provided in Table 8.9, the curriculum development team can assess the extent to which the proposed texts support the course objectives.

The following criteria are important to consider when selecting or developing instructional materials:

1. Be level appropriate: Ensure that materials are suitable for students' specific language proficiency levels.
2. Align with course objectives: Ensure that materials support the intended learning outcomes.
3. Be appropriate to the curriculum type: Tailor materials to the specific curriculum approach (e.g., skills-based versus task-based).
4. Be accessible and affordable: Consider both usability and availability and ensure that students can easily find and afford the materials.

Table 8.9 Sample Chart for Mapping Textbook Contents to Objectives

Textbook Title:			
Objective #	Units or pages addressing the objectives	Is the objective sufficiently addressed?	Gaps that need to be filled with supplemental material

5. Require minimal additional resources: Evaluate whether materials can be used with readily available equipment or if they require photocopying or specialized tools, including technology.
6. Be authentic and meaningful: Choose materials that engage students and reflect real-life contexts to enhance relevance.
7. Encourage critical thinking: Assess whether materials promote critical thinking and reflection on language use and cultural contexts.
8. Be up-to-date and relevant: Ensure that materials reflect current trends, issues, and interests that resonate with students to make learning more engaging and applicable.
9. Be sensitive to students' sociocultural context: Select materials that respect and reflect the cultural and social backgrounds of students.
10. Be inclusive of diverse backgrounds: Ensure that materials represent a range of perspectives, experiences, and varieties of English to foster an inclusive learning environment.

Themes. Similar to the selection and evaluation of books, themes are also an integral aspect of the curriculum, often determined through needs or situation analyses, especially if the program adopts a theme-based approach to curriculum and instruction. For example, the needs analysis conducted for the high-beginner adult ESL course discussed in Chapter 7 and referenced earlier in this chapter identified key communicative needs related to everyday interactions, specifically in areas such as public transportation, healthcare, and school communications. The curriculum can be structured into thematic units that emphasize these areas to allow for focused instruction on essential vocabulary and linguistic structures. This allows students to produce and utilize the language in real-life contexts. Furthermore, themes can reflect a teacher's or program's overall philosophy regarding teaching and learning. For instance, a posthumanist approach, which emphasizes the interconnectedness of humans, nonhumans, and the environment, may inform the selection of themes that promote ethical reflection and global awareness—such as environmental sustainability or animal rights. These themes encourage learners to engage critically with the world, thereby extending learning beyond mere language acquisition.

For successful implementation of themes at the meso level, a program may establish a set of themes that align with its goals and the needs of its student population. Subsequently, it can identify or create corresponding materials—textbooks, course packets, novels, and articles—that support these themes and curriculum objectives. To foster meaningful and coherent learning, instructional activities and assessments should also be designed around the course themes. For example, if the theme revolves around personal or social topics such as family structure and friendship, a writing assignment could ask students to compare and contrast different types of families.

If there are themes established for certain courses or levels of English proficiency, the curriculum development activity may involve identifying materials and assessments that support these themes (see the ENGL 010 example in the subsequent section). Course teachers can create theme-based instructional activities and materials tailored to their students' needs, which can then be added to the previously mentioned inventory of resources. Regardless of whether the curriculum is theme based, organizing learning around themes, topics, or genres is essential for contextualizing learning and making it more meaningful. Ongoing feedback from students can further enhance the relevance of these themes and ensure that the curriculum remains responsive to their evolving needs.

Topics. *Topics* here refers to the specific day-to-day content of the course, including skills, knowledge, and readings. A curriculum development activity can provide insights into key topics, knowledge, and skills, as well as the progression necessary to achieve student learning outcomes over the course duration. Tyler (1949/2013) offered key criteria for effective organization of knowledge and skills in curriculum development, which include:

- *Continuity* ensures that students have recurring opportunities to learn specific objectives over time.
- *Sequence* emphasizes that new knowledge builds on existing knowledge, progressing from broad concepts to deeper understanding.
- *Integration* involves connecting skills and knowledge learned in other courses to create a cohesive learning experience.

As noted earlier, the teacher should have the autonomy to select, detail, and arrange the specifics of their courses. Students can also have a voice in choosing course topics (as well as themes) if a negotiated curriculum model is adopted at the micro and/or meso level. This information is typically compiled in a syllabus to inform students of course contents, progression, and expectations. Coordination and collaboration among teachers can ensure systematic and consistent practices (this will be discussed further in the next chapter, "Curriculum Implementation"). When selecting topics, it is important to consider the same criteria recommended for the selection or creation of materials, such as relevance, level of suitability, engagement, cultural sensitivity, representation, and inclusion. Additionally, flexibility in adapting topics based on student feedback and emerging interests can keep the curriculum dynamic and responsive to learners' needs.

Learning Experiences. Learning experiences reflect how all previous curriculum elements interconnect and unfold in the classroom to facilitate learning. They encompass the activities, methodologies, and assessments that enable students to engage meaningfully with the curriculum. Specifying learning experiences during a curriculum development process can be challenging due to various factors at the nano level, such as individual teaching styles and students' diverse learning preferences and personalities, as well as micro-level contexts like classroom dynamics and environment.

However, a curriculum development activity at the meso level may outline the instructional methodologies that facilitate effective implementation based on the philosophical, theoretical, and empirical foundations established during the curriculum conceptualization phase. This may involve identifying opportunities for interactive and meaningful learning, such as collaborative projects, tasks that mirror real language use, and field trips. For specific curriculum types (e.g., task-based or genre-based), it is essential that key principles and procedures are outlined for successful implementation.

To nurture effective learning experiences, the following general guiding principles should be considered during curriculum development and implementation:

- Learner-centered approach: Prioritize the needs, interests, and preferences of students to create engaging and relevant learning experiences.
- Flexibility and adaptability: Utilize teaching methods that align with the curriculum type and objectives to enhance

learning effectiveness while also allowing for adjustments based on student feedback and classroom observations.

- Scaffolding: Provide structured support that gradually increases in complexity, helping students build on their existing knowledge and skills while developing independence in their learning.
- Differentiated instruction: Tailor instruction to meet diverse student needs, varying content, process, and product based on individual readiness, interests, and learning profiles.
- Active engagement: Design learning experiences that encourage active participation and collaboration among students to promote deeper understanding and involvement in the learning process.
- Authenticity: Utilize real-world contexts and tasks to make learning relevant and applicable to students' goals.
- Integration of skills: Promote the interconnection of language skills within learning experiences to provide a holistic approach to language acquisition.
- Formative assessment: Use ongoing assessments to monitor student progress and adjust teaching strategies to meet evolving learning needs.
- Supportive environment: Foster a safe space that encourages risk-taking, enhances confidence and belonging, and promotes mutual respect among students.

Final Remarks on Curriculum Development

At the conclusion of a curriculum development activity at the meso level, it is beneficial for the faculty (if feasible) to review the work resulting from the curriculum development process, which should then be incorporated into the curriculum guide recommended in Chapter 5. For newly designed curricula, conducting a pilot implementation can be advantageous to assess effectiveness and make any necessary updates before full-scale adoption. Documentation, along with regular review and revision of the curriculum, is also crucial not only for continuous improvement but also for ensuring that the curriculum evolves from and reflects actual classroom experiences.

Course Planning and Sample Curriculum Development Project

Course planning is an important element of curriculum development. The extent of course planning depends on the products that emerge from the curriculum development activities at the meso level, typically specified in the program's curriculum guide or manual. These guides can be descriptive or prescriptive. A descriptive curriculum guide provides a general framework of objectives and/or SLOs and perhaps other guiding information for instruction, materials, and assessments. In contrast, a prescriptive curriculum guide may prescribe specific components of the curriculum for a given course (e.g., content, assessments, and instructional methods). In some educational contexts, the only available piece of information about a course may be objectives or SLO statements. This requires teachers to navigate the different phases of curriculum development for their assigned course. In many cases, due to time limitations and lack of training in curriculum development, the textbook becomes the de facto curriculum (Ornstein, 1994).

Regardless of whether the available curriculum information is descriptive, prescriptive, or textbook based, it is important for successful implementation that teachers plan their assigned courses—or make sense of and interpret existing plans or textbooks by drawing on the knowledge, measures, and tools presented in the CPDIE framework as appropriate. Naturally, the fluidity of curriculum leads to it being "defined, redefined and negotiated at a number of levels and in a number of arenas" (Goodson, 1994, p. 17). The following discussion highlights an instructor's undertaking of course planning in an educational context in which the curriculum is relatively descriptive. The example provided showcases various curriculum elements and procedures discussed in this chapter and emphasizes curriculum conceptualization, planning, and development.

The Context

The example provided in this subsection highlights a preparatory academic writing course for non-native English-speaking (NNES) students, offered as part of a first-year writing program (FYWP) at a U.S. university. This course will be referred to as ENGL 010. It serves as a prerequisite for some NNES students before taking the university's required undergraduate composition course, with enrollment determined by a student's placement test score.

Curriculum design at the university level is generally descriptive rather than prescriptive. In many cases, course instructors have the liberty to choose their course themes, topics, materials, types of assignments, assessment procedures, and instructional methods. Some instructors might choose to adopt or modify a syllabus created by a colleague, which usually outlines the various components of the curriculum. Others may depend largely on the textbook or devise their own curriculum. For ENGL 010, the available resources included the course catalog description (which outlines the focus of the course, the student population, and placement and progression requirements), the SLOs for the required undergraduate composition course (for which ENGL 010 prepares students), and the FYWP's philosophy and expectations for writing instruction and assessment. The FYWP emphasizes rhetorical and genre awareness and requires three writing projects with multiple drafts for this course. The student population in ENGL 010 is diverse, representing various parts of the world.

Curriculum Conceptualization

The philosophical articulation and theoretical framework of the FYWP regarding the teaching and learning of writing, along with the larger curriculum (i.e., course sequencing and focus) and the course instructor's values and beliefs about L2 teaching and learning, guided the development of the ENGL 010 curriculum. Figure 8.2 captures some of the philosophical and theoretical foundations of ENGL 010.

As illustrated in Figure 8.2, the conceptualization of ENGL 010 embodies a blend of constructivist and socio-cognitive theories, supported by social reconstructionist and posthumanist philosophies. The curriculum emphasizes meaningful and contextualized learning, where students actively engage in constructing their knowledge and advocating for social, economic, and environmental issues as global citizens. Building on aspects of schema theory (Piaget & Inhelder, 1969) and threshold concepts (Meyer & Land, 2003), the curriculum development process focused on identifying key threshold concepts and sequencing knowledge and skills to enable students to draw upon and apply their prior knowledge and experiences (this approach is reflected in the progression of topics and the writing projects outlined below). The planning and development of the ENGL 010 curriculum were guided by the following considerations:

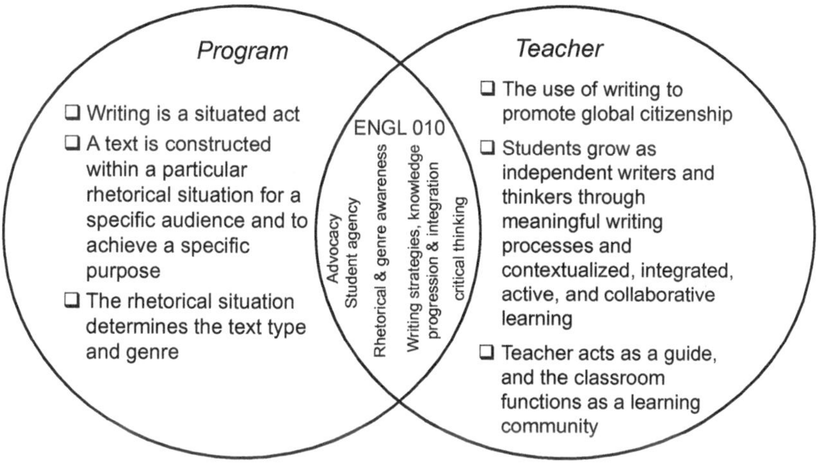

Figure 8.2. Curriculum Conceptualization: The Philosophical and Theoretical Bases of ENGL 010

- Designing meaningful writing projects that provide students with opportunities to:
    - Self-select and write about topics that resonate with them.
    - Develop writing processes tailored to their writing needs, abilities, and learning styles.
    - Experience, apply, and expand their knowledge and skills in context.
    - Approach writing with confidence and ease by breaking it into manageable phases and drawing on strategies and resources to navigate each phase effectively, make informed decisions, and be able to problem-solve.
- Identifying a theme focused on global issues to:
    - Create meaningful learning experiences.
    - Raise awareness of global, ecological, and social issues.
    - Enable students to explore, advocate for, and devise solutions to issues they care about.

- Locating theme-related texts that represent diverse genres, text types, and linguistic and cultural backgrounds.
- Determining and then sequencing the knowledge and skills necessary for students to develop academic writing skills and understand rhetorical concepts by:
    - Starting with fundamental knowledge to reinforce and build on what students already know.
    - Progressing from less to more complex topics (i.e., lower to higher cognitive skills).
- Incorporating ongoing needs assessments to monitor individual needs and allow students to communicate their preferences, goals, and priorities.
- Establishing an evaluation system that emphasizes feedback, learning, and growth.
- Fostering an inclusive learning environment where each student feels valued and comfortable sharing ideas, learning together, and supporting one another as writers.

Curriculum Planning

To collect information on the course, its context, and the targeted student population in preparation for curriculum development, the curriculum planning phase involved the following procedures.

Communicating with Course Instructors

One of the initial steps involved discussing the course with instructors who had previously taught it. These communications allowed the course instructor to ask questions, understand how others had approached this course, and gather insights into students' abilities and needs.

Collecting and Analyzing Course Syllabi

Another early procedure involved collecting ten syllabi for ENGL 010. These syllabi were obtained either from former instructors or accessed through the program's instructor Blackboard site, which contains sample syllabi for all composition courses and other relevant resources. The syllabi detailed all curriculum elements, including the course theme, writing project descriptions, and course schedule. Analyzing the syllabi provided valuable insights into the nature and length of writing assignments. Some instructors focused on unique themes such as fashion, technology, and health, while others adopted more generic themes that emphasized writing as a process or writing in college. Since there are no set SLOs for this course, many instructors aligned their SLOs with those of the core composition course that ENGL 010 prepares students for, which emphasizes rhetorical and genre awareness, as well as argumentation. A few instructors created their own SLOs, incorporating specific outcomes related to reading strategies, grammatical accuracy, and writing skills like paraphrasing and summarizing.

Examining the Larger Curriculum

Rather than developing the ENGL 010 curriculum in isolation, planning it in relation to the subsequent core composition course situated ENGL 010 within a broader curriculum context, enabling informed decisions and meaningful choices. This procedure involved examining the SLOs of the core composition course, sample content, and students' writing projects. The instructor's experience with developing and teaching the core composition curriculum was particularly valuable in informing the ENGL 010 development.

Surveying the Students

Another important planning procedure involved gathering some information about each student through an "About Me Survey." This survey included personal questions (e.g., preferred names, languages spoken, and other courses taken alongside ENGL 010), as well as questions about students' experiences and attitudes toward academic writing, perceptions of their writing abilities and time management skills, writing goals and priorities, topics of interest, and any additional information they wished to share. The survey was sent to registered students about a week before the semester began, after the class roster became available. Although this step occurred after establishing the main components of the curriculum (such as the course theme, SLOs, and major writing assessments), it proved helpful for planning instructional activities and getting to learn about the students before meeting them.

Investigating Potential Course Themes and Topics

The planning phase also involved extensive research on how to incorporate and center the curriculum around current issues that are critical to the world while remaining varied and not too narrow to account for diverse student interests. The outcome of this research is presented in the "Curriculum Development" subsection below.

Conducting Initial Needs Assessments

Initial needs assessment activities during the first week of class provided further understanding of students' abilities, needs, goals, and expectations. These activities included mini reflections on their academic writing experiences and free writing tasks related to the course theme (e.g., topic preferences). It is important to note that these shorter writing tasks also served as diagnostic assessments. The writing of one of the students, for instance, demonstrated that she was ready and would benefit from moving to the core composition course. Ongoing needs assessments were crucial for shaping the curriculum throughout the semester.

Curriculum Development

Informed by the curriculum conceptualization and planning phases, the curriculum development phase involved identifying what students will learn, how they will demonstrate their learning, and which theme, materials, topics, learning experiences, and instructional activities will facilitate this process. The following information highlights some of the key outcomes of the curriculum development phase.

SLOs

In terms of student learning outcomes (this educational context requires only SLOs and no course objectives), the course instructor chose to align the SLOs with those of the core composition course for which ENGL 010 serves as a preparatory course. As shown in Table 8.10, the SLOs are designed to be flexible and broad, outlining the overarching knowledge and skills students are expected to develop by completing this course. The formulation of the SLOs was guided by Bloom's Taxonomy and the guidelines for crafting SLOs discussed in this chapter.

The Theme

The curriculum development process involved finalizing the course theme and determining how it would be guided. The course instructor decided to use the United Nations Sustainable Development Goals (SDGs) as a framework to guide topics and readings and to contextualize writing assignments. As can be seen in Table 8.11, the SDGs encompass 17 goals

Table 8.10 ENGL 010 Student Learning Outcomes (SLOs)

Upon completion of this course, students will be able to:
1. Read varied text types across different genres by applying critical reading strategies. 2. Identify the elements of the rhetorical situation including appeals when deconstructing and constructing texts. 3. Plan, draft, revise, and edit own writing by employing a process approach that incorporates peer and instructor feedback. 4. Compose evidence-based arguments to support claims. 5. Make connections and synthesize information across multiple texts. 6. Construct coherent, cohesive, and well-supported and organized texts.

Table 8.11 An Overview of the ENGL 010 Curriculum

Course Sub-Title/Theme:
Toward Global Citizenship Through Writing
Course Description:
While the world thrives on technological advancements, communications, and connectivity; poverty, persistent struggles such as poverty, hunger, pollution, inequality, and limited access to healthcare (and the list goes on) remain prevalent in this modern day and time. As global citizens, we can alleviate some of these challenges by being conscious, raising awareness, and taking action. In this class, using the United Nations' Sustainable Development Goals (SDGs) as a framework for discussion and writing, we will tackle different social justice, environmental, and economic issues. Consisting of 17 goals to be accomplished by 2030, the SDGs are "an urgent call" to action as global citizens to better the life of all individuals, rebuild a more just and equitable society, and protect our planet. We will read and analyze texts in various genres on such topics and engage in the writing process to construct summary-response essays, a proposal argument, a multimodal campaign product, and a reflection. These activities will enhance your critical reading skills, rhetorical knowledge, and academic writing skills.

that address social issues, environmental and ecological matters, and economic development and innovation. This framework provides students with diverse topics to select from based on their interests, preferences, and values. It is important to note that some of the initial needs assessment activities during the first week aimed to connect the students with the theme, expose them to the 17 SDGs, and encourage them to reflect on and discuss which goals they perceive as priorities and why.

Summative Assessments

Another important initial step in the curriculum development process was deciding on the types of summative assessments that would allow students to demonstrate the course SLOs, engage with the course theme meaningfully, raise awareness of the global issues reflected in the SDGs, and explore ways to address these challenges. Based on this rationale and the FYWP's requirements of three writing projects, the end results were three writing portfolios distributed across the 16-week semester: the Summary-Response Portfolio, the Argument Portfolio, and the Reflection Portfolio. These portfolios are discussed further below in relation to the SLOs and the associated knowledge and skills.

Knowledge and Skills

The curriculum development process involved mapping the course SLOs to the summative assessments outlined above and identifying sub-knowledge and skills that students would need to approach these writing assignments confidently and demonstrate their level of accomplishment of the SLOs. Adopting a spiral approach to curriculum development (Bruner, 1960), the course instructor chose knowledge and skills that would build on one another, progressing from less to more complex.

In the first few weeks of the semester, students are introduced to fundamental knowledge, skills, and strategies that enable them to read, comprehend, summarize, analyze, and identify the rhetorical elements of a given text (e.g., author, text type, genre, primary and secondary audience, purpose, context, and the rhetorical appeals used by the author). Building on this foundational knowledge, the course then progresses to more complex writing tasks that require students to research, synthesize, argue, persuade, and create a multimodal text. Tables 8.12 and 8.13 highlight two sample summative assessments that demonstrate these knowledge and skills.

Table 8.12 Sample Curriculum Development Product I: Summative Assessment, Corresponding SLOs, and Focus of Instruction

	The Summary-Response Portfolio: *Cover Letter, Summary-Response 1, and Summary-Response 2*	
Highlights from the Assignment Description	The *Summary-Response Portfolio* will consist of two summary-response essays based on texts related to our course theme representing different genres. For summary-response 1, you will select an academic, professional, or news article to read, summarize, and respond to. For summary-response 2, you will select a TED Talk video to watch, take notes on, summarize, and respond to. A collection of articles and TED Talks will be available for you to select from in Blackboard. Your two summary-response essays must be written about two *different* genres (e.g., "Summary-Response 1 Essay: An Op-ed Article" and "Summary-Response 2 Essay: A TED Talk"). After the completion of the two summary-response essays, you will create a portfolio containing clean final drafts and the earlier drafts of summary-response 1 and 2 as well as a cover letter addressed to the course instructor. In the cover letter, you will discuss your experience navigating the two different texts and genres: how you tackled each content, what points you decided to capture in your summary and why, what strategies you used to respond to the text claims and why, and what differences and similarities you observed between these texts (e.g., the author's rhetorical choices, type of arguments, appeals, and sequencing of ideas).	**SLO #:** 1, 2, 3, 6 **Focus of Instruction and Formative Assessment** *(examples)*: ✓ active, critical, and rhetorical reading strategies ✓ main idea/thesis, supporting details, and major vs. minor details ✓ genre conventions: academic, professional, and news articles and TED Talks ✓ phases of the writing process approach (e.g., pre-writing tasks, drafting, peer feedback . . .) ✓ summarizing, paraphrasing, citing, and APA style ✓ response techniques ✓ academic essays: structure and organization ✓ summary-response essays ✓ rhetorical analysis ✓ letter writing and conventions

Table 8.13 Sample Curriculum Development Product II: Summative Assessment, Corresponding SLOs, and Focus of Instruction

	The Argument Portfolio: *Proposal Argument, Campaign Product, and Campaign Product Commentary*	
Highlights from the Assignment Description	For Writing Project 2, you will select one issue related to the 17 SDGs to investigate and then propose effective ways that you think will help in its realization. This writing project will consist of three deliverables. *Proposal Argument:* In your proposal argument (3–4 pages), research one of the existing issues that the goal is targeting, offer a detailed discussion of the current situation, describe what the problem is including its causes and effects, and then identify solutions for this problem. These solutions (2–3 solutions) can be a combination of existing efforts that are being made to alleviate this problem and your own solutions. In the solution section, include a discussion of the feasibility and effectiveness of each solution. This type of assignment involves argumentation and persuasion as you need to describe the issue in a way that would make your audience care about it and then convince them to take a particular course of action by proposing viable solutions. To accomplish this purpose, you need to make logical claims, support your arguments with evidence from a minimum of 5 credible sources cited in APA style, address potential counterarguments, and then refute those arguments.	**SLOs #:** 1, 2, 3, 4, 5, 6 **Focus of Instruction and Formative Assessment** *(examples)*: ✓ *reinforcing and building on the earlier knowledge and skills* ✓ elements of an argument (e.g., claim, evidence, and reasoning) ✓ formulating arguments ✓ types of claims and evidence ✓ rhetorical appeals ✓ logical fallacies ✓ addressing counterarguments ✓ researching, locating, and evaluating sources ✓ synthesizing information ✓ proposal argument essays: language, structure, and organization ✓ features of multimodal texts ✓ designing multimodal texts

Table 8.13 (*Continued*)

	The Argument Portfolio: *Proposal Argument, Campaign Product, and Campaign Product Commentary*	
	Campaign Product: Using the research and ideas from your proposal argument, you will create a campaign product to raise public awareness about the issue and offer ways to contribute to the realization of your SDG. Your raising awareness campaign product can be an infographic flyer (e.g., using Canva or a poster template in PowerPoint) or a 3-minute video combining text, visuals, and sound. Regardless of the medium you choose, your product should (1) incorporate some *background information* to generate awareness of the existing issue using concrete, concise, and impactful information such as statistics, facts, or vivid descriptions of current conditions; and (2) outline specific *actions* that individuals, communities, and/or governments can take to solve or alleviate the problem. For your campaign product to have a strong impact, it is important to make thoughtful and careful design decisions (i.e., presentation of information, font size and type, colors, imagery, and so on). *Campaign Product Commentary*: Write a 2-page commentary detailing the rhetorical and design choices you made while constructing your product. More specifically, discuss what your purpose is; how you attempt to achieve this purpose, who your audience is (primary and secondary); what rhetorical appeals you used to convince your audience, why you chose those appeals, organization, visuals, style, and tone you employed to present your content; and how effective your choices are in bringing awareness to the problem and persuading your audience to take action.	

The Writing Process and Feedback

The curriculum development process included identifying how writing would be scaffolded, monitored, and evaluated. To emphasize growth over grades, the instructor broke the writing process into several phases. To build schema, students engage in various *pre-writing* activities that involve reading, discussing, researching, brainstorming, and planning. If graded, these tasks contribute minimally to the overall grade as formative assessments. The drafting phase includes at least three drafts, each scaffolded as follows:

1. Rough draft: Building on the outline that they create during the pre-writing phase, students start a rough draft as homework.
2. In-class workshop: Students expand on their rough draft during an in-class writing workshop. During this workshop, the instructor provides oral feedback on preliminary ideas and facilitates peer feedback.
3. Peer feedback: Students read each other's drafts and provide written feedback, noting strengths and areas for improvement. They then pair up and take turns to discuss their papers, rationalizing their rhetorical choices and seeking specific feedback from their partner as needed.
4. Revisions: After peer feedback, students revise their drafts and submit a complete draft for instructor feedback. The feedback is interactive instead of corrective, focusing on guiding questions and positive reinforcement. This draft is graded on completion and timely submission. Students make revisions and submit a final draft.
5. Final draft: Students incorporate instructor feedback into their final draft, which is graded using a rubric that is accessible from the start and referenced throughout the writing process. Before final submission, the instructor may conduct a lesson on language-focused topics to help students address recurring issues, such as sentence structure and mechanics, during the editing process. The final draft carries the highest weight in course grades, and students can make additional edits when compiling their project portfolio.

Materials

The selection of course materials involved identifying texts that address varied topics related to the 17 SDGs, represent different genres (e.g., peer-reviewed journal articles, news articles, editorials, op-eds, web articles by professional organizations, and TED Talks), and expose students to a wide range of types of texts with different purposes (e.g., to inform or to argue/persuade). Locating texts that focus on, for example, social and environmental issues as well as economic development and innovation in diverse parts of the world while representing different varieties of English (especially for the TED Talk videos) were also part of the search criteria. This included research articles from peer-reviewed journals; reports and conceptual texts by international organizations such as the United Nations and The World Bank; news articles from various news outlets (which students had full access to through their institution) such as *The New York Times* , *Al Jazeera*, *All Africa*, *Global Voices,* and *The Guardian*; as well as under ten-minute, theme-related TED Talk videos.

Two resources that were particularly helpful in identifying theme-related academic articles of reasonable length were *The Conversation* (which publishes shorter articles such as research briefs and commentaries) and *Nature* (a multidisciplinary scientific journal). An extensive list of academic, professional, and news articles, along with TED Talk videos, was compiled and made available on the course Blackboard site. Students were also presented with a collection of news media and other sources to explore themselves and encouraged to seek additional or alternative materials when needed. Table 8.14 highlights some sample texts, their genres, and the relevant SDGs that they address (the course instructor attempted to align the topics of the texts with the SDGs).

Instructional Topics

One of the final steps in the curriculum development phase for this course involved identifying the weekly instructional topics, formative assessments, due dates for the different drafts of the writing projects, and other related course elements. After brainstorming and mapping, the information was organized into a course calendar to visualize the timeframe, sequence, and pace needed to cover all the identified knowledge and skills within the 16 weeks of the semester. It is important to note that while this may seem like the final step in the curriculum development

Table 8.14 Sample ENGL 010 Theme-Related Texts

Text Title and Author	Genre/Text Type	Text Focus/SDG #
Op-Ed: Climate Change is a Big Problem. Citizens Must Demand Many Small Solutions (Harvey & Gillis, 2022), *Los Angeles Times*	Newspaper, *opinion article*	13 Climate Action
Op-ed: Three Priorities for Climate Action (Bahous, 2023), *UN Women*	Web article (organization), *op-ed*	13 Climate Action 5 Gender Equality
How Poverty Affects the Brain (Storrs, 2017), *Nature*	Academic journal, *research briefs*	1 No Poverty 3 Good Health & Well-Being
Less Stuff, More Happiness (Hill, 2011), *TED Talk*	TED Talk	12 Responsible Consumption & Production
Environmentalism or Greenwashing? Responses of South African Value Chain Actros to Plastic Straw Marine Pollution (Chitaka, 2021), *South African Journal of Science*	Academic journal, *research study*	13 Climate Action
The Quest to Address the Global Sanitation Crisis (Nature Water, 2023), *Nature Water*	Academic journal, *editorial*	6 Clean Water & Sanitation
How I Brought a River, and My City, Back to Life (Chaouni, 2014), *TED Talk*	TED Talk	11 Sustainable Cities & Communities 9 Industry, Innovation, & Infrastructure
The Reporting System That Sexual Assault Survivors Want (Ladd, 2016), *TED Talk*	TED Talk	3 Good Health & Well-Being 10 Reduced Equalities 16 Peace, Justices, & Strong Institutions
How Climate Change is Affecting Mental Health in Some of the Caribbean's Indigenous Communities (Stewart, 2023), *Global Voices*	News media, *news story*	3 Good Health & Well-Being 13 Climate Action

phase, it should remain a work in progress, continually updated during implementation to reflect students' needs.

Final Remarks

The discussion above outlined some of the procedures undertaken by a course instructor to plan a course in a context where curriculum development is descriptive rather than prescriptive. Acting as a curriculum developer, the instructor utilized knowledge, measures, and tools from the CPDIE framework that were deemed suitable. The outcomes of the curriculum development phase were compiled into a course syllabus detailing the course theme, the rationale behind it, and how it would frame the writing activities. The syllabus also outlined the SLOs, course texts and resources, assessment criteria and the breakdown of grades, details on the three writing projects and the grading rubrics, program and course policies, and the tentative course calendar.

In brief, this chapter has explored key elements of the curriculum development phase, emphasizing the importance of a systematic approach that intertwines conceptualization, planning, and development. Through thoughtful consideration of curriculum objectives, assessment methods, and necessary content and instructional strategies, programs and teachers can create effective and cohesive curricula tailored to their specific contexts. The detailed example provided aimed to illustrate an authentic curriculum development process and its resulting components.

After you read, consider the following questions:

1. In the previous chapter, you were asked to select a course to plan by applying the procedures covered during the curriculum planning phase. What will students need to know and be able to do to meet the goal(s) of your course? Create a list of knowledge and skills first, and then refer to Bloom's Taxonomy to identify the domains of knowledge that your course objectives/outcomes fit within. Select appropriate verbs to articulate what students should be able to do in your objective and outcome statements.
2. Brainstorm forms of summative assessment that are appropriate for assessing the attainment of student learning outcomes that you identified in your response to the first question. Create a chart to map the objectives to the outcomes

and then to summative assessments. Ensure that the outcomes are measurable, and adjust them as necessary. Additionally, consider ways to monitor learning for your identified objectives and outcomes using formative assessments and add these to the chart.

3. Based on your response to the previous questions, outline the types of content and experiences needed to facilitate effective learning of course objectives and outcomes in light of the curriculum theoretical framework. What course themes do you believe would best engage learners and facilitate learning? Why? What specific topics and materials would support these themes?
4. Review the discussion of the sample curriculum development process for ENGL 010 presented in this chapter. Which model(s) of curriculum development do you believe the process aligns with? Why?

Chapter 9

Curriculum Implementation

Before you read, reflect on the following questions:

1. What are the key elements of effective lesson planning?
2. What are the differences between curriculum objectives and instructional objectives?
3. What strategies or best practices can support the effective implementation of curriculum development plans?
4. In what ways can collaboration among educators enhance the effectiveness of curriculum implementation at both the micro and meso levels?

This chapter first discusses aspects of curriculum implementation, including lesson planning and instructional objectives, and then highlights measures at the micro and meso levels to support instruction and ensure curriculum effectiveness.

CPDIE: Curriculum Implementation Phase

Curriculum implementation is the most crucial part of the language curriculum cycle, where all plans and concepts become a reality. The relationship between the different components of the curriculum cycle—conceptualization, planning, development, implementation, and review—is reciprocal. Curriculum conceptualization guides planning while both inform development. The outcomes of development then guide implementation. In turn, what emerges from curriculum implementation apprises the earlier phases of the curriculum cycle and provides input for the review phase to enhance the interconnectedness among the different phases. The review leads back to conceptualization (often on a smaller scale), and the process is commenced again. However, certain phases may receive more focus due to factors that might arise at the nano, micro, meso, macro, or supra level, necessitating modifications and updates to the curriculum.

Establishing practices that facilitate the flow of information throughout the curriculum cycle benefits each phase by maintaining interconnectedness and coherence. The subsequent sections of this chapter will explore the implementation phase of the CPDIE framework by highlighting elements of lesson planning, outlining guiding principles for effective teaching, and suggesting practices at the meso level for enriching instruction and maximizing curriculum effectiveness.

Lesson Planning

Thoughtful lesson planning is important to ensure that the planned curriculum aligns with the implemented curriculum and vice versa. The Center for Applied Linguistics (2008) defines a lesson as "a unified set of activities that focuses on one teaching objective at a time" (p. 29). Using the established curriculum objectives and/or SLOs as a framework and foundation for lesson planning, the teacher interprets and extracts instructional objectives that are essential for achieving curriculum objectives/SLOs.

Instructional Objectives

Instructional objectives break down a curriculum objective into smaller, discrete units of knowledge needed to accomplish an outcome. For instance, if a student learning outcome aims to enable students to be able to "Prepare and give effective oral presentations," the teacher needs to identify what students need to accomplish this outcome. Such an outcome may require various abilities for students to prepare the content of the presentation and deliver it effectively, including:

- knowledge and skills in information literacy (e.g., researching, reading, evaluating, summarizing, synthesizing, and citing information),
- knowledge of the topic (e.g., clear and logical elaborations),
- verbal communication skills (e.g., comprehensible pronunciation, intonation, pausing, pacing, tone, and voice projection),

- non-verbal communication skills (e.g., posture, movement, facial expressions, and eye contact),
- digital media skills (i.e., using media tools or platforms to design content effectively with proper font size and type, colors, text, and visuals), and
- question-handling skills.

The use of needs assessment is essential to identify what instructional objectives a lesson should focus on (e.g., pronunciation) and to what extent (e.g., what features of pronunciation students need to work on). Identifying and *strategically* sequencing the knowledge and skills that students need to achieve course outcomes allows for building on, reinforcing, and utilizing existing knowledge and skills when approaching new information.

Instructional objectives are precise and short term and function as a vehicle that enables the students to work toward accomplishing curriculum objectives/outcomes. Communicating the instructional objectives of a lesson explicitly to the students helps activate their existing knowledge and direct their focus. Just as with writing curriculum objectives, it is important to avoid vague verbs that can be interpreted differently, such as *know* and *understand*. It is unclear what these two abstract verbs entail. Using concrete verbs such as *identify*, *differentiate*, *list*, or *construct* provides more meaning and specificity to what an instructional activity intends to achieve.

Instructional objectives are also versatile and can communicate and differentiate between task objectives and language objectives in a task-based language teaching curriculum. For example, a lesson may be developed around a series of tasks in which students produce a restaurant review on an online platform. Based on the assumptions about task-based language teaching (i.e., focusing purely on performing the main task or also incorporating explicit language tasks), a lesson may include task-focused instructional objectives such as the ability "To evaluate and comment on dining experiences." In addition, depending on the emphasis placed on generating awareness of the linguistic knowledge needed for this task, instructional objectives may also include language objectives that target specific areas, such as:

- Grammar knowledge: *Students will be able to use varied adjectives to describe taste, atmosphere, service, and prices.*

- Writing skills: *Students will be able to produce complex sentences using relative clauses. Students will be able to construct clear and focused topic sentences.*
- Vocabulary: *Students will be able to identify and use descriptive and dining-related words.*

Similarly, in a content-based instruction context that is content-driven (rather than language-driven) (Met, 1999), instructional objectives specify the linguistic knowledge that supports content learning, which is the ultimate goal of the lesson. This is particularly important in content-area teaching that adopts sheltered instruction to help English language learners develop the academic language needed to acquire content knowledge. Effective lesson planning in such contexts should align instructional objectives (typically consisting of content objectives and language objectives) with curriculum objectives and/or content area standards (Echevarria & Short, 2010). The following examples from Himmel (2012) illustrate the extraction of content and language objectives from two U.S. Common Core State Standards (2010):

- Content area standard for 4th-grade math: *Draw and identify lines and angles, and classify shapes by properties of their lines and angles.*
  - Content Objective: *Students will be able to classify triangles based on their angles.*
  - Language Objective: *Students will be able to read descriptions of triangles and their angles.*
- Content area standard for 9th-grade English Language Arts: *Write arguments to support claims in an analysis of substantive topics or texts, using valid reasoning and relevant and sufficient evidence. Provide a concluding statement or section that follows from and supports the argument presented.*
  - Content Objective: *Students will be able to draft a conclusion paragraph for their expository essay.*
  - Language Objective: *Students will be able to use transitional phrases (e.g.,* as a result*) in writing.*

Instructional Activities

At the micro level, lesson planning is a smaller but continuous curriculum development activity that requires making strategic decisions to ensure all curricular elements are interconnected and support one another. The identified instructional objectives guide the selection and planning of activities, materials, and equipment needed to facilitate instruction and achieve these objectives. When planning a lesson, it is important to identify and predict factors that can impede or contribute to its success—just like a smaller-scale situation analysis. This includes the media resources and materials needed and how to access and use them. For instance, to conduct the task-based lesson on restaurant reviews (referenced earlier), the teacher might select authentic genre-based materials such as menus and online restaurant reviews to help develop awareness of both genre and linguistic features. During lesson planning, the teacher needs to assess the situation to determine what is feasible. For example:

- Will physical copies be available to students?
- Does the classroom have a computer and projector to display online content?
- Will the final product be in digital or written format?
- Do all students have the means and skills to produce digital content?
- How will the task be scaffolded? Are outline templates or vocabulary handouts needed to support students in approaching the task?
- To promote authentic language use, will students be asked to dine at a restaurant and then write a review? Is this requirement convenient and feasible for each student?
- To allow flexibility, can the task be based on a previous dining experience?
- Should students choose between dining at a restaurant or writing about a recent experience?
- If dining out is feasible, should students do this in pairs or groups to incorporate post-tasks that allow students to compare and contrast their dining experiences or restaurant reviews?

These are some decisions that the teacher needs to make when selecting and arranging the learning experiences and aligning them with the intended objectives or outcomes. Thoughtful consideration of the type, sequence, and pace of instructional activities is essential for purposeful teaching and learning. Table 9.1 displays general questions to guide the planning of instructional activities.

Table 9.1 Guiding Questions for the Planning of Instructional Activities

1. What activities will be meaningful to the students and effective in facilitating learning?
2. What nano-level factors related to students (e.g., prior knowledge, interests, learning styles, and socio-emotional factors) should be considered when planning instructional activities?
3. Will the teaching of new knowledge be explicit through teacher explanations or implicit through scaffolded discovery learning (i.e., deductive vs. inductive learning)?
4. Will there be opportunities for individual, pair, and group work? What specific tasks will students work on in each format?
5. What is the best way to group students (i.e., random grouping, selective grouping based on personalities or levels of English proficiency, or student-selected groups)? How many students will be per group? Will there be specific roles assigned to each member of the group (e.g., facilitator, note-taker, researcher, timekeeper, and/or reporter)?
6. What procedures or materials can boost students' motivation and engagement?
7. What resources are available at the micro (classroom), meso (program), and/or macro (community) levels to support teaching and learning? How can these resources be effectively utilized?
8. How will learning be monitored? What methods of formative assessments will be used? Will there be opportunities for self-assessment or self-reflection?

Sample Lesson Planning

Table 9.2 presents a sample lesson plan for the ENGL 010 course that was discussed in the previous chapter to illustrate aspects of curriculum conceptualization, planning, and development. This lesson occurs early in the semester to equip students with the knowledge and skills needed to be able to read, summarize, and respond to texts, preparing them for the summary-response writing that will take place in the following weeks.

Table 9.2 Curriculum Implementation: A Sample Lesson Plan for ENGL 010

Course	**English 010: Introduction to Academic Writing**
Target Students & Context	College students at the upper intermediate level of English proficiency (equivalent to B2 in the CEFR Global Scale). First-Year Writing Program at a U.S. university
Topic	Reading and Analyzing Texts
Student Learning Outcomes	1. Students will be able to (SWBAT) read varied text types in different genres by applying critical reading strategies. 2. SWBAT identify the elements of the rhetorical situation, including appeals when deconstructing and constructing texts.
Instructional Objectives	• SWBAT apply reading techniques, such as annotating, summarizing, questioning, predicting, and making inferences, to identify and analyze the rhetorical elements of a text, main ideas, supporting details, relationships between ideas, organizational patterns, and use of evidence and appeals.
Prior Knowledge	In the two previous class sessions: • Students were introduced to the rhetorical situation and its elements (i.e., the circumstances surrounding the construction of a text such as its author(s), context, purpose, text type, medium, and audience), as well as the types of appeals commonly used by authors (i.e., logos, pathos, and ethos). The speech "I Have a Dream," by Martin Luther King Jr., was used to demonstrate a rhetorical situation and break down its elements.

(*Continued*)

Table 9.2 (*Continued*)

Course	English 010: Introduction to Academic Writing
	• Students learned active, critical, and rhetorical reading strategies (including paraphrasing techniques) and applied these strategies by reading and annotating the article "Eat Green: Our Everyday Food Choices Affect Global Warming and the Environment," by the Natural Resources Defense Council (Kaplan, 2010). The teacher modeled her interaction with the text by explaining the thought process behind her annotations. Students also had the opportunity to discuss the text in small groups, summarizing its main points and discussing its rhetorical elements, the authors' use of appeals, and connections to the SDGs. • Students were introduced to the concept of genre. Using inductive teaching techniques, they examined different sets of texts from (1) online news outlets, (2) peer-reviewed journals, and (3) professional organizations to identify shared features and differences in conventions, style, and organization. The class then discussed how authors respond to a rhetorical situation using a fitting genre. To illustrate this, the teacher used an example of a ransom letter written in three different styles (from the article "Navigating Genres" by Kerry Dirk, 2010) and had students vote on which style was more fitting for the genre of ransom letters and the rhetorical situation.

Table 9.2 (*Continued*)

<table>
<tr><th>Course</th><th colspan="2">English 010: Introduction to Academic Writing</th></tr>
<tr><td>Time Period</td><td colspan="2">1 hour and 15 minutes</td></tr>
<tr><td>Teaching Procedures</td><td>Approximate Time</td><td>Materials & Resources</td></tr>
<tr><td>1. As a warm-up activity and a quick review, students answer questions about different rhetorical concepts and types of reading strategies</td><td>10 mins.</td><td>Computer and projector
Kahoot</td></tr>
<tr><td>2. Teacher introduces students to the article “Math Teachers Hold a Bias against Girls When the Teachers Think Gender Equality Has Been Achieved.” Individually, students preview the text and scan for information that provides context about its rhetorical elements (e.g., Who are the authors? What are their credentials? When and where was the article published? Who is the intended audience? What do you think the purpose is? What can be inferred about the text just by reading its title?)</td><td>5 mins.</td><td>Blackboard and Google Docs
Text by Copur-Gencturk et al. (2023) published in The Conversation
A link to the online article and a Google Doc (with a copy of the article for easier annotation in the next step) are available through Blackboard.</td></tr>
</table>

(*Continued*)

Table 9.2 (*Continued*)

Course	English 010: Introduction to Academic Writing	
3. Students work individually to annotate the article. In addition to highlighting/underlining, students are asked to add a marginal comment for each paragraph to identify its purpose and main idea (in their own words); highlight words that signal any patterns of development; and note any questions or reactions they have (e.g., points that they find new, interesting, relatable, unclear, unconvincing, or those that they agree/disagree with).	20 mins.	A summary of the five-step reading process posted on Blackboard from a chapter that students read and answered related questions on as homework: Chapter 2 "From Reading to Writing" from *Models for Writers: Short Essays for Composition* (Rosa & Eschholz, 2012)
4. Using a graphic organizer, students deconstruct the text by identifying its thesis (overall main idea), main ideas, and major supporting details. Students then pair up to compare and rationalize their graphic organizers. As a class, the teacher and students discuss how to differentiate and identify these elements of a text (e.g., common patterns of development in writing, signal words, and paragraph structure . . .)	20 mins.	A graphic organizer template in Google Docs available in Blackboard Students have the option to create their own visualizations of the article instead

Table 9.2 (*Continued*)

Course	English 010: Introduction to Academic Writing	
5. Working collaboratively in groups, students discuss, analyze, and respond to specific questions about the article related to rhetorical elements, genre features, main ideas, claims and use of reasoning and evidence, overall effectiveness, and personal reactions. Some sample questions are: • What is the text type and genre? What are some features of this genre? How does the text cite other sources? • What types of rhetorical appeals are employed in this article? • How effective are the authors in making their points clear? Why? • What is your own experience or reaction to the topic discussed in the article? After discussions, groups share their answers with the class, and the teacher comments and invites further discussion.	20 mins.	Blackboard and Google Docs Students respond to the questions in the Google Docs file

(*Continued*)

Table 9.2 (*Continued*)

Course	**English 010: Introduction to Academic Writing**	
Homework and Follow-up: Write a one-paragraph summary of the text (due before next class, submission through Blackboard). *In the following class, students will learn about summary writing features and structure then revise their preliminary summaries based on the new guidelines.*		

As noted in Chapter 5, it is important for lesson plans and activities to be documented and stored, including their successes and areas for improvement, so they can be utilized in future teaching sessions and shared as resources with other instructors. Information that emerges from the implemented curriculum (e.g., lesson plans, summative assessment details, rubrics, instructional activities, and students' work) also becomes an asset for curriculum review, revision, and development. This information can be used to enhance the curriculum and enrich the curriculum guide, resulting in plans that align with and reflect actual practice.

Supportive Practices for Curriculum Implementation

The TESOL International Association (n.d.) outlines six principles for effective language teaching. According to these principles, *exemplary* teachers (1) know their students, (2) create conditions for language learning, (3) design high-quality language lessons, (4) adapt lesson delivery as needed, (5) monitor and assess language development, and (6) engage and collaborate within a community of practice. The discussion in this book so far has revolved around knowledge and practices that promote principles 1 to 5. This subsection highlights ways to foster engagement and collaboration in line with principle 6. Before discussing meso-level practices for nurturing a community of practice, important practices that promote teachers' personal growth and development will be highlighted. It goes without saying that such practices are the seeds for cultivating curriculum success and effective teaching.

Deliberate, Reflective Practices at the Micro Level

How can a teacher pursue, attain, or maintain *exemplary* teaching? Referring back to the six TESOL principles, all outlined conditions necessitate deliberate practice. ***Deliberate practice***, a term coined by psychologist Anders Ericsson and his colleagues (1993), shows that high levels of achievement or performance do not solely depend on experience or intrinsic talent. Instead, "superior performance reflects primarily acquired skills and other attributes attained as the result of extended training and practice" (Ericsson, 1998, p. 75). When planning and teaching become deliberate (i.e., purposeful) rather than routine (i.e., monotonous), teachers systematically seek ways to enhance the teaching and learning experience. They are intentional in their planning and actively seek ways to monitor, assess, and adapt to their students' needs.

Deliberate practice involves self-awareness, commitment, and dedication to continuous improvement. Through this process, teachers identify areas for growth and strategies for enhancement. Kyndt et al. (2016) identified several informal practices that contribute to teachers' professional development, including:

- reading professional literature and consulting resources;
- conducting observations;
- seeking feedback from colleagues;
- collaborating with other teachers (e.g., through discussions, meetings, joint projects, and mentoring);
- self-reflecting on and analyzing their own practices;
- experimenting and learning by doing (e.g., testing novel curricular activities);
- sharing materials, resources, ideas, and practices; and/or
- engaging in curriculum-related and extracurricular activities (e.g., serving on committees).

Engagement in these practices has been shown to enhance teachers' subject knowledge, pedagogical skills, and professional identity (Kyndt et al.,

2016). Similarly, Dunn and Shriner (1999) identified activities that reflect deliberate practices in teaching, including careful planning of materials and instructional strategies (both written and mental) and evaluating student progress through various formal and informal methods. They noted, "the frequent and mindful engagement in these activities, prompting cycles of teaching—evaluation—revision, may be what accounts for expertise" (Dunn & Shriner, 1999, p. 631).

Research in the ELT literature emphasizes the importance of reflective practices for ESL/EFL instructors' professional development (Farrell, 2011, 2014, 2015, 2018; Richards & Farrell, 2011; Richards & Lockhart, 1994). Reflection serves as a vital form of deliberate practice. As Farrell (2018) noted, reflective practice allows teachers to step back from repetitive tasks, enabling them to understand their actions and seek improvements, which can help them escape routine and prevent burnout. He further explained that reflective practice is realized "when teachers consciously take on the role of reflective practitioner and subject their own beliefs about teaching and learning to critical analysis, take full responsibility for their actions in the classroom, and continue to improve their teaching practice" (p. 1). This process entails systematically gathering data about their teaching through various methods to "develop a deeper understanding of their teaching, assess their professional growth, develop informed decision-making skills, and become proactive and confident in their teaching" (Farrell, 2018, p. 2). Some of these methods may include:

- keeping a teaching journal to record and regularly reflect on classroom events;
- seeking advice and discussions with trusted colleagues;
- joining a teacher development group for mutual support;
- carrying out classroom observations, either by being observed by others or by recording their own teaching sessions;
- conducting action research on curriculum and instructional issues;
- exploring teacher roles and identities through conceptual reflection; and/or
- examining their personal beliefs about teaching and learning in relation to actual classroom practices.

Engagement in professional development, whether through formal conferences and training workshops or informal collaboration, can have a profound impact on teaching practices and curriculum effectiveness.

Community of Practice at the Meso Level

As previously noted, an educational program can play a significant role in optimizing curriculum and instruction. This can be facilitated through establishing opportunities for coordination, involvement, systematized assessment, and internal professional development.

Coordination

Collaboration in curriculum planning and assessment can be fostered through effective coordination. Depending on the program's structure, opportunities for instructor coordination can be integrated throughout the semester. In a coordination system, when multiple sections of the same course exist, a teacher with substantial experience can be designated as the course coordinator or lead, a role that can rotate in future sessions. The coordinator acts as a resource and promotes regular communication among instructors. Scheduled coordination meetings at the beginning, middle, and end of the semester allow teachers to discuss curriculum plans and clarify ambiguities. Meeting notes can document specific issues and curriculum innovations, informing future reviews and revisions. From experience, teachers often continue to communicate daily outside these meetings to collaboratively create theme-related materials, activities, and assessments.

In multi-level language programs, a coordination system ensures strong horizontal alignment among courses, enriching the learning experience by connecting and reinforcing knowledge across different classes. For example, in a high intermediate level comprising three courses—Reading, Academic Writing, and Listening and Speaking—if students explore a topic related to artificial intelligence in the Reading class, that same topic can be integrated into the Academic Writing class for writing assignments. Additionally, in the Listening and Speaking class, students can engage in discussions and listening activities centered around the same theme. This approach not only facilitates vocabulary recycling across different language skills but also provides students with repeated, contextualized exposure to the topic through various modes of input and output.

Establishing systems for curriculum coordination—conceptually planned during the phases of curriculum conceptualization, planning, and development—promotes smooth and effective execution during implementation. It also ensures that students receive consistent and equitable learning experiences. Coordination does not necessitate that all activities be aligned daily; rather, it encourages ongoing communication and collaboration among teachers, fostering a supportive environment for exchanging ideas and feedback. Little (1990) described this nature of collaboration and collegiality as follows:

> Through routine sharing, teaching is presumably made less private, more public. In principle, the pool of ideas and methods is expanded. The coordination of teachers' work and students' careers is made possible in ways that cannot be achieved through other forms of collegial contact. By making the ordinary materials of their work accessible to one another, teachers expose their ideas and intentions to others. Unlike periodic advice-giving, which tends to atomize and fragment teachers' grasp of their own and others' practice, widespread sharing may reveal an entire pattern of choices with regard to curriculum and instruction. Further, the ground is laid for productive discussion and debate regarding curricular and instructional priorities. (p. 518)

Involvement

Teacher involvement in program-related matters can take various forms and may differ across educational programs based on factors such as availability, appointment type, teaching load, and compensation. Typically, participation in these activities is regarded as a service to the institution and can be recognized in teacher evaluations. Ideally, programs should create systematic opportunities for teachers to enhance the teaching and learning experience by serving on committees or joining working groups. As Nicholls and Nicholls (1972/2018) noted, "participation in co-operative curriculum development activities can lead to a greatly increased professionalism in teachers" (p. 18).

Establishing committees focused on curriculum, assessment, and materials and inviting instructors to join can yield benefits at the nano, micro, and meso levels. At the nano level, committee service can deepen teachers' knowledge in the field, enhance critical skills, facilitate research collaboration, showcase capabilities, and "open the door to opportunities to pursue administrative jobs" (Levine, 2014, p. 685). At the micro and meso levels, faculty committees not only cultivate a community of practice and a sense of belonging but can also lead to curriculum innovations and improved teaching practices. Additionally, forming working groups as needed to pursue specific goals, such as exploring inclusive teaching strategies, is another way to promote collaboration, involvement, and best practices.

Systematized Assessment Practices

Establishing unified assessment procedures within a program can enhance transparency, validity, and reliability, providing valuable data for curriculum evaluation, review, and revision. This is particularly important for high-stakes assessments such as placement and diagnostic tests as well as summative achievement exams. Following a program's protocol for student level or course placement, carrying out diagnostic testing during the first day or week of instruction is essential to ensure proper placement and to give teachers valuable insights into specific student needs. Diagnostic exams are typically outcome based, reflecting the knowledge and skills students are expected to master by the end of the course. During coordination meetings, teachers can discuss potential misplacements and identify specific needs to inform instructional planning.

Given that summative assessments are high stakes—determining the extent of a student's success in meeting intended outcomes—it is crucial that systematic and unified measures are established to guide their creation, administration, implementation, and interpretation. These measures may include coauthored or peer-reviewed final exams (Elturki, 2020). In the peer review process, the test author seeks feedback from another instructor, who reviews and takes the exam to ensure clarity and alignment with the intended outcomes and then provides constructive feedback to the author.

When utilizing authentic assessments, such as final presentations, involving other instructors in the evaluation process using a rubric enhances interrater reliability and ensures consistent and fair grading. Similarly, evaluating students' final written products, whether papers or portfolios, should involve multiple instructors for the same reasons. For courses with multiple sections, norming sessions can be particularly beneficial. During these sessions, instructors collaboratively grade several exams or papers using a rubric, discuss acceptable and unacceptable responses, and establish a consensus on how to address poorly constructed questions or partial answers (Elturki, 2020).

Lastly, aggregating and interpreting student achievement data can provide valuable insights into the quality of assessments, curriculum, and instruction. Conducting item analysis (Siri & Freddano, 2011) is one effective method, wherein test questions are matched to specific learning outcomes and incorrect responses are analyzed to identify problematic questions. Incorporating these measures can yield important insights into the effectiveness of the curriculum and instructional practices.

Internal Professional Development

A substantial body of research demonstrates a positive association among teacher professional development, effective pedagogical practices, and student success (Darling-Hammond et al., 2017). Many educational programs often encourage and financially support formal professional development opportunities, such as attending conferences and joining professional organizations. In addition to these formal avenues, the following list outlines other accessible ways to promote professional development at the meso level to foster a community of practice, promote professional growth, and encourage collaboration (Elturki, 2021b).

Literature Group Meetings. To keep abreast of current research trends, literature group meetings can be scheduled each semester for instructors to discuss selected readings. These readings may focus on emerging topics or issues of shared interest, such as alternative assessment methods. Instructors should be invited to suggest articles for discussion, enhancing their engagement and contributing to their deliberate practice.

Instructor-Facilitated Presentations. Recognizing that "every teacher, whether new or veteran, has something he or she can offer" (Matherson & Windle, 2017, p. 31), programs can incorporate opportunities for instructors to present their teaching practices. This could include sharing teaching tips, technology resources, or instructional activities during informal sessions, such as lunchtime brown bags. Contributions to internal professional development can be acknowledged in performance evaluations to incentivize participation.

Peer Observations. Encouraging peer teaching observations is another effective way to foster professional development and reflective practice. Instructors can arrange observations with colleagues to gain feedback on new techniques or activities they are trying.

Pre- and Post-Conference Sharing Sessions. Conducting pre-conference sharing sessions enables instructors who will be presenting at professional conferences to rehearse their presentations and obtain feedback. Similarly, post-conference sharing sessions provide an opportunity for those who attended a conference to share insights and highlights from their favorite sessions with colleagues.

To conclude this chapter, effective curriculum implementation requires strategic planning of one's own course and lessons guided by the overall curriculum framework. Because of the reciprocal nature of curriculum construction, what emerges from the curriculum implementation phase can be used to optimize the overall curriculum framework so that the planned curriculum is well aligned with the implemented curriculum and the actual learning experiences. Continuous improvement, along with fostering collaboration and professional growth, is essential for successful curriculum implementation, teacher development, and, ultimately, student success.

After you read, consider the following questions:

1. Building on your curriculum development plan from Chapter 7, select one objective/outcome to plan a lesson for. In your lesson plan, include the following:
   a. The specific objective/outcome you are targeting
   b. Corresponding instructional objectives
   c. Materials and resources needed
   d. Type and sequence of instructional activities
2. In two to three paragraphs, provide a rationale for the choices you made in your lesson plan, including the theoretical foundations that support your decisions. Briefly describe your students and the curriculum context, and explain how these factors influenced your planning. Reference any educational theories or models that informed your decisions.
3. Reflect on your personal learning experiences. What were some positive and negative aspects? Based on these reflections, what do you think are the key characteristics of a positive learning experience?

4. Recall at least three teaching events and describe what you typically do before, during, and after you teach a lesson. What recurring patterns and themes can you identify in your practices? How can you rationalize these practices? In other words, what informs your teaching practice?
5. Evaluate and reflect on your teaching practices in light of the six TESOL principles for exemplary teachers. How do your practices align or diverge from these principles? Provide specific examples from your own teaching to illustrate your reflections.
6. What types of professional growth activities are you currently seeking, would like to pursue, or are available to you? How do these align with your goals as an educator? Consider both formal and informal opportunities for growth.

Chapter 10

Curriculum Evaluation

Before you read, reflect on the following questions:

1. How often should a curriculum be evaluated?
2. Why is periodic evaluation of the curriculum important?
3. How can curricula be reviewed and revised? What does the process look like?
4. What kind of information can benefit curriculum review and revision?

This chapter focuses on the curriculum evaluation phase within the CPDIE framework. It highlights the importance of curriculum evaluation at both the meso and micro levels and discusses strategies for systematically reviewing and strengthening the interconnectedness among curricular elements to maximize curriculum effectiveness.

CPDIE: The Curriculum Evaluation Phase

In both mainstream education and the ELT field, all models and approaches to curriculum development discussed in Chapter 4—whether emphasizing the pre-identification of objectives or advocating for the curriculum to evolve from teaching situations—agree on the importance of evaluation. Tyler (1949/2013) described curriculum evaluation as:

> A process for finding out how far learning experiences as developed and organized are actually producing the described results and the process of evaluation will involve identifying the strengths and weaknesses of the plans. This helps to check the validity of the basic hypotheses upon which the instructional program has been organized

> and developed, and it also checks the effectiveness of particular conditions that are being used to carry forward the instructional program. As a result of evaluation[,] it is possible to note in what aspects the curriculum is effective and in what respects it needs improvement. (p. 105)

Curriculum evaluation serves varied purposes at different levels of context. Generally, we make sense of our lived experiences to help us with decision-making when planning future experiences. In curriculum and instruction, we think, plan, develop, and then implement. What is next? We repeat the cycle. It is the nature of the teaching profession. We use implementation experiences to rethink, replan, and redevelop. By nature, it is a continuous, cyclical process, sought both for course and program improvements. The curriculum evaluation phase in the CPDIE framework brings the curriculum full circle and ties together the components of the curriculum.

Curriculum Evaluation at the Micro and Meso Levels

At the nano and micro levels, teachers assess the effectiveness of their teaching and learning experiences, identifying areas for improvement and making necessary adjustments to lesson plans, instructional activities, materials, assessments, and/or classroom management strategies. Emphasizing a more human-centered approach to evaluation, as discussed by Quintero Polo (2003), this process is viewed not just as a technical measurement against predetermined goals but as an ongoing and meaningful aspect of classroom life. It reflects the experiences and emotions of both teachers and students. This holistic and contextualized approach to evaluation prioritizes the lived experiences of those involved in the teaching and learning process, allowing educators to make more informed decisions that genuinely reflect the dynamics of the classroom and support effective teaching and learning. As described by Quintero Polo (2003), curriculum evaluation signifies the conclusion of one cycle and the initiation of the next, serving as a vital tool for aiding decision-making in the new cycle. It informs adjustments to the curriculum, fostering continuous improvement in both practice and outcomes.

At the meso level, educational programs review their practices to ensure continuous improvement and confirm that the curriculum effectively meets student needs while aligning with broader educational goals.

The CIPP (Context, Input, Process, Product) Model for Evaluation (Stufflebeam, 2003) provides a comprehensive framework for this level of evaluation. It emphasizes evaluating the environment in which a program operates (context evaluation), the resources and strategies necessary to meet program goals (input evaluation), the teaching and learning processes involved in implementation (process evaluation), and the outcomes achieved by the program (product evaluation). This holistic approach ensures that all aspects of the curriculum are aligned and effective in achieving desired educational outcomes.

As highlighted by the UNESCO International Bureau of Education, regular evaluations of the curriculum are essential to ensure it is "fit for its intended purposes; inclusive; relevant; consistent with broader societal goals" (Stabback, 2016, p. 40). Systematic curriculum evaluation at the meso level enables informed decision-making and fosters a culture of transparency, accountability, and continuous improvement. It allows for adaptability in response to evolving educational trends, student demographics, and societal needs. Additionally, it promotes teacher reflection and professional growth while providing a means to document best practices, thus creating a repository of successful practices for future reference.

Using a critical lens, the essential question whether at both micro or meso level is: Has the totality of the teaching and learning experience effectively achieved the intended learning goals? Curriculum evaluation provides an opportunity to validate the different components of the curriculum and strengthen their interconnectedness. This may involve clarifying or modifying course objectives, outcomes, content, materials, or instructional methods in response to specific situational factors, including evolving student needs. It also provides an opportunity to document what emerges through practice, as curriculum serves "in a sense as a retrospective account" (Richards, 1984, p. 36). Indeed, some researchers, including Stenhouse (1975, p. 4), assert that curriculum "can only be specified in full retrospectively" or after instruction has taken place.

Logistics for Curriculum Evaluation

This section discusses the logistics of curriculum evaluation, review, and revision, focusing on systematic practices at the program level that are teacher led or facilitated. Individual teachers can adapt these procedures to inform their course reviews and future planning.

Prerequisites and Expectations

A Written Plan

Depending on the nature, size, and structure of the educational program, curriculum reviews should occur periodically. Accrediting agencies, such as CEA, require documented reviews of various program components. CEA's Program Development, Planning, and Review Standard 2 (2022) states that programs must regularly review and revise their components and maintain written plans to guide this process. Such plans may specify when and how curricula are reviewed, who participates in the process, and what materials, including evidence, are needed. This plan can be integrated into the curriculum guide or manual proposed in Chapter 5.

Curriculum Reviewers

The importance of teacher involvement in curriculum-related matters has been emphasized several times throughout this book simply because teachers are the implementers of the planned curriculum. They interact with the curriculum on a regular basis, translate it into practice, and observe how students learn and grow. Effective curriculum evaluation necessitates that teachers report, interpret, and analyze data to make informed decisions about areas that need improvement. At the meso level, teachers should have systematic opportunities to work collaboratively toward maximizing curriculum effectiveness and coherence. Carrying out such work, as commented by Nicholls and Nicholls (1972/2018), allows teachers to reappraise their work and enhance their professional knowledge.

Materials and Data

The curriculum evaluation process is evidence based. Just as curriculum development draws from various data sources (Table 10.1), similar information can guide curriculum review and revision. Drawing on similar data sources discussed in Chapter 7, post-curriculum and instruction needs analysis—such as student surveys, interviews, teacher observations, and assessment data—can highlight areas for improvement. This feedback may provide insights into course objectives, knowledge and skills, topics, textbooks, instructional activities, assessments, teaching methods, classroom atmosphere, sense of belonging, and overall engagement.

Table 10.1 Materials and Data for Curriculum Evaluation, Review, and Revision

Source	**Brief Description**
Input from teachers	Observations and interactions with students, teaching observations, and coordination meetings
Formal student evaluations	End-of-course student evaluations and program surveys
Needs and situation analysis	Various sources and methods discussed in Chapter 7
Assessment data	Data collected through assessments
Insights from professional development	Information from literature group meetings or other training sessions
Findings from action research	Relevant findings, if available
Relevant standards, benchmarks, or policies	Standards and regulations that need to be accounted for
Overall curriculum document	The main curriculum guide, document, or syllabi
Curriculum review guide	A guide outlining the goals, tasks, and expectations for the curriculum review process
Tools or materials	Materials like Bloom's Taxonomy and mapping charts to assist with the review
Documentation forms	Forms to document and rationalize changes recommended or made to the curriculum

Furthermore, analyzing student achievement data can be a crucial indicator of how effectively the curriculum and instruction have met the intended learning outcomes. The UNESCO International Institute for Educational Planning (2023) underscores that "learning data, in conjunction with other dimensions of quality such as context, teaching and learning environment, and learner characteristics, can reveal the factors that most affect learning outcomes" (para. 2). Such data is also an essential aspect of accountability, compliance, and quality assurance, particularly in relation to accreditation processes and program quality assessments. Institutions often rely on this data to demonstrate that they meet established standards and expectations set by accrediting bodies, ensuring they provide a high-quality educational experience. Additionally, assessment feedback can inform the curriculum cycle, allowing for the clarification and modification of course objectives and instructional methods, thereby providing a "fresh starting-point for further development" (Nicholls & Nicholls, 1972/2018, p. 22). For the purpose of curriculum evaluation, this data should be systematically compiled and aggregated at the program level, potentially by an assessment coordinator or another designated role. Compiling and aggregating student achievement data in percentages, pass rates, and graphs allows for horizontal and vertical comparisons of courses across the curriculum. Over time, this data can reveal patterns and trends in student achievement of intended outcomes across different courses, enabling inferences about areas of strength and weakness in the curriculum.

The Evaluation and Review Process

The timing and frequency of curriculum reviews should be determined at the meso level in a written plan. Ad hoc review sessions can be scheduled as needed to address emerging issues. Depending on program size and roles, a curriculum committee or designated personnel may prepare materials for review sessions. The following outlines key measures to consider pre-, during, and post-review sessions (Elturki, 2022).

Pre: Preparation and Planning

Planning for a curriculum review session begins with defining the scope and purpose of the review activity:

- Identify which courses will be reviewed and the reasons for their selection.
- Determine whether the entire curriculum will be assessed, and, if so, why.
- Decide if the session will focus on a specific curricular element (e.g., objectives, assessments, instructional materials, or instructional activities)

Clear goals should be established to define what needs to be accomplished. Following this, the data and tools required for the review process should be identified based on these intended goals. Review teams should be formed, ideally consisting of instructors with experience teaching the specific courses under review. Finally, a detailed description of the specific tasks, guiding questions, and timelines for the review should be prepared.

During: Evaluation and Review Work

A brief meeting can be held to ensure the review teams understand their tasks and what needs to be accomplished. Working in groups, the review teams discuss and analyze the datasets provided and any available input to help them make informed decisions. For instance, data gathered from item analysis (refer to "Systematized Assessment Practices" in Chapter 9) conducted by individual teachers as part of their assessment procedures can be utilized to identify specific knowledge gaps. Additionally, an analysis of student achievement data may reveal a low pass rate in a specific course or language skill, highlighting areas that require further investigation. The review teams collaborate to identify potential reasons behind trends in the data, such as vague or problematic course objectives, insufficient opportunities for knowledge reinforcement, ineffective materials, or issues with the teaching methods. Once these factors are assessed, the teams can work on recommending revisions.

In a comprehensive curriculum review session, these teams should evaluate both the relationships among curricular elements of a single course (i.e., horizontal alignment or course coherence) and the connections between courses across the educational program, known as vertical alignment. To illustrate this process, consider a multi-level language curriculum conducting a comprehensive review of the lower and intermediate levels (Levels 1, 2, and 3). As depicted in Figure 10.1, the curriculum evaluation process consists of two phases: horizontal and vertical review. In the initial phase, teams of three to five members will be formed, each assigned to review a specific level by examining its specific courses: Academic Writing (AW), Academic Reading (AR), and Academic Listening and Discussion (ALD). This horizontal review enables team members to analyze how well these courses align with one another to ensure coherence in objectives, instructional methods, and assessments within that level. Once the horizontal review is complete, the teams will regroup to form new teams that include a representative from each course across all levels. This structure will facilitate a vertical review to ensure the progression from Level 1 to Level 3 is smooth and logical. During this phase, team members can discuss how the skills

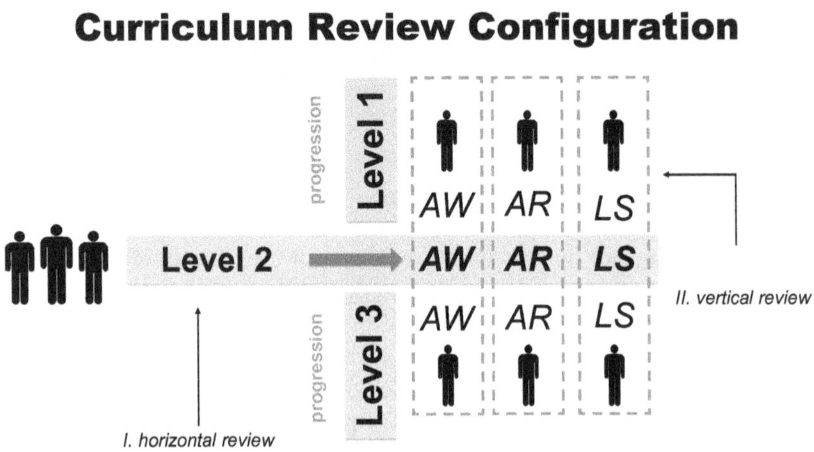

Figure 10.1. Framework for Horizontal and Vertical Evaluation of Multi-Level Curricula

and knowledge acquired in earlier levels (e.g., Level 1 and Level 2) support the learning objectives of the subsequent levels (e.g., Level 3). This collaborative approach fosters continuity in the curriculum and helps identify any gaps or redundancies that may exist in the overall program. By employing both horizontal and vertical review processes, the teams will provide a comprehensive evaluation of the curriculum, which can lead to well-informed revisions that enhance both coherence within levels and continuity across levels.

Any major revisions or changes need to be justified based on evidence and aligned with the program's philosophical beliefs and theoretical assumptions. Finally, these proposed revisions can be shared and negotiated during an all-faculty meeting.

Post: Curriculum Updates and Implementation

When there is consensus on the aspects of the curriculum that require revision, the curriculum guide can be updated accordingly. Documenting the nature, reasons, and basis of any major revisions is essential for future reference. The timing of implementing the revised curriculum depends on the extent of the changes and the time required to update or create materials. In cases where a curriculum innovation or major change is introduced, piloting the revised curriculum allows for testing its practicality and effectiveness prior to program-wide implementation.

Curriculum Evaluation in Practice

Insights from the ELT Literature

This subsection highlights some ELT literature that discusses curriculum evaluation as a critical component of course design and revision processes. These examples emphasize the importance of ensuring that the curriculum effectively meets student needs and aligns with desired outcomes.

The Case of the EGP Curriculum

MacPherson (2019) emphasized the importance of course evaluation in his discussion on the development and implementation of the General English course for Japanese students at Nagasaki Junshin Catholic University (highlighted in Chapter 8, Table 8.2). MacPherson asserted that effective evaluation could lead to curriculum enhancements that are responsive to learners' needs. Key components of MacPherson's evaluation approach included collecting feedback from students at both the midpoint and conclusion of the course. This feedback addressed the relevance and practicality of the topics covered, the complexity of the language used, students' motivation to continue learning English, and suggestions for course improvement. This data, combined with initial needs analysis surveys, diagnostic testing, formative and summative assessment results, and teachers' self-evaluations, has been crucial for informing decisions on revisions to enhance the course.

The Case of the ESP Curriculum

Similar to MacPherson (2019), Edwards (2000) detailed the process of developing and implementing his ESP business course for senior bankers in Germany (highlighted in Chapter 8, Table 8.1). The curriculum was assessed using a range of methods including test results, interviews, discussions, and other informal means. The data gathered indicated improvements in fluency and speaking confidence, suggesting that the course achieved its intended goals. Positive feedback from educational experts led to the course's indefinite extension. The course successfully incorporated different teaching methods to accommodate diverse student learning styles and addressed specific needs.

However, some issues identified in the evaluation process included a lack of technology, such as video recording tools, which limited opportunities for self-evaluation and reflection on student performance. Additionally, access to authentic data from within the bank was also challenging, which restricted the depth of practical application and real-world relevance. Furthermore, reliance on outdated frameworks for needs analysis proved impractical, highlighting the need for more adaptable approaches in course design. Edwards (2000) suggested that effective ESP curriculum development should leverage the teacher's practical experience and insights from students themselves, rather than strictly adhering to explicit directives for needs analysis. He also emphasized that the curriculum could benefit from the selective and efficient adaptation of authentic texts from media and available ESP textbooks to enhance both its relevance and development efficiency.

The Case of the EAP Curriculum

A study by Smith and colleagues (2022) exemplifies innovative methodologies to inform the evaluation of the EAP listening and speaking curricula. The researchers conducted a triangulated needs analysis—incorporating document analysis, interviews, observations, and questionnaires—to assess the academic oral communication needs of EAP students at the English Language Institute at the University of Hawai'i at Mānoa. They then used the findings to evaluate the effectiveness of the existing listening and speaking curricula and instructional practices. The curriculum evaluation phase involved examining syllabi from the past semesters and gathering input from instructors and administrators through interviews. Their systematic comparison of the needs analysis findings and the SLOs identified several areas of alignment and discrepancy.

The evaluation revealed that the existing curricula and instruction effectively addressed specific academic listening strategies outlined in the SLOs, with a focus on lecture comprehension, integration of lecture information, and analytical skills. These objectives were achieved through instructional techniques such as note-taking, vocabulary development, and extensive listening practice. Additionally, the evaluation indicated that less time was dedicated to notetaking compared to other activities like listening diaries. The researchers noted that this approach aligns with the needs analysis findings, which showed that students regarded notetaking as a manageable task requiring minimal practice, whereas lecture preparation and vocabulary tasks were deemed essential for improving lecture comprehension.

However, the evaluation also identified limitations in opportunities for skill development in Q&A sessions and exposure to the North

American participatory lecturing style, indicating a need for enhanced teaching strategies. Furthermore, while the need for interaction with native speakers was addressed to some extent through guest speaker assignments, these were inconsistently implemented and did not adequately target students' comprehension-related challenges. To address this gap, it was recommended that participating in discussions with native speakers be added as a sub-goal of the SLOs. Discrepancies were also observed regarding discussion leading, which, although emphasized in the SLOs, did not rank highly in student feedback. It was noted that focusing on discussion participation rather than leading may better support students. Finally, while the SLOs aimed for students to deliver accurate oral presentations, the curriculum lacked explicit preparation for responding to audience questions, which was recommended to be added as a sub-goal of the SLOs to enhance students' abilities to handle questions. This research underscores the value of a robust needs analysis in informing curriculum evaluation and improvement and highlights its critical role in aligning educational programs with student needs.

The Case of the Tailored Curriculum

In their study on revising an existing curriculum using needs analysis data, Tabari and Rahimy (2021) detailed efforts to tailor the prerequisite General English course at the Ayandegan Institute of Higher Education in Tonekabon, Iran. To inform the revision, the researchers administered a needs analysis questionnaire that collected information on learners' demographics, target and present needs, preferences, objectives, and learning strategies. This data revealed that the standard curriculum primarily focused on reading comprehension while neglecting speaking and listening skills. It also suffered from limited instructional time, generic materials that did not align with learner needs, an inconsistent evaluation process, and ineffective use of available technology.

In response, the revision process led to a tailored curriculum that integrated all four language skills to respond to students' needs. Key changes included increased instructional time, prioritization of speaking skills based on the needs analysis to align course goals with student interests, and the adoption of a communicative, task-based textbook complemented by a workbook, audio materials, and audio-visual resources to support diverse learning styles. A unified final exam was implemented to ensure consistent assessment across different classes.

Teacher feedback on the tailored curriculum was largely positive, particularly regarding the suitability of the textbook, the extended course duration, and the unified assessment system. However, some teachers noted that the curriculum still fell short in preparing students for real-life language use and that English was not the primary medium of instruction. The researchers attributed these ongoing challenges, common in EFL contexts, to students' lack of interest in English, negative prior experiences, resistance to using English, and insufficient listening and speaking skills. These findings highlight that curriculum improvements are a continuous process that must occur periodically to enhance learning experiences and address persistent and emerging challenges.

The Case of the Post-Colonial Curriculum

In her book ***Post-colonial Curriculum Practices in South Asia: Building Confidence to Speak English*** Attanayake (2020) discusses the curriculum design process of "A Confidence Building Course to Speak English." Her research revealed that Language Attitude Anxiety (LAA) is prevalent among English language learners in post-colonial countries such as Sri Lanka, India, Pakistan, and Bangladesh. This anxiety often stems from negative experiences and societal attitudes toward English-speaking abilities. Prejudice against those who do not meet language expectations significantly contributes to LAA, resulting in a lack of confidence that manifests as fear, uncertainty, and shyness in speaking English. To address these challenges, the course is designed to foster positive attitudes and build confidence in English speaking, thereby reducing LAA.

The curriculum design for this course is grounded in Cummins' (2000) Basic Interpersonal Communication Skills (BICS), which focuses on the language skills necessary for everyday social interactions. The course utilizes materials developed through Speech Act Theory (Bach & Harnish, 1979) to categorize speech functions and employ Cooperative Language Learning as its core teaching methodology. This approach involves students in speaking activities through group and pair work. A key emphasis is placed on creating a safe environment where learners can build confidence in their speaking abilities without experiencing negative emotions. This is facilitated by, for example, avoiding overcorrection, mandatory performance, competition, individual tasks, and grammar rules. Additionally, the curriculum design incorporates opportunities for periodic formative assessment to monitor students' confidence levels. Summative assessment is performance based and emphasizes confidence rather than language proficiency. Aligned with the course objectives and teaching methodology, students perform plays in groups for their final assessment. They actively participate in selecting themes and developing scripts with teacher assistance. While grading student performances is generally discouraged, if necessary, the criteria should not include English language proficiency.

Attanayake (2020) offers a framework for evaluating language courses that prioritize confidence building over proficiency. She emphasizes that student feedback should be the primary source for course evaluation, with teacher insights serving as supplementary data. In the pre-evaluation phase, learners assess suggested materials, teaching methodologies, and assessment methods in relation to the course objectives. This phase also includes evaluating students' confidence levels as a pre-test before instruction to compare with results at the course's end. The in-course evaluation allows for adjustments based on learners' needs; however, Attanayake notes that implementing changes can be particularly challenging in an intensive course without disrupting instruction flow. The post-evaluation phase is crucial for assessing the effectiveness of the course materials, teaching methodologies, and assessment strategies in building students' confidence to speak English. This evaluation can utilize learner questionnaires, interviews, teacher journals, and teaching observations. Attanayake's course design process carefully aligns curricular elements to foster language confidence in post-colonial settings, ultimately transforming anxiety into assurance in students' English-speaking abilities. This approach highlights the vital role of evaluation as a continuous feedback mechanism that informs instructional practices and empowers learners to take ownership of their learning.

Insights from the Curriculum Project ENGL 010

This subsection revisits the "Course Planning and Sample Curriculum Development Project" (ENGL 010) presented in Chapter 8, which emphasized curriculum conceptualization, planning, and development. The following discussion will concentrate on the evaluation phase. It will highlight the course instructor's review and revision of certain curriculum elements after its implementation.

To recap, ENGL 010 is a preparatory academic writing course for NNES students offered as part of the FYWP at a U.S. university. Guided by the SLOs of the core composition course that students will advance to upon completing ENGL 010, as well as the FYWP's conceptual perspectives on writing and the requirements of at least three writing projects, the instructor adopted the United Nations' Sustainable Development Goals (SDGs) as a framework for writing. For more details on the rationale and course elements, please refer to Chapter 8.

Monitoring and Documenting

The instructor implemented a variety of strategies to document and evaluate the curriculum. These included varied formative assessments, such as mini writing tasks, pair and group work, and one-on-one conferences focused on early drafts of each writing project. These strategies facilitated monitoring of students' progress, their understanding of course concepts, and their writing skill development. Additionally, the three portfolios, which included multiple drafts of each writing project along with grading rubrics, played a crucial role in documenting students' growth. Students also wrote a final reflection detailing their experiences in the course, challenges faced, skills acquired, and areas for further improvement.

Beyond student-focused assessments, the instructor engaged in ongoing reflection throughout the semester, taking notes on the content covered each week. For instance, utilizing the track-changes feature in Microsoft Word, she annotated the detailed 16-week course calendar, which outlined weekly topics and instructional activities. After implementing an instructional activity or material, she would reflect on students' interactions with it and make any necessary adjustments to improve clarity and effectiveness.

Evaluation

Based on the collected evidence referenced above, student input, and the instructor's evaluation of the first iteration of the ENGL 010 course, several issues were identified that needed to be addressed in the curriculum review and revision process. One major issue was the progression of the writing projects and the skills needed to navigate each. During the curriculum development phase, the instructor established three writing projects to prepare students for the SLOs of the core composition course while aligning with the course theme. Writing Project 1 (WP1), the Summary-Response Portfolio, required students to write two summary-response essays on texts from different genres, followed by a cover letter detailing their rhetorical choices. Although most students' final drafts met the assignment requirements, the task presented significant challenges, especially as it was the first writing assignment of the semester. Discussing other authors' texts involves several complex skills, including reading comprehension, summarization, paraphrasing, citation, analysis, and response, all of which must be integrated into a cohesive academic essay. While these topics were covered in the early weeks of the course, the instructor felt that students needed more time to expand and reinforce these skills. They also needed to fully grasp the fundamental knowledge necessary for writing cohesive, coherent, and well-supported academic essays before attempting to summarize and respond to others' texts. To address this, the instructor concluded that students required additional foundational skills to navigate such assignments successfully.

Major Revisions

To support students' development of writing skills and build confidence, the instructor made some revisions to the progression of topics and writing projects. Drawing on her experience teaching novice multilingual writers, she concluded that beginning with a personally meaningful writing task would be more accessible for learners than engaging with external sources. However, the task still needed to emphasize essential academic writing features. Accordingly, the first two writing projects were adjusted, and the progression of knowledge and skills was revised (Figure 10.2). The instructor emphasized the diagnostic writing task completed during the second week of the semester. Initially, this informal task aimed to help assess students' writing skills and see their work without using artificial intelligence tools like ChatGPT. Although it remained a formative assessment with minimal grading, it received more emphasis. During Week 1 of the semester, lessons focused on familiarizing students with the SDGs and reading strategies. As homework at the end of Week 1 (Figure 10.2), students were asked to identify an SDG they believe should be a priority and explain why. Provided with a pre-writing planning sheet, students outlined their chosen SDG and why they thought it should be prioritized. Using this sheet, students had class time the following week to write an essay. Since this was a diagnostic assessment, it was made clear to the students that they should not stress about it and should do their best as it would not affect their course grades.

In the revised curriculum, the Academic Essay was added as the first writing project (WP1) to expand and build on the diagnostic essay (Table 10.2). The rationale was to allow students to develop essential academic writing skills, such as formulating effective thesis statements and supporting details, enhancing their reading skills, and building background knowledge of the SDGs through engaging with reading and applying reading strategies. This writing assignment also served as a tool for students to apply the topics covered during lessons and to experience the phases of writing as a process. To clarify this last point further, after covering a writing concept (e.g., thesis statements, topic sentences, and supporting details), students would revisit their essays to assess (or add) such elements in their writing and make any necessary adjustments based on what they had learned. To facilitate this process, the instructor created a Google Drive folder for each student, linked in Blackboard, containing their work. One of the items in this folder was a working draft of WP1 to facilitate the revision and application of the concepts and skills covered in a given lesson.

In the revised version of the ENGL 010 curriculum, the first four weeks focused on providing students with opportunities to express their thoughts about the SDGs through the construction of an academic essay. During this period, students built their understanding of key academic writing features, such as clarity, unity, and support, by applying these concepts to their own writing. As part of the revision process, the instructor identified an open-source textbook that concisely covered essential topics such as structuring, paragraphing, and style. She decided to adopt

Table 10.2 Sample Revision: A Preview of the Academic Essay Prompt

Writing Project 1 aims to familiarize you with the components of academic essays, the phases of the writing process, essay unity, source integration, sentence structure and mechanics, as well as the United Nations' Sustainable Development Goals (SDGs). This will be facilitated by building on what you have written for the diagnostic essay during Week 2. We will revisit your diagnostic essay to revise and edit it by applying the knowledge and skills covered early in the semester. The diagnostic writing prompt required the following:

As homework: *Read the United Nations' 17 SDGs and identify one goal you believe is the most urgent in your local context (e.g., community, town/city, or country). Reflect on what you have experienced or seen in relation to the issue that this goal targets. Outline three reasons that make this goal a priority.*

In-class: *Write an essay explaining your priority SDG by discussing the three reasons. Your essay should include an introduction with background information about the SDG and a thesis statement outlining the three reasons. Each reason should be discussed in a separate paragraph, with clear explanations and examples. Finally, add a conclusion paragraph that summarizes your key points.*

selected chapters from this resource for the course. Each week, students were assigned a chapter to read outside of class and then asked to respond to multiple-choice questions about the chapter on Blackboard. These mini-quizzes aimed to ensure that students completed the readings and reinforced the concepts discussed. Hence, students could take the quizzes twice and keep their highest score.

In the revised curriculum, students were introduced to summary and response skills in Week 5. Instead of a Summary-Response Portfolio consisting of three pieces (two summary-response essays and a cover letter), the instructor streamlined this assignment into a single Summary-Response Essay (WP2). This change was made to accommodate the newly added Academic Essay as WP1, which took up the first four weeks of the course. Following the completion of the Summary-Response Essay, the curriculum shifts its focus to argumentation, similar to the first iteration of the course. Students then worked on their Argument Proposal and Campaign Product (WP3). The course still concludes with a Reflective Essay (WP4).

It is important to note that the revisions made to the curriculum—specifically in terms of the nature and order of the writing projects and the progression of topics—proved effective. By equipping students with essential foundational academic skills early in the semester, they were better prepared to navigate more complex assignments later on.

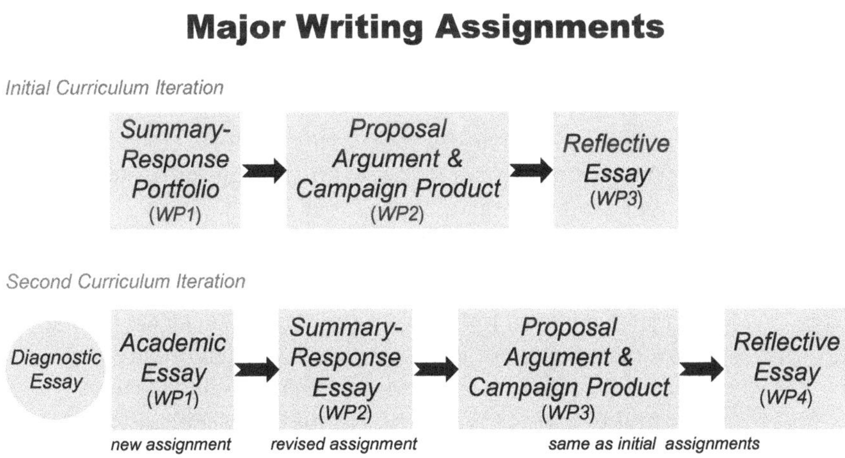

Figure 10.2. Sample Revision: Progression and Type of Writing Assignments

Students felt more comfortable and ready to approach the summary-response writing assignment when it was introduced later in the semester, compared to when it was the first assignment.

This iterative process, adopted by the course instructor continuously to monitor, evaluate, and document necessary revisions during the initial implementation of the curriculum, facilitated the identification of issues and led to prompt adjustments in the second iteration of the course. This proactive approach ensures that the curriculum is responsive to learner needs and effectively supports their writing development.

To conclude, cyclical evaluation of the curriculum informs its conceptualization, planning, development, and implementation. This process ensures curriculum alignment and effectiveness in meeting the curriculum's intended purposes and responding to the needs of the student population. Integrating periodic and systematic opportunities for curriculum review and revision at the meso level brings instructors together to share innovations and collaborate on enhancing the totality of the teaching and learning experience. At the micro level, individual instructors need to monitor, assess, and reflect on the implemented curriculum to identify areas for improvement, make necessary revisions, and ensure it remains responsive and effective. Whether at the meso or micro levels, systematic curriculum evaluation, review, and revision are vital for continuous improvements and optimizing student learning and success.

After you read, consider the following questions:

1. How is the curriculum evaluated, reviewed, and revised in your educational context? What does the process look like?
2. Retrieve a lesson that you have written before. How did it go? What evidence can help you answer this question? What changes can be made to improve the lesson?
3. You are part of a curriculum review team evaluating a listening and speaking course for young adult learners at the intermediate level. Input from students and teachers indicates a lack of engagement in course topics and materials. How would you approach this review? What specific data can inform the process? What steps should be taken to identify issues and recommend revisions?

4. You teach in a multi-level EFL institute with six levels of English proficiency. The goal is to prepare students for higher education in English-medium institutions. Student achievement data indicates inconsistencies in performance across levels. How will a program-wide curriculum review session be arranged to ensure coherence and meaningful progression? How will you structure the teams? Create a curriculum review plan/agenda outlining the review goals, data and tools, and tasks, including guiding questions.

References

Abdollahzadeh, E., & Baniasad, S. (2010). Ideologies in the imported English textbooks: EFL learners and teachers' awareness and attitude. *Journal of English Language Teaching and Learning, 53*(217), 1–17.

Agosti, C. I., & Bernat, E. (Eds.). (2018). *University pathway programs: Local responses within a growing global trend.* Springer International Publishing.

Ahmed, K. (2011). Casting Arabic culture as the "other": Cultural issues in the English curriculum. In, C. Gitsaki (Ed.), *Teaching and learning in the Arab world* (pp. 119–137). Peter Lang Publications. https://doi.org/10.3726/978-3-0351-0201-7

Akbari, Z. (2015). Current challenges in teaching/learning English for EFL learners: The case of junior high school and high school. *Procedia-Social and Behavioral Sciences, 199*, 394–401. https://doi.org/10.1016/j.sbspro.2015.07.524

Alemdar, M. & Aytaç, A. (2002). The impact of teachers' educational philosophy tendencies on their curriculum autonomy. *Journal of Pedagogical Research, 6*(1), 270–284. https://dx.doi.org/10.33902/JPR.2022.166

Alharbi, A. O. (2022). Issues with communicative language teaching implementation in Saudi Arabia concerning the government policy, teachers, and students: Two decades of research. *Arab World English Journal, 13*(2), 412–423. https://dx.doi.org/10.24093/awej/vol13no2.28

Ali, M. M. (2010). Revisiting English language teaching (ELT) curriculum design: How appropriate is Bangladesh higher secondary level national ELT curriculum as a learner-centred one? *IIUC Studies, 7*, 283–296. https://banglajol.info/index.php/IIUCS/article/view/12494

Ali, M., & Walker, A. L. (2014). "Bogged down" ELT in Bangladesh: Problems and policy: Investigating some problems that encumber ELT in an EFL context. *English Today, 30*(2), 33–38. https://doi.org/10.1017/S0266078414000108

Allen, J. P., & Widdowson, H. G. (1974). Teaching the communicative use of English. *International Review of Applied Linguistics in Language Teaching, 12*(1), 1–21.

Allen, P. (1977). Structural and functional models in language teaching. *TESL Talk, 8*(1), 5–15.

Altinyelken, H. K. (2010). Curriculum change in Uganda: Teacher perspectives on the new thematic curriculum. *International Journal of Educational Development, 30*(2), 151–161. https://doi.org/10.1016/j.ijedudev.2009.03.004

Alvi, M. (2016). *A manual for selecting sampling techniques in research.* Munich Personal RePEc Archive. https://mpra.ub.uni-muenchen.de/70218/

Anderson, L. W., Krathwohl, D. R., Airasian, P. W, Cruikshank, K. A., Mayer, R. E, Pintrich, P. R., Raths, J., & Wittrock, M. C. (2001). *A taxonomy for learning, teaching, and assessing: A revision of Bloom's taxonomy of educational objectives: Complete edition.* Longman.

Anthony, E. M. (1963). Approach, method and technique. *English Language Teaching 17*(2), 63–67. https://doi.org/10.1093/elt/XVII.2.63

Antoine, A., Mason, R., Mason, R., Palahicky, S. & Rodriguez de France, C. (2018). *Pulling together: A guide for curriculum developers.* BCcampus. https://opentextbc.ca/indigenizationcurriculumdevelopers/

Aqel, I. M. (2013). The effect of using grammar-translation method on acquiring English as a foreign language. *International Journal of Asian Social Science, 3*(12), 2469–2476. https://archive.aessweb.com/index.php/5007/article/view/2596

Arias-Contreras, C., & Moore, P. J. (2022). The role of English language in the field of agriculture: A needs analysis. *English for Specific Purposes, 65,* 95–106. https://doi.org/10.1016/j.esp.2021.09.002

Atkinson, D. (2002). Toward a sociocognitive approach to second language acquisition. *The Modern Language Journal, 86*(4), 525–545. https://doi.org/10.1111/1540-4781.00159

Attanayake, A. (2020). *Post-colonial curriculum practices in South Asia: Building confidence to speak English.* Routledge. https://doi.org/10.4324/9781351129800

Auerbach, E. R. (1992). *Making meaning, making change: Participatory curriculum development for adult ESL literacy.* Center for Applied Linguistics. https://files.eric.ed.gov/fulltext/ED356688.pdf

Ausubel, D. P., Novak, J. D., & Hanesian, H. (1978). *Educational psychology: A cognitive view* (2nd ed.). Holt, Rinehart and Winston.

Azarnoosh, M., & Kargozari, H. R. (2018). In A. Faravani, M. Zeraatpishe, M. Azarnoosh, & H. R. Kargozari (Eds.), *Issues in syllabus design* (pp. 135–140). Sense Publishers. https://doi.org/10.1163/9789463511889_012

Bach, K., & Harnish, R. M. (1979). *Linguistic communication and speech acts.* MIT Press.

Bachman, L. F., & Palmer, A. S. (1996). *Language testing in practice: Designing and developing useful language tests.* Oxford University Press.

Bahous, S. (2023, September 1). Op-ed: Three priorities for climate action. UN Women. https://www.unwomen.org/en/news-stories/op-ed/2023/09/op-ed-three-priorities-for-climate-action

Bandura, A. (1977). *Social learning theory.* Prentice-Hall.

Bandura, A. (1997). *Self-efficacy: The exercise of control.* Macmillan.

Baratta, A. (2018). "I speak how I speak:" A discussion of accent and identity within teachers of ELT. In B. Yazan & N. Rudolph (Eds.), *Criticality, teacher identity, and (in)equity in English language teaching: Issues and implications* (pp. 163–178). Springer. https://doi.org/10.1007/978-3-319-72920-6_9

Bärenfänger, O., & Tschirner, E. (2008). Language educational policy and language learning quality management: The common European framework of reference. *Foreign Language Annals, 41*(1), 81–101. https://doi.org/10.1111/j.1944-9720.2008.tb03280.x

Basturkmen, H. (2009). Commenting on results in published research articles and masters dissertations in language teaching. *Journal of English for Academic Purposes, 8*(4), 241–251. https://doi.org/10.1016/j.jeap.2009.07.001

Basturkmen, H. (2010). *Developing courses in English for specific purposes.* Springer.

Basturkmen, H. (2012). A genre-based investigation of discussion sections of research articles in Dentistry and disciplinary variation. *Journal of English for Academic Purposes, 11*(2), 134–144. https://doi.org/10.1016/j.jeap.2011.10.004

Basturkmen, H. (2024). Learning a specialized register: An English for Specific Purposes research agenda. *Language Teaching*, 1–12. https://doi.org/10.1017/S0261444823000472

Battiste, M. (2009). Naturalizing Indigenous knowledge in Eurocentric education. *Canadian Journal of Native Education, 32*(1), 5–18. https://doi.org/10.14288/cjne.v32i1.196482

Baykut, S., Erbil, C., Ozbilgin, M., Kamasak, R., & Bağlama, S. H. (2022). The impact of the hidden curriculum on international students in the context of a country with a toxic triangle of diversity. *The Curriculum Journal, 33*(2), 156–177. https://doi.org/10.1002/curj.135

Beane, J. (1997). *Curriculum integration: Designing the core of democratic education.* Teachers College Press.

Beauchamp, G. A. (1964). Developing curriculum theory. *The High School Journal, 48*(1), 7–12. https://www.jstor.org/stable/40368000

Beauchamp, G. A. (1972). Basic components of a curriculum theory. *Curriculum Theory Network, 3*(10), 16–22. https://www.jstor.org/stable/1179213

Beauchamp, G. A. (1975). *Curriculum theory* (3rd ed.). The Kagg Press.

Beauchamp, G. A. (1982). Curriculum theory: Meaning, development, and use. *Theory into Practice, 21*(1), 23–27. https://doi.org/10.1080/00405848209542976

Belcher, D. (2009). What ESP is and can be: An introduction. In D. Belcher (Ed.), *English for specific purposes: Theory and practice* (pp. 1–20). University of Michigan Press.

Belcher, D. D. (2006). English for specific purposes: Teaching to perceived needs and imagined futures in worlds of work, study, and everyday life. *TESOL Quarterly, 40*(1), 133–156. https://doi.org/10.2307/40264514

Bemis, K. A., & Schroeder, G. B. (1969). *The writing and use of behavioral objectives.* The U.S. Department of Health, Education, and Welfare, Office of Education. https://eric.ed.gov/?id=ED033881

Benesch, S. (1996). Needs analysis and curriculum development in EAP: An example of a critical approach. *TESOL Quarterly, 30*(4), 723–738. https://doi.org/10.2307/3587931

Benesch, S. (1999a). Rights analysis: Studying power relations in an academic setting. *English for Specific Purposes, 18*, 313–327. https://doi.org/10.1016/S0889-4906(98)00011-8

Benesch, S. (1999b). Thinking critically, thinking dialogically. *TESOL Quarterly, 33*(3), 573–580. https://doi.org/10.2307/3587682

Benesch, S. (2001). *Critical English for Academic Purposes: Theory, politics and practice.* Lawrence Erlbaum Associates Inc.

Berman, A., Garcia, B., Nam, B., Chu, S., & Quek, F. (2016). Toward a making community of practice: The social aspects of elementary classroom-based making. *Proceedings of the 6th Annual Conference on Creativity and Fabrication in Education, USA*, 9–16. https://doi.org/10.1145/3003397.3003399

Bertrand, Y. (2003). *Contemporary theories and practice in education* (2nd ed.). Atwood Publishing.

Bhatia, V. K. (1993). *Analyzing genre: Language use in professional settings.* Longman.

Bhatia, V. K. (2010). Interdiscursivity in professional communication. *Discourse & Communication, 4*(1), 32–50. https://doi.org/10.1177/1750481309351208

Bhatia, V. K. (2019). Genre as interdiscursive performance in English for professional communication. In K. Hyland & L. Wong (Eds), *Specialised English* (pp. 36–49). Routledge.

Biber, D. (2006). *University language: A corpus-based study of spoken and written registers.* John Benjamins Publishing Company.

Biber, D. (2009). A corpus-driven approach to formulaic language in English: Multi-word patterns in speech and writing. *International Journal of Corpus Linguistics, 14*(3), 275–311. https://doi.org/10.1075/ijcl.14.3.08bib

Biber, D., Conrad, S., & Cortes, V. (2004). If you look at . . . : Lexical bundles in university teaching and textbooks. *Applied Linguistics, 25*(3), 371–405. https://doi.org/10.1093/applin/25.3.371

Bloom, B. S., Engelhart, M. D., Furst, E. J., Hill, E. J., & Krathwohl, D. R. (1956). *Taxonomy of educational objectives: The classification of educational goals.* David McKay Company.

Bloomfield, L. (1935). Linguistic aspects of science. *Philosophy of Science, 2*(4), 499–517. https://doi.org/10.1086/286392

Bloomfield, L. (1942). *Outline guide for the practical study of foreign languages.* Linguistic Society of America at the Waverly Press.

Bobbitt, F. (1918). *The curriculum.* The Cambridge Press.

Bobbitt, F. (1924). *How to make a curriculum.* The Cambridge Press.

Bocanegra-Valle, A. (2016). Needs analysis for curriculum design. In K. Hyland & P. Shaw, *The Routledge handbook of English for academic purposes* (pp. 560–576). Routledge.

Boomer, G. (1982). *Negotiating the curriculum: A teacher-student partnership.* Ashton Scholastic.

Boomer, G., Lester, N., Onore, C., & Cook, J. (Eds.), (1992). *Negotiating the curriculum: Educating for the 21st century.* Falmer Press.

Boozer, A., & Carlson, D. L. (2015). Planning backward to go forward: Examining preservice teachers' use of backward design to plan and deliver instruction. *Teacher Education and Practice, 28*(4), 522–548.

Brameld, T. (1965). Anthropotherapy—toward theory and practice. *Human Organization, 24*(4), 288–293. https://www.jstor.org/stable/44125350

Brameld, T. (1965). *Education as power.* Rinehart and Winston.

Brau, B., Fox, N., & Robinson, E. (2022). Behaviorism. In R. Kimmons (Ed.), *Education research.* EdTech Books. https://edtechbooks.org/education_research/behaviorismt

Breen, M. P. (1985). The social context for language learning—a neglected situation? *Studies in Second Language Acquisition, 7*(2), 135–158. https://doi.org/10.1017/S0272263100005337

Breen, M. P., & Candlin, C. N. (1980). The essentials of a communicative curriculum in language teaching. *Applied Linguistics, 1*(2), 89–112. https://doi.org/10.1093/applin/I.2.89

Breen, M. P., & Littlejohn, A. (Eds.). (2000). *Classroom decision-making: Negotiation and process syllabuses in practice*. Cambridge University Press.
Brindley, G. (1989). The role of needs analysis in adult ESL programme design. In R. K. Johnson (Ed.), *The second language curriculum* (pp. 63–78). Cambridge University Press. https://doi.org/10.1017/CBO9781139524520
Brinton, D. M., Snow, M. A., & Wesche, M. B. (1989). *Content-based second language instruction*. Newbury House Publishers.
British Council. (2022). *Borderless classroom models–From virtual mobility to real results*. TeachingEnglish by British Council. https://www.teachingenglish.org.uk/news-and-events/world-teachers-day/2022/borderless-classroom-models-virtual-mobility-real-results
Bron, J., Bovill, C., van Vliet, E., & Veugelers, W. (2016). Negotiating the curriculum: realizing student voice. *Social Educator, 34*(1), 39–54. https://eprints.gla.ac.uk/120635/
Brooks, M. (1987). Curriculum development from a constructivist perspective. *Educational Leadership, 44*(4), 63–67. https://files.ascd.org/staticfiles/ascd/pdf/journals/ed_lead/el_198612_brooks.pdf
Brooks, M. (2014). Content-based curricular development: guidelines for designing effective content-based instructed courses. *CELE Journal* (22), 16–34. https://cir.nii.ac.jp/crid/1520572359895213312
Brown, H. D. (2002). English language teaching in the "post-method" era: Toward better diagnosis, treatment, and assessment. In J. Richards & W. Renandya (Eds.), *Methodology in language teaching: An anthology of current practice* (pp. 9–18). Cambridge University Press. doi:10.1017/CBO9780511667190.003
Brown, H. D., & Lee, H. (2015). *Teaching by principles: An interactive approach to language pedagogy* (4th ed.). Pearson Education.
Brown, H. D., & Bradford, A. (2017). EMI, CLIL, & CBI: Differing approaches and goals. In P. Clements, A. Krause, & H. Brown (Eds.), *Transformation in language education* (pp. 328–334). Japan Association for Language Teaching.
Brown, J. D. (1995). *The elements of language curriculum: A systematic approach to program development*. Heinle & Heinle.
Brown, J. D. (2009). Foreign and second language needs analysis. In M. H. Long, & C. J. Doughty (Eds.), *Handbook of language teaching* (pp. 269–293). Wiley-Blackwell.
Brown, J. D. (2012). EIL curriculum development. In L. Alsagoff, S. L. McKay, G. Hu, & W. A. Renandya (Eds.), *Principles and practices for teaching English as an international language* (pp. 147–167). Routledge.
Brumfit, C. J. (1979). Notional syllabuses—a reassessment. *System, 7*(2), 111–116. https://doi.org/10.1016/0346-251X(79)90033-2
Bruner, J. S. (1960). *The process of education*. Harvard University Press.
Bruner, J. S. (1966). *A theory of instruction*. Harvard University Press.
Bui, G., & Tai, K. W. (2022). Revisiting functional adequacy and task-based language teaching in the GBA: Insights from translanguaging. *Asian-Pacific Journal of Second and Foreign Language Education, 7*(40), 1–14. https://doi.org/10.1186/s40862-022-00160-7
Bumen, N. T., Cakar, E., & Yildiz, D. G. (2014). Curriculum fidelity and factors affecting fidelity in the Turkish context. *Educational Sciences: Theory and Practice, 14*(1), 219–228. https://files.eric.ed.gov/fulltext/EJ1038715.pdf

Burbules, N. C. (2000). The limits of dialogue as a critical pedagogy. In TrifonasP. P., *Revolutionary pedagogies: Cultural politics, instituting education, and the discourse of theory* (pp. 251–273). Routledge.

Butler, Y. G. (2011). The implementation of communicative and task-based language teaching in the Asia-Pacific region. *Annual Review of Applied Linguistics*, *31*,36–57. https://doi.org/10.1017/S0267190511000122

Cabrera, M. D. P. M. (2014). Textbook use training in EFL teacher education. In J. D. D. M. Agudo (Ed.), *English as a foreign language teacher education: Current perspectives and challenges* (pp. 267–286). Brill.

Canagarajah, A. S. (1999). *Resisting linguistic imperialism in English teaching*. Oxford University Press.

Canagarajah, A. S. (2002). Globalization, methods and practice in periphery classrooms. In D. Block & D. Cameron. (Eds.), *Globalization and language teaching* (pp. 134– 150). Routledge.

Canagarajah, S. (2011). Translanguaging in the classroom: Emerging issues for research and pedagogy. *Applied Linguistics Review, 2*(2011), 1–27. https://doi.org/10.1515/9783110239331.1

Caniglia, G., John, B., Bellina, L., Lang, D. J., Wiek, A., Cohmer, S., & Laubichler, M. D. (2018). The glocal curriculum: A model for transnational collaboration in higher education for sustainable development. *Journal of Cleaner Production, 171*, 368–376. https://doi.org/10.1016/j.jclepro.2017.09.207

Carroll, J. B. (1965). The contributions of psychological theory and educational research to the teaching of foreign languages. *The Modern Language Journal*, *49*(5), 273–281. https://doi.org/10.2307/322133

Casal, J. E., & Kessler M. (2023). Rhetorical move-step analysis. In M. Kessler & C. Polio (Eds.), *Conducting genre-based research in applied linguistics: A methodological guide* (pp. 82–104). Routledge. https://doi.org/10.4324/9781003300847-7

CEA standards for English language programs and institutions. (2022). *Commission on English Language Program Accreditation*. https://cea-accredit.org/images/2022_docs_and_handbooks/2022_CEA_Standards.pdf

Center for Applied Linguistics. (2008). *Practitioner toolkit: Working with adult English language learners*. https://www.cal.org/caela/tools/program_development/prac_toolkit.html

Center for Applied Special Technology (CAST). (2018). *Universal design for learning guidelines version 2.2*. http://udlguidelines.cast.org

Center for Applied Special Technology (CAST). (n.d.). *UDL tips for assessment*. https://www.cast.org/binaries/content/assets/common/publications/downloads/cast-udltipsforassessment-20200920-a11y.pdf

Chastain, K. (1971). *The development of modern-language skills: Theory to practice*. Center for Curriculum Development.

Chaouni, A. (2014, March). *How I brought a river, and my city, back to life* [Video]. TED Conferences. https://www.ted.com/talks/aziza_chaouni_how_i_brought_a_river_and_my_city_back_to_life

Cheung, A. C. K., & Man Wong, P. (2012). Factors affecting the implementation of curriculum reform in Hong Kong: Key findings from a large-scale survey study.

International Journal of Educational Management, 26(1), 39–54. https://doi.org/10.1108/09513541211194374

Cheung, D., & Wong, H. (2002). Measuring teacher beliefs about alternative curriculum design. *The Curriculum Journal, 13*(2), 225–248. https://doi.org/10.1080/09585170210136868

Ching, G. S. (2021). Academic identity and communities of practice: Narratives of social science academics career decisions in Taiwan. *Education Sciences, 11*(388), 1–17. https://doi.org/10.3390/educsci11080388

Chitaka, T. Y. (2021). Environmentalism or greenwashing? Responses of South African value chain actors to plastic straw marine pollution. *South African Journal of Science, 117*(7/8). https://doi.org/10.17159/sajs.2021/9042

Cho, J., & Allen, T. (2005). "Backward" curriculum design and assessment: What goes around comes around, or haven't we seen this before? *Taboo, 9*(2), 105–122. https://files.eric.ed.gov/fulltext/EJ795704.pdf

Chomsky, N. (1964). The development of grammar in child language: Discussion. *Monographs of the Society for Research in Child Development, 29*(1), 35–42. https://doi.org/10.2307/1165753

Chomsky, N. (1978). *Topics in the theory of generative grammar.* De Gruyter Mouton. https://doi.org/10.1515/9783110903843

Chomsky, N. (1986). *Knowledge of language: Its nature, origin, and use.* Praeger.

Chowdhury, R., & Kamal, M. (2014). Balancing conformity and empowerment: Critical needs analysis in an EAP course at Dhaka University. In I. Liyanage & T. Walker (Eds.), *English for Academic Purposes (EAP) in Asia* (pp. 79–92). SensePublishers. https://doi.org/10.1007/978-94-6209-752-0_6

Christison, M., & Murray, D. E. (2014). *What English language teachers need to know: Designing curriculum.* Routledge.

Clarke, M. A. (1983). The scope of approach, the importance of method, and the nature of technique. In J. E. Alatis, H. H. Stern, & P. Strevens (Eds.), *Applied linguistics and the preparation of second language teachers: Toward a rationale* (pp. 106–115). Georgetown University Press. https://repository.library.georgetown.edu/bitstream/handle/10822/555476/GURT_1983.pdf?sequence=1

Common Core State Standards. (2010). *Common core state standards for math and English language arts.* https://learning.ccsso.org/common-core-state-standards-initiative

Copur-Gencturk, Y., Thacker, I., & Cimpian, J. (2024, October 28). U.S. math teachers view student performance differently based on race and gender. *The Conversation.* https://theconversation.com/us-math-teachers-view-student-performance-differently-based-on-race-and-gender-241418

Connor, U. (2000). Variation in rhetorical moves in grant proposals of US humanists and scientists. *Text & Talk, 20*(1), 1–28. https://doi.org/10.1515/text.1.2000.20.1.1

Cook, V. (2001). Using the first language in the classroom. *Canadian Modern Language Review, 57*(3), 402–423. https://doi.org/10.3138/cmlr.57.3.402

Corcoran, C. (2014). Chinese learning styles: Blending Confucian and Western theories. *Journal of Instructional Pedagogies, 13.* https://eric.ed.gov/?id=EJ1060088

Cornbleth, C. (1988). Curriculum in and out of context. *Journal of Curriculum and Supervision, 3*(2), 85–96. https://files.ascd.org/staticfiles/ascd/pdf/journals/jcs/jcs_1988winter_cornbleth.pdf

Cornbleth, C. (1990). *Curriculum in context.* The Flamer Press.
Counts, G. S. (1932). *Dare the school build a new social order?* Southern Illinois University Press.
Coxhead, A. (2000). A new academic word list. *TESOL Quarterly, 34*(2), 213–238. https://doi.org/10.2307/3587951
Coxhead, A., & Demecheleer, M. (2018). Investigating the technical vocabulary of plumbing. *English for Specific Purposes, 51*, 84–97. https://doi.org/10.1016/j.esp.2018.03.006
Crittenden, B. (1979). Product or process in curriculum evaluation? *New Education, 1*(2), 35–51.
Cummins, J. (2000). *Language, power and pedagogy: Bilingual children in the crossfire.* Multilingual Matters.
Cummins, J. (2008). BICS and CALP: Empirical and theoretical status of the distinction. In B. Street & N. H Hornberger (Eds.), *Encyclopedia of language and education* (2nd ed., Vol. 2, pp. 71–83). Springer.
Cunningham, T., Gannon, J., Kavanagh, M., Greene, J., Reddy, L., & Whitson, L. (2007). Theories of learning and curriculum design: Key positionalities and their relationships. *Level 3, 5*(1), 1–25. https://arrow.tudublin.ie/level3/vol5/iss1/6
Dahm, M. R., Slade, D., Brady, B., Goncharov, L., & Chien, L. (2022). Tracing interpersonal discursive features in Australian nursing bedside handovers: Approachability features, patient engagement and insights for ESP training and working with internationally trained nurses. *English for Specific Purposes, 66*, 17–32. https://doi.org/10.1016/j.esp.2021.10.002
Danner, R. B., & Ofuani, F. N. (2022). The influence of educational philosophies and learning theories on language teaching and learning in English as a second learning context. *Rivers State University Journal of Education, 25*(1), 69–81. https://www.rsujoe.com.ng/index.php/joe/article/view/97
Darling-Hammond, L., Hyler, M. E., & Gardner, M. (2017). *Effective teacher professional development.* Learning Policy Institute.
De Los Reyes, R. A. (2018). Translanguaging in multilingual third grade ESL classrooms in Mindanao, Philippines. *International Journal of Multilingualism, 16*(3), 302–316. https://doi.org/10.1080/14790718.2018.1472268
Dearden, J. (2014). *English as a medium of instruction–a growing global phenomenon: Phase 1 interim report April 2014.* British Council. https://www.britishcouncil.es/sites/default/files/british_council_english_as_a_medium_of_instruction.pdf
Demarest, A. B. (2015). *Place-based curriculum design: Exceeding standards through local investigations.* Routledge.
D'Emidio-Caston, M., & Crocker, E. (1987). *Montessori education: A humanistic approach for the 1990s* (ED314212). ERIC. https://files.eric.ed.gov/fulltext/ED314212.pdf
Dewey, J. (1910). *How to think.* D. C. Heath & Company.
Dewey, J. (1938). *Experience and education.* Macmillan Company.
Dirk, K. (2010). Navigating genres. In C. Lowe & P. Zemliansky (Eds.), *Writing spaces: Readings on writing* (Vol. 1, pp. 249–262). Parlor Press.

Doiz, A., Lasagabaster, D., & Sierra, J. M. (Eds.). (2012). *English-medium instruction at universities: Global challenges.* Multilingual Matters.

Dong, J., & Lu, X. (2020). Promoting discipline-specific genre competence with corpus-based genre analysis activities. *English for Specific Purposes, 58*, 138–154. https://doi.org/10.1016/j.esp.2020.01.005

Dressen-Hammouda, D. (2025). Ethnography in ESP. In S. Starfield & C. A. Hafner (Eds.), *The handbook of English for specific purposes* (2nd ed., pp. 599–618). John Wiley & Sons.

Dube, B., & Campbell, E. (2023). Borderless curriculum in the post-human era: Reflections on the United States of America and South African initial teacher pedagogical practices. *Journal of Curriculum Studies Research, 5*(1), 34–43. https://doi.org/10.46303/jcsr.2023.4

Dube, B., Mahlomaholo, S., Setlalentoa, W., & Tarman, B. (2023a). Creating sustainable learning environments in the era of the posthuman: Towards borderless curriculum. *Journal of Curriculum Studies Research, 5*(1), i–x. https://doi.org/10.46303/jcsr.2023.1

Dube, B., Mosia, M., & Moreeng, B. (2023b). Re-envisioning scholarship of teaching and learning with data analytics and a borderless curriculum in a troubled world. *Curriculum and Teaching Dialogue, 15*(1), 27–40. https://doi.org/10.38159/ehass.20234121%0d

Dudley-Evans, T. & St. John, M. J. (1998). *Developments in English for specific purposes: A multidisciplinary approach.* Cambridge University Press.

Dueñas, M. (2003). A description of prototype models for content-based language instruction in higher education. *Bells: Barcelona English Language and Literature Studies, 12*, 1–11 https://www.raco.cat/index.php/Bells/article/view/82923

Dunn, T. G., & Shriner, C. (1999). Deliberate practice in teaching: What teachers do for self-improvement. *Teaching and Teacher Education, 15*(6), 631–651. https://doi.org/10.1016/S0742-051X(98)00068-7

Đurović, Z. (2021). Corpus linguistics methods for building ESP word lists, glossaries and dictionaries on the example of a marine engineering word list. *Lexikos, 31*, 259–282. http://dx.doi.org/10.5788/31-1-1647

Dweck, C. S. (2006). *Mindset: The new psychology of success.* Random House.

Echevarria, J., & Short, D. (2010). Programs and practices for effective sheltered content instruction. In D. Dolson & L. Burnham-Massey, *Improving education for English learners: Research-based approaches* (pp. 250–321). California Department of Education.

Edwards, F. (2011). Teaching and learning together: Making space for curriculum negotiation in higher education. *Waikato Journal of Education, 16*(3), 143–156. https://doi.org/10.15663/wje.v16i3.41

Edwards, N. (2000). Language for business: Effective needs assessment, syllabus design and materials preparation in a practical ESP case study. *English for Specific Purposes, 19*(3), 291-296. https://doi.org/10.1016/S0889-4906(98)00029-5

Eisner, E. W. (1979). *The educational imagination: On the design and evaluation of school programs.* Macmillan Publishing Co.

Eiss, A. F., & Harbeck, M. B. (1969). *Behavioral objectives in the affective domain.* National Science Supervises Association. https://eric.ed.gov/?id=ED028101

Ellili-Cherif, M., & Hadba, H. M. (2017). Fidelity to and satisfaction with prescribed curriculum in an Arab educational context: ESL teachers' perspective. *The Curriculum Journal, 28*(3), 367–388. https://doi.org/10.1080/09585176.2016.1240885

Elliott, J., & Norris, N. (Eds.). (2012). *Curriculum, pedagogy and educational research: The work of Lawrence Stenhouse.* Routledge. https://doi.org/10.4324/9780203818114

Ellis, G., & Sinclair, B. (1989). *Learning to learn English: A course in learner training.* Cambridge University Press.

Ellis, N. C. (2019). Essentials of a theory of language cognition. *The Modern Language Journal, 103*, 39–60. https://doi.org/10.1111/modl.12532

Ellis, R. (1993). The structural syllabus and second language acquisition. *TESOL Quarterly, 27*(1), 91–113. https://doi.org/10.2307/3586953

Ellis, R. (2003). *Task-based learning and teaching.* Oxford University Press.

Ellis, R. (2019). Towards a modular language curriculum for using tasks. *Language Teaching Research, 23*(4), 454–475. https://doi.org/10.1177/1362168818765315

Ellis, R. (2021). A short history of SLA: Where have we come from and where are we going? *Language Teaching, 54*(2), 190–205. doi:10.1017/S0261444820000038

Ellsworth, E. (1992). Why doesn't this feel empowering? Working through the repressive myths of critical pedagogy. In C. Luke & J. Gore (Eds), *Feminisms and critical pedagogy* (pp. 90–119). Routledge.

Elturki, E. (2020). A systematic process for assessing assessment. *English Teaching Forum, 58*(4), 12–21. https://americanenglish.state.gov/files/ae/resource_files/etf_58_4_pg12-21.pdf

Elturki, E. (2021a). Writing within the disciplines: An exploratory study of writing in graduate pathway programs and the shifting role of the English for Academic Purposes curriculum. *Pedagogies: An International Journal, 18*(2), 135–152. https://doi.org/10.1080/1554480X.2021.1975542

Elturki, E. (2021b, September). In-house professional development: Opportunities for teachers. *English teaching professional* (136), 40–42. https://www.modernenglishteacher.com/in-house-professional-development

Elturki, E. (2022). A framework for navigating the review and revision of the ELT curriculum. *English Language Teacher Education and Development, 25*, 38–46.

Emans, R. (1966). A proposed conceptual framework for curriculum development. *The Journal of Educational Research, 59*(7), 327–332. https://doi.org/10.1080/00220671.1966.10883370

Endeley, M. N. & Zama, M. A. (2021). *Perspectives in curriculum studies.* Spears Media Press.

English, F. W. (2000). *Deciding what to teach and test: Developing, aligning, and auditing the curriculum.* Corwin Press.

English, F. W., & Kaufman, R. A. (1975). *Needs assessment: A focus for curriculum development.* Association for Supervision and Curriculum Development. https://eric.ed.gov/?id=ED107619

Ericsson, K. A. (1998). The scientific study of expert levels of performance: General implications for optimal learning and creativity. *High Ability Studies, 9*(1),75–100. https://doi.org/10.1080/1359813980090106

Ericsson, K. A., Krampe, R. T., & Tesch-Römer, C. (1993). The role of deliberate practice in the acquisition of expert performance. *Psychological Review*, *100*(3), 363–406. https://psycnet.apa.org/doi/10.1037/0033-295X.100.3.363

Ertmer, P. A., & Newby, T. J. (2013). Behaviorism, cognitivism, constructivism: Comparing critical features from an instructional design perspective. *Performance Improvement Quarterly*, *6*(4), 43–71. https://doi.org/10.1002/piq.21143

Evans, R. W. (2010). The (unfulfilled) promise of critical pedagogy. In S. Totten & J. Pedersen (Eds.), *Teaching and studying social issues: Major programs and approaches* (pp. 233–249). Information Age Publishing.

Ewald, J. D. (1999). Comments on Graham Crookes and Al Lehner's "Aspects of process in an ESL critical pedagogy teacher education course": A plea for published reports on the application of a critical pedagogy to "language study proper." *TESOL Quarterly*, *33*(2), 275–279. https://doi.org/10.2307/3587722

Ewer, J. R., & Latorre, G. (1967). Preparing an English course for students of science. *ELT Journal*, *21*(3), 221–229. https://doi.org/10.1093/elt/XXI.3.221

Fang, F. (2018). Glocalization, English as a lingua franca and ELT: Reconceptualizing identity and models for ELT in China. In B. Yazan & N. Rudolph (Eds.), *Criticality, teacher identity, and (in)equity in English language teaching: Issues and implications* (pp. 23–40). Springer. https://doi.org/10.1007/978-3-319-72920-6_2

Farrell, T. S. (2018). Reflective practice for language teachers. In J. I. Liontas & M. DelliCarpini (Eds.), *The TESOL encyclopedia of English language teaching*, (Vol. 1, pp. 1–6). Wiley Blackwell.

Farrell, T. S. C. (2007). *Reflective language teaching: From research to practice*. Continuum Press.

Farrell, T. S. C. (2011). Exploring the professional role identities of experienced ESL teachers through reflective practice. *System*, *66*, 1–9. https://doi.org/10.1016/j.system.2011.01.012

Farrell, T. S. C. (2014). *Reflective practice in ESL teacher development groups: From practices to principles*. Palgrave Macmillan.

Farrell, T. S. C. (2015). *Promoting teacher reflection in second language education:A framework for TESOL professionals*. Routledge.

Farrell, T. S., & Kennedy, B. (2019). Reflective practice framework for TESOL teachers: One teacher's reflective journey. *Reflective Practice*, *20*(1), 1–12.

Feldman, J. (2020). The role of professional learning communities to support teacher development: A social practice theory perspective. *South African Journal of Education*, *40*(1), 1–8. https://hdl.handle.net/10520/EJC-1c030389d7

Feuerherm, E., & Oshio, T. (2020). Conducting a community-based ESOL programme needs analysis. *ELT Journal*, *74*(3), 327–337. https://doi.org/10.1093/elt/ccaa011

Fien, J. (1992). Understanding the macro-context of teaching environmental education: A case study from Queensland, 1989-1991. *Australian Journal of Environmental Education*, *8*, 77–114. doi:10.1017/S0814062600003323

Finney, D. (2002). The ELT curriculum: A flexible model for a changing world. In J. C. Richards & W. A. Renandya (Eds.), *Methodology in language teaching: An anthology of current practice* (pp. 69–79). Cambridge University Press.

Firth, A., & Wagner, J. (1997). On discourse, communication, and (some) fundamental concepts in SLA research. *The Modern Language Journal, 81*(3), 285–300. https://doi.org/10.1111/j.1540-4781.1997.tb05480.x

Flinders, D. J., Noddings, N., & Thornton, S. J. (1986). The null curriculum: Its theoretical basis and practical implications. *Curriculum Inquiry, 16*(1), 33–42. https://doi.org/10.2307/1179551

Flowerdew, J., & Wan, A. (2006). Genre analysis of tax computation letters: How and why tax accountants write the way they do. *English for Specific Purposes, 25*(2), 133–153. https://doi.org/10.1016/j.esp.2005.03.005

Flowerdew, J., & Wan, A. (2010). The linguistic and the contextual in applied genre analysis: The case of the company audit report. *English for Specific Purposes, 29*(2), 78–93. https://doi.org/10.1016/j.esp.2009.07.001

Flowerdew, L. (2005). An integration of corpus-based and genre-based approaches to text analysis in EAP/ESP: Countering criticisms against corpus-based methodologies. *English for Specific Purposes, 24*(3), 321–332. https://doi.org/10.1016/j.esp.2004.09.002

Flowerdew, L. (2012). Needs analysis and curriculum development in ESP. InB. Paltridge & S. Starfield (Eds.), *The handbook of English for specific purposes* (pp. 325–346). Wiley-Blackwell.

Flowerdew, L. (2013). Needs analysis and curriculum development in ESP. InB. Paltridge & S. Starfield (Eds.), *The handbook of English for specific purposes* (pp. 325–346). Wiley-Blackwell.

Forman, R. (2014). How local teachers respond to the culture and language of a global English as a foreign language textbook. *Language, Culture and Curriculum, 27*(1), 72–88. https://doi.org/10.1080/07908318.2013.868473

Fosnot, C. (1996). Constructivism: A Psychological theory of learning. In C. Fosnot (Ed.), *Constructivism: Theory, perspectives, and practice* (pp.8–33). Teachers College Press.

Fosnot, C. T. & Perry, S. (2005). Constructivism: A psychological theory of learning. In C. T. Fosnot (Ed.), *Constructivism: Theory, perspectives, and practice* (2nd ed.,pp. 8–38). Teachers College Press.

Fraiberg, S. (2018). Multilingual and multimodal practices at a global startup: Toward a spatial approach to language and literacy in professional contexts. *English for Specific Purposes, 51*, 55–68. https://doi.org/10.1016/j.esp.2018.03.003

Freire, P. (1970). *Pedagogy of the oppressed* (M. B. Ramos, Trans.). Herder and Herder. (Original work published 1968).

Fries, C. C. (1945). *Teaching and learning English as a foreign language*. University of Michigan Press.

Fries, C. C. (1957). Structural linguistics and language teaching. *The Classical Journal, 52*(6), 265–268. https://www.jstor.org/stable/3294807

Frydenberg, G. (1982). Designing an ESP reading skills course. *ELT Journal, 36*(3), 156–163. https://doi.org/10.1093/elt/36.3.156

Fryer, D. L. (2012). Analysis of the generic discourse features of the English-language medical research article: A systemic-functional approach. *Functions of Language, 19*(1), 5–37. https://doi.org/10.1075/fol.19.1.01fry

Gabel, S. (2002). Some conceptual problems with critical pedagogy. *Curriculum Inquiry, 32*(2), 177–201. https://doi.org/10.1111/1467-873X.00222

Galante, A., & Piccardo, E. (2022). Teaching pronunciation: Toward intelligibility and comprehensibility. *ELT Journal, 76*(3), 375–386. https://doi-org.proxy.cc.uic.edu/10.1093/elt/ccab060

Galloway, N., & Numajiri, T. (2019). Global Englishes language teaching: Bottom-up curriculum implementation. *TESOL Quarterly, 54*(1), 118–145. https://doi.org/10.1002/tesq.547

Galloway, N., & Rose, H. (2021). English medium instruction and the English language practitioner. *ELT Journal, 75*(1), 33–41. https://doi.org/10.1093/elt/ccaa063

Gamson, D.A. & Eckert, S.A. (2019). Standards, instructional objectives, and curriculum design: A complex relationship. *Phi Delta Kappan, 100*(6), 8–12. https://kappanonline.org/standards-instructional-objectives-curriculum-design-gamson-eckert-anderson/

García, O., Lin, A. M. Y. (2017). Translanguaging in bilingual education. In O. García, A. Lin, & S. May (Eds.), *Encyclopedia of language and education: Bilingual and multilingual education* (3rd ed., pp. 117–130). Springer. https://doi.org/10.1007/978-3-319-02258-1_9

García-Mateus, S., & Palmer, D. (2017). Translanguaging pedagogies for positive identities in two-way dual language bilingual education. *Journal of Language, Identity & Education, 16*(4), 245–255. https://doi.org/10.1080/15348458.2017.1329016

Gardner, H. (1983). *Frames of mind: The theory of multiple intelligences.* Basic Books.

Gardner, H. (1987). The theory of multiple intelligences. *Annals of Dyslexia, 37*,19–35. https://www.jstor.org/stable/23769277

Gardner, H. (1993). *The theory of multiple intelligences: The theory in practice.* Basic Books.

Ghorbani, M. R. (2009). ELT in Iranian high schools in Iran, Malaysia and Japan: Reflections on how tests influence use of prescribed textbooks. *Reflections on English Language Teaching, 8*(2), 131–139.

Giroux, H. (2001). *Theory and resistance in education: Towards a pedagogy for the opposition* (2nd ed.). Greenwood Publishing Group.

Giroux, H. (2002). Teachers as transformatory intellectuals. *EDucate, 1*(2), 46–49. https://www.itacec.org/afed/document/henry_giroux_2_ok.pdf

Glatthorn, A., Boschee, F., Whitehead, M., & Boschee, B. F. (2019). *Curriculum leadership: Strategies for development and implementation* (5th ed.). Sage Publications.

Goodlad, J. I. & Richter, M. N. (1966). *The development of a conceptual system for dealing with problems of curriculum and instruction.* U.S. Department of Health, Education and Welfare. https://files.eric.ed.gov/fulltext/ED010064.pdf

Goodlad, J. I. (1967). The humanistic curriculum. *Music Educators Journal, 53*(7), 91–95. https://doi.org/10.2307/3391034

Goodlad, J. I. (1968). The future of learning and teaching. *AV Communication Review, 16*(1), 5–15. http://www.jstor.org/stable/30217418

Goodlad, J. I. (1981). Curriculum development beyond 1980. *Educational Evaluation and Policy Analysis, 3*(5), 49–54. https://doi.org/10.3102/01623737003005049

Goodlad, J. I. (1994). *What schools are for* (2nd ed.). Phi Delta Kappa Educational Foundation.

Goodlad, J. I. (Ed.). (1979). *Curriculum inquiry: The study of curriculum practice.* McGraw-Hill.

Goodson, I. F. (1994). *Studying curriculum: Cases and methods.* Teachers College Press.

Gottschalk, F., & Weise, C. (2023, August). *Digital equity and inclusion in education: An overview of practice and policy in OECD countries* (OECD Education Working Paper No. 299). https://dx.doi.org/10.1787/7cb15030-en

Gouëdard, P., Pont, B., Hyttinen, S., & Huang, P. (2020). *Curriculum reform: A literature review to support effective implementation.* Organisation for EconomicCo-operation and Development. https://dx.doi.org/10.1787/efe8a48c-en

Gouin, F. (1892). *The art of teaching and studying languages* (H. Swan & V. Betis, Trans). George Philip and Son.

Grabe, W. & Stoller, F. L. (1997). Content-based instruction: Research foundations. In M. A. Snow and D.M. Brinton (Eds.), *The content-based classroom: Perspectives on integrating language and content* (pp. 5–21). Addison Wesley Longman.

Grabe, W., & Stoller, F. L. (2011). *Teaching and researching reading* (2nd ed.). Pearson Education.

Graves, K. (2000). *Designing language courses: A guide for teachers.* Heinle & Heinle.

Graves, K. (2008). The language curriculum: A social contextual perspective. *Language Teaching, 41*(2), 147–181. https://doi.org/10.1017/S0261444807004867

Graves, K., & Garton, S. (2017). An analysis of three curriculum approaches to teaching English in public-sector schools. *Language Teaching, 50*(4), 441–482. doi:10.1017/S0261444817000155

Green, M. F. (2021). In search of curricular coherence. *International Journal of Teaching and Learning in Higher Education, 33*(1), 100–109. https://files.eric.ed.gov/fulltext/EJ1338433.pdf

Grider, C. (1993). *Foundations of cognitive theory: A concise review* (ED372324). ERIC. https://files.eric.ed.gov/fulltext/ED372324.pdf

Guillén-Galve, I., & Bocanegra-Valle, A. (Eds.). (2021). *Ethnographies of academic writing research: Theory, methods, and interpretation* (Vol. 1). John Benjamins Publishing Company.

Gvelesiani, I. (2023). Teaching ESP—new strategies and approaches. *Journal of Research in Higher Education, 7*(1), 25–39. https://www.ceeol.com/search/article-detail?id=1130937

Hall, C. J., Wicaksono, R., Liu, S., Qian, Y., & Xiaoqing, X. (2013). *English reconceived: Raising teachers' awareness of English as a "plurilithic" resource through an online course.* British Council. https://www.teachingenglish.org.uk/sites/teacheng/files/D053%20Raising%20teachers%20awareness%20of%20English_ONLINE%20FINAL.pdf

Hall, G., & Cook, G. (2012). Own-language use in language teaching and learning. *Language Teaching, 45*(3), 271–308. doi:10.1017/S0261444812000067

Ham, M., & Dekkers, J. (2019). What role do teachers' beliefs play in the implementation of educational reform? Nepali teachers' voice. *Teaching and Teacher Education, 86*, 1–9. https://doi.org/10.1016/j.tate.2019.102917

Hansen, R. E. (1995). Five principles for guiding curriculum development practice: The case of technological teacher education. *Journal of Industrial Teacher Education*, 32(2), 30–50. https://scholar.lib.vt.edu/ejournals/JITE/v32n2/hansen.html

Haque, E. (2007). Critical pedagogy in English for Academic Purposes and the possibility for "tactics" of resistance. *Pedagogy, Culture & Society*, *15*(1), 83–106. https://doi.org/10.1080/14681360601162311

Harasim, L. M. (2012). *Learning theory and online technology*. Routledge.

Harmer, J. (1983). *The practice of English language teaching*. Longman.

Harmer, J. (2003). Popular culture, methods and context. *ELT Journal, 57*(3),288–294. https://doi.org/10.1093/elt/57.3.288

Harvey, H., & Gillis, J. (2022, September 18). Op-Ed: Climate change is a big problem. Citizens must demand many small solutions. *Los Angeles Times*. https://www.latimes.com/opinion/story/2022-09-18/climate-change-citizen-action-building-codes-energy-efficiency

Harwood, N., & Hadley, G. (2004). Demystifying institutional practices: Critical pragmatism and the teaching of academic writing. *English for Specific Purposes*, *23*(4), 355–377. https://doi.org/10.1016/j.esp.2003.08.001

Hass, G. (1987). *Curriculum planning: A new approach* (5th ed.). Allyn & Bacon.

Helmer, K. A. (2013). Critical English for academic purposes: Building on learner, teacher, and program strengths. *Journal of English for Academic Purposes*, *12*(4), 273–287. https://doi.org/10.1016/j.jeap.2013.08.003

Herrera, S. G., & Murry, K. G. (2011). *Mastering ESL and bilingual methods: Differentiated instruction for culturally and linguistically diverse (CLD) students*(2nd ed.). Allyn & Bacon.

Hill, G. (2011, March). *Less stuff, more happiness* [Video]. TED Conferences.https://www.ted.com/talks/graham_hill_less_stuff_more_happiness

Hilliard, A. D. (2014). A critical examination of representation and culture in four English language textbooks. *Language Education in Asia*, *5*(2), 238–252.

Himes, H., & Schulenberg, J. (2013, September). Theoretical reflections: Theory and philosophy should always inform practice. *Academic Advising Today, 36*(3). ps://advisingtheory.wordpress.com/2013/09/04/theoretical-reflections-theory-and-philosophy-should-always-inform-practice/

Himmel, J. (2012). *Language objectives: The key to effective content area instruction for English learners*. Colorín Colorado. https://www.colorincolorado.org/article/language-objectives-key-effective-content-area-instruction-english-learners

Hitchcock, C., Meyer, A., Rose, D., & Jackson, R. (2002). Providing new access to the general curriculum: Universal design for learning. *Teaching Exceptional Children*, *35*(2), 8–17. https://doi.org/10.1177/004005990203500201

Holliday, A. R., & Cooke, T. M. (1982). An ecological approach to ESP. In A. Waters (Ed.), *Issues in ESP* (pp. 124–143). University of Lancaster.

Holt, B. J., & Hannon, J. C. (2006). Teaching-learning in the affective domain. *Strategies*, *20*(1), 11–13. https://doi.org/10.1080/08924562.2006.10590695

hooks, b. (1994). *Teaching to transgress: Education as the practice of freedom*. Routledge.

Howatt, A. P. R. (1984). *A history of English language teaching*. Oxford University Press.

Huang, H. Y., & Wible, D. (2024). Situating EAP learners in their disciplinary classroom: How Taiwanese engineering majors "read" their textbooks. *English for Specific Purposes, 74*, 85–102. https://doi.org/10.1016/j.esp.2024.01.003
Huang, Q., & Yu, Q. J. (2023). Towards a communication-focused ESP course for nursing students in building partnership with patients: A needs analysis. *English for Specific Purposes, 70*, 57–69. https://doi.org/10.1016/j.esp.2022.11.006
Huang, S. H. (2016). Communicative language teaching: Practical difficulties in the rural EFL classrooms in Taiwan. *Journal of Education and Practice*, *7*(24),186–202. https://eric.ed.gov/?id=EJ1112915
Huang, S. H., & Yang, L. C. (2020). English for general purposes (EGP) at a Taiwanese university: A mix-methodological analysis of students' perspectives. *Tsing Hua Journal of Educational Research, 37*(1), 41–83. Doi:10.6869/THJER.202006_37(1).0002
Hübner, N., Savage, C., Gräsel, C., & Wacker, A. (2021). Who buys into curricular reforms and why? Investigating predictors of reform ratings from teachers in Germany. *Journal of Curriculum Studies, 53*(6), 802–820. https://doi.org/10.1080/00220272.2020.1870714
Huh, S. (2006). A task-based needs analysis for a business English course. *Second Language Studies, 24*(2), 1–64. http://www.infostays.com/sls/wp-content/uploads/2014/09/HuhSorin.pdf
Huhta, M., Vogt, K., Johnson, E., & Tulkki, H. (2013). *Needs analysis for language course design: A holistic approach to ESP*. Cambridge University Press.
Hunkins, F. P., & Hammill, P. A. (1994). Beyond Tyler and Taba: Reconceptualizing the curriculum process. *Peabody Journal of Education*, *69*(3), 4–18. https://www.jstor.org/stable/1492885
Hutchinson, T., & Waters, A. (1987). *English for specific purposes: A learning-centered approach*. Cambridge University Press. https://doi.org/10.1017/CBO9780511733031
Hyland, K. (2002). Specificity revisited: How far should we go now? *English for Specific Purposes, 21*(4), 385–395. https://doi.org/10.1016/S0889-4906(01)00028-X
Hyland, K. (2003). Genre-based pedagogies: A social response to process. *Journal of Second Language Writing, 12*(1), 17–29. https://doi.org/10.1016/S1060-3743(02)00124-8
Hyland, K. (2006). *English for academic purposes: An advanced resource*. Routledge.
Hyland, K. (2008). As can be seen: Lexical bundles and disciplinary variation. *English for Specific Purposes, 27*(1), 4–21. https://doi.org/10.1016/j.esp.2007.06.001
Hyland, K. (2011). Disciplines and discourses: Social interactions in the construction of knowledge. In D. Starke-Meyerring, A. Paré, N. Artemeva, M. Horne, &L. Yousoubova (Eds.), *Writing in knowledge societies* (pp. 193–214). Parlor Press.
Hyland, K. (2018). Sympathy for the devil? A defence of EAP. *Language Teaching, 51*(3), 383–399. doi:10.1017/S0261444818000101
Hyland, K. (2022). English for specific purposes: What is it and where is it taking us? *ESP Today, 10*(2), 202–220. https://doi.org/10.18485/esptoday.2022.10.2.1
Hymes, D.H. (1972). On communicative competence. In J. B. Pride & J. Holmes (Eds.), *Sociolinguistics: Selected readings* (pp. 269–293). Penguin.

Hyon, S. (2018). *Introducing genre and English for specific purposes.* Routledge.

Hyun, E. (2006). Transforming instruction into pedagogy through curriculum negotiation. *Journal of Curriculum and Pedagogy, 3*(1), 136–164. https://doi.org/10.1080/15505170.2006.10411587

Ibrahim, H. B. (2022). Implementing backward design to foster intercultural communicative competence in textbook-based curricula: A proposed framework for English language practitioners. *Intercultural Communication Education, 5*(1), 1–16.

Illeris, K. (2016). *Learning, development and education: From learning theory to education and practice.* Routledge. https://doi.org/10.4324/9781315620565

Irving, P. W., McPadden, D., & Caballero, M. D. (2020). Communities of practice as a curriculum design theory in an introductory physics class for engineers. *Physical Review Physics Education Research, 16*(2), 1–31. https://doi.org/10.1103/PhysRevPhysEducRes.16.020143

Jackson, P. W. (1992). Conceptions of curriculum and curriculum specialists. In P. Jackson (Ed.), *Handbook of research on curriculum* (pp. 3–40). MacMillan.

Jacob, M. M., Sabzalian, L., Jansen, J., Tobin, T. J., Vincent, C. G., & LaChance, K. M. (2018). The gift of education: How Indigenous knowledges can transform the future of public education. *International journal of multicultural education, 20*(1), 157–185. https://doi.org/10.18251/ijme.v20i1.1534

James, M. (2012). An alternative to the objectives model: The process model for the design and development of curriculum. In J. Elliott & N. Norris (Eds.), *Curriculum, pedagogy and educational research: The work of Lawrence Stenhouse*(pp. 61–83). Routledge.

Jarvis, P. (2006). *Lifelong learning and the learning society: Towards a comprehensive theory of human learning.* Routledge.

Jenks, A. (2016). *It's in the syllabus.* Society for Cultural Anthropology https://culanth.org/fieldsights/its-in-the-syllabus

Jeon, J. H. (2009). Reflecting critical pedagogy: Its application to EFL contexts and criticism. *English Language & Literature Teaching, 15*(3), 59–81. https://koreascience.kr/article/JAKO200917357306455.page

Johns, T. F. (1994). From printout to handout: Grammar and vocabulary teaching in the context of data-driven learning. In T. Odlin (Ed.), *Perspectives on pedagogical grammar* (pp. 293–313). Cambridge University Press.

Johnson, D. C., Peterson, A. D., Spears, A., & Vest, J. (2017). Investigating "understanding by design" in the national music education standards: Perspectives and practices of music teacher educators. *Visions of Research in Music Education, 30*(1), 1–25. https://opencommons.uconn.edu/vrme/vol30/iss1/5/

Johnston, B. (1999). Putting critical pedagogy in its place: A personal account. *TESOL Quarterly, 33*(3), 557–565. https://doi.org/10.2307/3587680

Jonassen, D. H. (1991). Evaluating constructivistic learning. *Educational Technology, 31*(9), 28–33. https://www.jstor.org/stable/44401696

Jonassen, D. H. (1994). Thinking technology: Toward a constructivist design model. *Educational Technology, 34*(4), 34–37. https://www.learntechlib.org/p/171050/

Jones, S. (2016). How does classroom composition affect learning outcomes in Ugandan primary schools? *International Journal of Educational Development, 48*, 66–78. https://doi.org/10.1016/j.ijedudev.2015.11.010

Jordan, R. R. (1997). *English for academic purposes: A guide and resource book for teachers.* Cambridge University Press.

Joseph Jeyaraj, J., & Harland, T. (2016). Teaching with critical pedagogy in ELT: The problems of indoctrination and risk. *Pedagogy, Culture & Society, 24*(4), 587–598. https://doi.org/10.1080/14681366.2016.1196722

Kachru, B. B. (1982). *The other tongue: English across cultures.* University of Illinois Press.

Kachru, B. B. (1984). World Englishes and the teaching of English to non-native speakers: Contexts, attitudes, and concerns. *TESOL Newsletter, 18*(5), 25–26.

Kachru, B. B. (1992a). Teaching world Englishes. In B. B. Kachru (Ed.), *The other tongue: English across cultures* (2nd ed., pp. 355–365). University of Illinois Press.

Kachru, B. B. (1992b). World Englishes: Approaches, issues and resources. *Language teaching, 25*(1), 1–14. doi:10.1017/S0261444800006583

Kanoksilapatham, B. (2005). Rhetorical structure of biochemistry research articles. *English for Specific Purposes, 24*(3), 269–292. https://doi.org/10.1016/j.esp.2004.08.003

Kanu, Y. (Ed.). (2011). *Integrating Aboriginal perspectives into the school curriculum: Purposes, possibilities, and challenges.* University of Toronto Press.

Kaplan, J. (2010, February 19). *Eat green: Our everyday food choices affect global warming and the environment.* Natural Resources Defense Council. https://www.nrdc.org/resources/eat-green-our-everyday-food-choices-affect-global-warming-and-environment

Karthika, V. K. (2024). The human, non-human affective entanglements:A posthuman perspective of an ESOL classroom. *Higher Education for the Future, 11*(2), 151–167. https://doi.org/10.1177/23476311241246634

Kearney, N. C., & Cook, W. W. (1961). Curriculum. In C. W. Harris (Ed.), *Encyclopedia of educational research* (pp. 358–365). Macmillan and American Educational Research Association.

Kearns, K. D., & Sullivan, C. S. (2011). Resources and practices to help graduate students and postdoctoral fellows write statements of teaching philosophy. *Advances in Physiology Education, 35*(2), 136–145.

Kelly, A. V. (2004). *The curriculum: Theory and practice* (5th ed.). Sage.

Kessler, M. (2020). A text analysis and gatekeepers' perspectives of a promotional genre: Understanding the rhetoric of Fulbright grant statements. *English for Specific Purposes, 60*, 182–192. https://doi.org/10.1016/j.esp.2020.07.003

Khan, A. B., Mansoor, H. S., & Manzoor, S. (2016). The effectiveness of grammar translation method in teaching and learning of English language at intermediate level. *International Journal of Institutional & Industrial Research, 1*(1), 22–25.

Kim, A. A., Molle, M., Kemp, J., & Cook, H. G. (2018). *Examination of identification and placement decisions made for K–12 English learners* (WCER Working Paper No. 2018–12). http://www.wcer.wisc.edu/publications/working-papers

Kim, H. (2011). Social and cultural issues in some EFL textbooks in Korea. *Science and Technology, 10*, 30–39. https://www.hpu.edu/research-publications/tesol-working-papers/2012/TESOL_WPS_2012_Kim.pdf

Kirkgöz, Y. (2019a). Ideology and culture in EFL textbooks in the era of globalization in Turkey. In A. Al-Issa & S. Mirhosseini (Eds.), *Worldwide English language education today: Ideologies, policies and practices* (pp. 102–116). Routledge.

Kirkgöz, Y. (2019b). Investigating the growth of English-medium higher education in Turkey and the Middle East region. In D. F. Staub (Ed.), *Quality assurance and accreditation in foreign language education: Global issues, models, and best practices from the Middle East and Turkey* (pp. 9–19). Springer.

Kitzman, A. (2009). Needs analysis: Remembering the vital step of curriculum design in general English. *近畿大学語学教育部紀要 [Kinki University Department of Language Education Bulletin]*, *9*(2), 83–98. https://kindai.repo.nii.ac.jp/records/13302

Kliebard, H. M. (1970). The Tyler rationale. *The School Review*, *78*(2), 259–272. https://www.jstor.org/stable/1084240

Kliebard, H. M. (1982). Curriculum theory as metaphor. *Theory into Practice*, *21*(1), 11–17. https://www.jstor.org/stable/1476704

Köksal, D., & Ulum, Ö. G. (2021). Analysis of cultural hegemony in touchstone EFL course book series. *The Reading Matrix: An International Online Journal*, *21*(1), 131–141. https://readingmatrix.com/files/24-o589r4hk.pdf

Kooli, C. (2019). The philosophy of education in the Sultanate of Oman: Between perennialism and progressivism. *American Journal of Education and Learning*, *4*(1), 36–49. https://ssrn.com/abstract=3690889

Krashen, S. D. & Terrell, T. D. (1983). *The natural approach: Language acquisition in the classroom*. Alemany Press.

Kubota, R. (2018). Critical approaches to second language writing. In J. I. Liontas (Ed.), *The TESOL Encyclopedia of English Language Teaching* (pp. 1–7). Wiley Blackwell. https://doi.org/10.1002/9781118784235.eelt0525

Kumaravadivelu, B. (1993). Maximizing learning potential in the communicative classroom. *ELT Journal*, 47, 12–21. https://doi.org/10.1093/elt/47.1.12

Kumaravadivelu, B. (1994). The postmethod condition: (E)merging strategies for second/foreign language teaching. *TESOL Quarterly*, *28*(1), 27–48. https://doi.org/10.2307/3587197

Kumaravadivelu, B. (2001). Toward a postmethod pedagogy. *TESOL Quarterly*, *35*(4), 537–560. https://doi.org/10.2307/3588427

Kumaravadivelu, B. (2006a). TESOL methods: Changing tracks, challenging trends. *TESOL Quarterly*, *40*(1), 59–81. https://doi.org/10.2307/40264511

Kumaravadivelu, B. (2006b). *Understanding language teaching: From method to postmethod*. Routledge.

Kurniawan, R., Miftah, M. Z., & Qamariah, Z. (2021). Grammar-translation method affects students' reading comprehension and motivation. *International Journal of Research on English Teaching and Applied Linguistics*, *1*(1), 7–15. http://dx.doi.org/10.30863/ijretal.v1i1.1194

Kuteeva, M., & McGrath, L. (2015). The theoretical research article as a reflection of disciplinary practices: The case of pure mathematics. *Applied Linguistics*, *36*(2), 215–235. https://doi.org/10.1093/applin/amt042

Kyndt, E., Gijbels, D., Grosemans, I., & Donche, V. (2016). Teachers' everyday professional development: Mapping informal learning activities, antecedents, and learning outcomes. *Review of educational research*, *86*(4), 1111–1150. https://doi.org/10.3102/0034654315627864

Ladd, J. (2016, February). *The reporting system that sexual assault survivors want* [Video]. TED Conferences. https://www.ted.com/talks/jessica_ladd_the_reporting_system_that_sexual_assault_survivors_want

Lado, R. & Fries, C. C. (1958). *English sentence patterns: Understanding and producing English grammatical structures an oral approach*. University of Michigan Press.

Lado, R. (1957). *Linguistics across cultures: Applied linguistics for language teachers.* University of Michigan Press.

Lado, R. (1964). *Language teaching: A scientific approach*. McGraw-Hill Companies.

Lantolf, J. P. (Ed.). (2000). *Sociocultural theory and second language learning*. Oxford University.

Lantolf, J. P., & Appel, G. (1994). Theoretical framework: An introduction to Vygotskian perspectives on second language research. In J. P. Lantolf & G. Appel (Eds.), *Vygotskian approaches to second language research* (pp. 1–32). Greenwood Publishing Group.

Lave, J., & Wenger, E. (1991). Situated learning: Legitimate peripheral participation. Cambridge University Press.

Le Grange, L., & Du Preez, P. (2023). Curriculum studies in the posthuman condition/posthuman curriculum (studies). *South African Journal of Higher Education*, *37*(5), 60–77. https://hdl.handle.net/10520/ejc-high_v37_n5_a5

Le, L. P. (2021). Teaching ESP in the 21st century. In M. K. Kabilan, R. M. R. Abdul Aziz, & J. A. Netto-Shek (Eds.), *Teaching and learning of English in the 21st century. Perspectives and practices from South East Asia* (pp. 281–306). Penerbit Universiti Sains Malaysia.

Leask, B. (2014). Internationalizing the curriculum and all students' learning. *International Higher Education*, (78), 5–6. https://doi.org/10.6017/ihe.2014.78.5798

Leaver, B. L., & Stryker, S. B. (1989). Content-based instruction for foreign language classrooms. *Foreign Language Annals*, *22*(3), 269–275. https://doi.org/10.1111/j.1944-9720.1989.tb02746.x

Lee, I. (2009). Situated globalization and racism: An analysis of Korean high school EFL textbooks. *Language and Literacy*, *11*(1), 1–14. https://doi.org/10.20360/G2F59N

Levine, A. (2014, February). Leveraging committee assignments for advancement. *Science*, 685–688. DOI: 10.1126/science.opms.r1400140

Li, J. (2016). The transmission of cultural values via EFL textbooks in China. *Journal of Educational Media, Memory, and Society*, *8*(2), 128–144. https://doi.org/10.3167/jemms.2016.080207

Li, L. C., Grimshaw, J. M., Nielsen, C., Judd, M., Coyte, P. C., & Graham, I. D. (2009). Evolution of Wenger's concept of community of practice. *Implementation Science*, 4, 1–8. https://doi.org/10.1186/1748-5908-4-11

Little, J. W. (1990). The persistence of privacy: Autonomy and initiative in teachers' professional relations. *Teachers College Record*, *91*(4), 509–536. https://doi.org/10.1177/016146819009100

Littlewood, W. (2007). Communicative and task-based language teaching in East Asian classrooms. *Language Teaching, 40*(3), 243–249. https://doi.org/10.1017/S0261444807004363

Littlewood, W. (2011). Communicative language teaching: An expanding concept for a changing world. In E. Hinkel (Ed.), *Handbook of research in second language teaching and learning* (Vol. 2, pp. 541–557). Routledge.

Llerena, C. L. A. (2020). The benefits of backward design in the English as a foreign language context. *Indonesian Journal of English Education, 7*(2), 145–158. http://www.jallr.com/index.php/JALLR/article/view/162

Long, M. H. (2005). Methodological issues in learner needs analysis. In M. H. Long (Ed.), *Second language needs analysis* (pp. 19–76). Cambridge University Press. https://doi.org/10.1017/CBO9781139524520

Long, M. H. (2014). *Second language acquisition and task-based language teaching.* John Wiley & Sons.

Lunenburg, F. C. (2011). Curriculum development: Inductive models. *Schooling, 2*(1), 1–8.

Macalister, J., & Nation, I. P. (2020). *Language curriculum design* (2nd ed.).Routledge.

MacDonald, J. B. (1971). Curriculum theory. *The Journal of Educational Research, 64*(5), 196–200. https://doi.org/10.1080/00220671.1971.10884138

Mackey, W. F. (1967). *Language teaching analysis.* Indiana University Press.

MacPherson, J. (2019). Assessing learner needs for general English course design. *純心人文研究* [Junshin Journal of Studies in Humanities], *25*, 141–155.

Madhya Pradesh Board of Secondary Education (MPBSE). (n.d.). *General English: Aims and objectives.* https://mpbse.nic.in/10th-2007-08/General_Language/English-10th.pdf

Maki, P. (2004). *Assessing for learning: Building a sustainable commitment across the institution.* Stylus Publishing.

Marsh, C. J. (Ed.). (1997). *Perspectives: Key concepts for understanding curriculum 1.* The Falmer Press.

Mart, C. T. (2013). The grammar-translation method and the use of translation to facilitate learning in ESL classes. *Journal of Advances in English Language Teaching, 1*(4), 103–105. https://european-science.com/jaelt/article/view/281

Maslow, A. H. (1943). A theory of human motivation. *Psychological Review, 50*(4), 370–396. https://doi.org/10.1037/h0054346

Matherson, L., & Windle, T. M. (2017). What do teachers want from their professional development? Four emerging themes. *Delta Kappa Gamma Bulletin, 83*(3), 28–32. https://www.dkg.org/DKGDocs/2017_Jour_83-3_Systems-to-Address-Quality-Teaching.pdf#page=28

Mayer, M., & Hicks, J. H. (1993). *Robert Maynard Hutchins: A memoir.* University of California Press.

Mayer, R. E. (2014). Cognitive theory of multimedia learning. In R. E. Mayer (Ed.), *The Cambridge handbook of multimedia learning* (2nd ed., pp. 43–71). Cambridge University Press.

Mayer, R. E., & Moreno, R. (1998). A cognitive theory of multimedia learning: Implications for design principles. *Journal of Educational Psychology, 91*(2),358–368. https://esoluk.co.uk/calling/pdf/chi.pdf

Mbembe, A. (2015). *Decolonizing knowledge and the question of the archive* [Lecture]. Wits Institute for Social and Economic Research. https://wiser.wits.ac.za/system/files/Achille%20Mbembe%20-%20Decolonizing%20Knowledge%20and%20the%20Question%20of%20the%20Archive.pdf

McCreary, M. (2022). Beyond backward design, or, by the end of this article, you should be able to imagine some alternatives to learning objectives. *To Improve the Academy: A Journal of Educational Development*, *41*(1), 68–91. https://doi.org/10.3998/tia.454

McCutcheon, G. (1982). What in the world is curriculum theory? *Theory into Practice*, *21*(1), 18–22. https://www.jstor.org/stable/1476705

McLaren, P. (2016). *Life in schools: An introduction to critical pedagogy in the foundations of education* (6th ed.). Routledge.

McLeod, S. (2024). *Albert Bandura's social learning theory*. Simply Psychology. Rederived February 10, 2024, from https://www.simplypsychology.org/bandura.html

McTighe, J., & Thomas, R. S. (2003). Backward design for forward action. *Educational Leadership*, *60*(5), 52–55. https://www.ascd.org/el/articles/backward-design-for-forward-action

McTighe, J., & Wiggins, G. P. (2012). *Understanding by design framework* [White paper]. Association for Supervision and Curriculum. http://www.ascd.org/ASCD/pdf/siteASCD/publications/UbD_WhitePaper0312.pdf

Meo, G. (2008). Curriculum planning for all learners: Applying universal design for learning (UDL) to a high school reading comprehension program. *Preventing School Failure: Alternative Education for Children and Youth*, *52*(2), 21–30. https://doi.org/10.3200/PSFL.52.2.21-30

Met. M. (1999). *Content-based instruction: Defining terms, making decisions*. The National Foreign Language Center. https://carla.umn.edu/cobaltt/modules/principles/decisions.pdf

Meyer, A., & Rose, D. H. (2000). Universal design for individual differences. *Educational leadership*, *58*(3), 39–43.

Meyer, J., & Land, R. (2003). Threshold concepts and troublesome knowledge: Linkages to ways of thinking and practicing within the disciplines. In C. Rust (Ed.), *Improving student learning theory and practice–10 years on* (pp. 412–424). Oxford Centre for Staff and Learning Development.

Mezirow, J. (1997). Transformative learning: Theory to practice. In P. Cranton (Ed.), *Transformative learning in action: Insights from practice* (pp. 5–12). Jossey-Bass.

Mezirow, J. (2018). Transformative learning theory. In K. Illeris (Ed.), *Contemporary theories of learning: Learning theorists . . . In their own words* (2nd ed, pp. 114–128). Routledge.

Mheta, G., Lungu, B. N., & Govender, T. (2018). Decolonisation of the curriculum: A case study of the Durban University of Technology in South Africa. *South African Journal of Education, 38*(4), 1–7. http://dx.doi.org/10.15700/saje.v38n4a1635

Michael, N. A., & Libarkin, J. C. (2016). Understanding by design: Mentored implementation of backward design methodology at the university level. *Bioscene: Journal of College Biology Teaching*, *42*(2), 44–52. https://[illegible]

Milawati, M. (2019). Grammar translation method: Current practice in EFL context. *Indonesian Journal of English Language Teaching and Applied Linguistics, 4*(1),187–196. http://ijeltal.org/index.php/ijeltal/article/view/437

Miller, L. R., Klassen, K., & Hardy, J. W. (2021). Curriculum design from theory to practice: Preparing Japanese students to study abroad using content-based language teaching. *The Curriculum Journal, 32*(2), 215–246. https://doi.org/10.1002/curj.68

Morgan, B. D. (1998). *The ESL classroom: Teaching, critical practice, and community development.* University of Toronto Press.

Morley, J., Robinett, B. W., Selinker, L., & Woods, D. (1984). ESL theory and the Fries legacy. *JALT Journal, 6*(2), 171–207. https://jalt-publications.org/jj/articles/2883-esl-theory-and-fries-legacy

Moskal, A., Loke, S., & Hung, N. (2016). Challenges implementing social constructivist learning approaches: The case of Pictation. *Proceedings of the Australasian Society for Computers in Learning in Tertiary Education Conference, Australia*, 446–454.

Munby, J. (1978). *Communicative syllabus design.* Cambridge University Press.

Muro, M., & Jeffrey, P. (2008). A critical review of the theory and application of social learning in participatory natural resource management processes. *Journal of Environmental Planning and Management, 51*(3), 325–344. https://doi.org/10.1080/09640560801977190

Murphy, E. (1997). *Constructivism: From philosophy to practice.* Educational Resources Information Center. https://eric.ed.gov/?id=ED444966

Mustafawi, E., & Shaaban, K. (2019). Language policies in education in Qatar between 2003 and 2012: From local to global then back to local. *Language Policy, 18*, 209–242. https://doi.org/10.1007/s10993-018-9483-5

Nateghian, N. (2024). English language needs of Iranian students of civil engineering: Are the courses aligned with workplace needs? *English for Specific Purposes, 76*, 122–135. https://doi.org/10.1016/j.esp.2024.08.002

Nation, I. P. & Macalister, J. (2010). *Language curriculum design.* Routledge.

Nature Water. (2023). The quest to address the global sanitation crisis. *Nature, 1*, 899. https://doi.org/10.1038/s44221-023-00165-7

Nevenglosky, E. A., Cale A. C., & Aguilar, S. P. (2019). Barriers to effective curriculum implementation. *Research in Higher Education Journal, 36*, 1–31. https://eric.ed.gov/?id=EJ1203958

Newton, R. R. (1970). Three trends in curriculum theory: A study of general curriculum development and its relation to religious education. *PACE, 1*,490–507. http://hdl.handle.net/2345/2439

Nicholls, A. & Nicholls, S. H. (2018). *Developing a curriculum: A practical guide.* Routledge. (Original work published 1972).

Nkambule, N. S., & Tang, C. W. (2023). Building a case for communities of practice as drivers of innovative teaching in English medium instruction context. *Higher Education*, 1–20. https://doi.org/10.1007/s10734-023-01032-w

Norris, J. M. (2016). Language program evaluation. *The Modern Language Journal, 100*(S1), 169–189. https://doi.org/10.1111/modl.12307

Null, W. (2011). *Curriculum: From theory to practice.* Rowman & Littlefield Publishers.

Nunan, D. (1988a). *Syllabus design.* Oxford University Press.

Nunan, D. (1988b). *The learner-centered curriculum: A study in second language teaching.* Cambridge University Press.

Nunan, D. (1991). *Language teaching methodology: A textbook for teachers.* Prentice-Hall.

Obilo, P. I., & Sangoleye, S. A. (2010). Curriculum implementation and the teacher: Challenges and way forward. *The 9th National Conference of the School of Social Sciences, Alvan Ikoku Federal College of Education, Owerri, Nigeria.*

OECD. (2019). *OECD Future of education and skills 2030 concept note.* https://www.oecd.org/education/2030-project/teaching-and-learning/learning/learning-compass-2030/OECD_Learning_Compass_2030_concept_note.pdf

OECD. (n.d.). *Future of education and skills 2030/2040.* OECD. https://www.oecd.org/en/about/projects/future-of-education-and-skills-2030.html

Ogwora, E. T., Kuria, G., Nyamwaka, E., & Nyakan, B. (2013). Philosophy as a key instrument in establishing curriculum, educational policy, objectives, goals of education, vision and mission of education. *Journal of Education and Practice, 4*(11), 95–101. https://www.iiste.org/Journals/index.php/JEP/article/view/6452

Ordoñez-Jasis, R., & Myck-Wayne, J. (2012). Community mapping in action: Uncovering resources and assets for young children and their families. *Young Exceptional Children, 15*(3), 31–45. https://doi.org/10.1177/1096250612451756

Ornstein, A. C. & Hunkins, F. B. (2018). *Curriculum foundations, principles, and issues* (7th ed.). Pearson Education.

Ornstein, A. C. & Levine, D. U. (1993). *Foundations of education* (5th ed.). Houghton Mifflin Company.

Ornstein, A. C. (1990). Philosophy as a basis for curriculum decisions. *The High School Journal, 74*(2), 102–109. https://www.jstor.org/stable/40364829

Ornstein, A. C. (1994). The textbook-driven curriculum. *Peabody Journal of Education, 69*(3), 70–85. http://www.jstor.org/stable/1492889

Ornstein, A. C., & Hunkins, F. P. (2018). *Curriculum: Foundations, principles, and issues* (7th ed.). Pearson Education.

O'Sullivan, M. C. (2002). Reform implementation and the realities within which teachers work: A Namibian case study. *Compare: A Journal of Comparativeand International Education, 32*(2), 219–237. https://doi.org/10.1080/03057920220143192

Paltridge, B., Starfield, S., & Tardy, C. M. (2016). *Ethnographic perspectives on academic writing.* Oxford University Press.

Pardo, B. S., & Díaz, M. A. (2020). A SWOT analysis of the communicative English language skills improvement programme: A tool for autonomous EFL learning. *Complutense Journal of English Studies, 28*, 109–120. https://dx.doi.org/10.5209/cjes.63845

Paris, D., & Alim, H. S. (Eds.). (2017). *Culturally sustaining pedagogies: Teaching and learning for justice in a changing world.* Teachers College Press.

Parkinson, J. (2017). The student laboratory report genre: A genre analysis. *English for Specific Purposes, 45*, 1–13. https://doi.org/10.1016/j.esp.2016.08.001

Pavlov, I. P. (1927). *Conditioned reflexes: An investigation of the physiological activity of the cerebral cortex* (G. V. Anrep, Trans.). Oxford University Press. (Original work published 1927).

Perez, D. (2022). *Social foundations of K-12 education.* Kansas State University Libraries. https://kstatelibraries.pressbooks.pub/dellaperezprojecs/

Philips, J. K. (2003). National standards for foreign language learning: Culture the driving force. In D. L. Lange & R. M. Paige (Eds.), *Culture as the core: Perspective on culture in second language* (pp. 161–171). Information Age Publishing.

Phượng, H. Á. (2022). *Borderless classroom model* [PowerPoint slides]. TeachingEnglish by British Council. https://www.teachingenglish.org.uk/sites/teacheng/files/2022-10/Borderless_Clasroom_model.pdf

Piaget, J. (1952). *The origins of intelligence in children* (M. Cook, Trans.). International University Press. (Original work published 1936).

Piaget, J., & Inhelder, B. (1969). *The psychology of the child* (H. Weaver, Trans.).Basic Books. (Original work published 1966).

Pinar, W. F. (1978). The reconceptualisation of curriculum studies. *Journal of Curriculum Studies, 10*(3), 205–214. https://doi.org/10.1080/0022027780100303

Prabhu, N. S. (1987). *Second language pedagogy.* Oxford University Press.

Pratt, D. (1994). *Curriculum planning: A handbook for professionals.* Harcourt Brace College Publishers.

Praveen, C. (2020). New ESL teacher for the new education policy: A SWOT Analysis. *Journal of English Language Teaching, 62*(1), 29–36. http://journals.eltai.in/index.php/jelt/article/view/JELT620108

Print, M. (1993). *Curriculum development and design* (2nd ed.). Routledge. https://doi.org/10.4324/9781003115328

Quintero Polo, Á. H. (2003). Teachers' informed decision-making in evaluation: Corollary of ELT curriculum as a human lived experience. *Colombian Applied Linguistics Journal* (5), 122–138. http://www.scielo.org.co/scielo.php?script=sci_arttext&pid=S0123-46412003000100008

Rabbidge, M. (2019). *Translanguaging in EFL contexts: A call for change.* Routledge.

Rahman, M. M., Islam, M. S., Karim, A., Chowdhury, T. A., Rahman, M. M., Seraj, P. M. I., & Singh, M. K. M. (2019). English language teaching in Bangladesh today: Issues, outcomes and implications. *Language Testing in Asia, 9*(1), 1–14. https://doi.org/10.1186/s40468-019-0085-8

Rahman, M. M., Johan, M., Selim, S. M. M., Singh, M. K. M., & Shahed, F. H. (2019). Teachers' beliefs and practices of implementing secondary English curriculum reform in Bangladesh: A phenomenological study. *Journal of Asia TEFL, 16*(2), 591–607. http://dx.doi.org/10.18823/asiatefl.2019.16.2.10.591

Ramaswamy, M., Marciniuk, D. D., Csonka, V., Colò, L., & Saso, L. (2021). Reimagining internationalization in higher education through the United Nations sustainable development goals for the betterment of society. *Journal of Studies in International Education, 25*(4), 388–406. https://doi.org/10.1177/10283153211031046

Richards, J. C. (1984). Language curriculum development. *RELC Journal, 15*(1),1–29. https://doi.org/10.1177/003368828401500101

Richards, J. C. (1990). *The language teaching matrix.* Cambridge University Press.

Richards, J. C. (1993). Beyond the text book: The role of commercial materials in language teaching. *RELC Journal, 24*(1), 1–14. https://doi.org/10.1177/003368829302400101

Richards, J. C. (2001). *Curriculum development in language teaching*. Cambridge University Press. https://doi.org/10.1017/CBO9780511667220

Richards, J. C. (2013). Curriculum approaches in language teaching: Forward, central, and backward design. *RELC Journal, 44*(1), 5–33. https://doi.org/10.1177/0033688212473293

Richards, J. C. (2017). *Curriculum development in language teaching* (2nd ed.). Cambridge University Press. https://doi.org/10.1017/9781009024556

Richards, J. C., & Farrell, T. S. (2011). *Practice teaching: A reflective approach*. Cambridge University Press.

Richards, J. C., & Lockhart, C. (1994). *Reflective teaching*. Cambridge University Press.

Richards, J. C., & Rodgers, T. S. (1982). Method: Approach, design, and procedure. *TESOL Quarterly, 16*(2), 153–168. https://doi.org/10.2307/3586789

Richards, J. C., & Rodgers, T. S. (2001). *Approaches and methods in language teaching* (2nd ed.). Cambridge University Press.

Richards, J. C., & Schmidt, R. (2011). *Longman dictionary of language teaching and applied linguistics* (4th ed.). Pearson.

Richards, J. C., Gallo, P. B., Renandya, W. A. (2001). Exploring teachers' beliefs and the processes of change. *The PAC Journal, 1*(1), 41–62.

Richterich, R. (1972). *A model for the definition of language needs of adults learning a modern language*. Council of Europe. https://eric.ed.gov/?id=ED082544

Richterich, R., & Chancerel, J. L. (1978). *Identifying the needs of adults learning a foreign language*. Prentice-Hall International.

Rivers, W. M. (1964). *The psychologist and the foreign language teacher*. University of Chicago Press.

Roehrig, G. H., & Kruse, R. A. (2005). The role of teachers' beliefs and knowledge in the adoption of a Reform-Based curriculum. *School Science and Mathematics, 105*(8), 412–422. https://doi.org/10.1111/j.1949-8594.2005.tb18061.x

Roehrig, G. H., Kruse, R. A., & Kern, A. (2007). Teacher and school characteristics and their influence on curriculum implementation. *Journal of Research in Science Teaching, 44*(7), 883–907. https://doi.org/10.1002/tea.20180

Rogers, C.R. (1969). *Freedom to learn*. Merrill.

Römer, U. (2011). Corpus research applications in second language teaching. *Annual Review of Applied Linguistics, 31*, 205–225. https://doi.org/10.1017/S0267190511000055

Rosa, A. F., & Eschholz, P. (2012). *Models for writers: Short essays for composition*(11th ed.). Bedford/St. Martin's.

Rose, D. H., Meyer, A., & Hitchcock, C. (2005). (Eds.). *The universally designed classroom: Accessible curriculum and digital technologies*. Harvard Education Press.

Rothman, J., & Slabakova, R. (2018). The generative approach to SLA and its place in modern second language studies. *Studies in Second Language Acquisition, 40*(2), 417–442. doi:10.1017/S0272263117000134

Salvia, J., Ysseldyke, J. E., & Bolt, S. (2007). *Assessment in special and inclusive education* (10th ed.). Houghton Mifflin Company.

Santoso, G. (2021). Model analysis (SWOT) of curriculum development from civic education at 21 century, 4.0 era in Indonesian. *International Journal of*

Entrepreneurship and Business Development, 4(2), 250–256. https://doi.org/10.29138/ijebd.v4i2.1221
Schiro, M. (2012). *Curriculum theory: Conflicting visions and enduring concerns.* Sage.
Schwartz, B. D., & Sprouse, R. A. (1998, October). Back to basics in generative second language acquisition research. *Proceedings of the Second Language Research Forum.* University of Hawai'i. http://www.nflrc.hawaii.edu/NetWorks/NW09/
Seals, C. A., Newton, J., Ash, M., & Nguyen, B. T. T. (2020). Translanguaging and task based language teaching: Crossovers and challenges. In L. Aghai, P. Sayer, J. L. Schissel, & Z. Tian (Eds.), *Envisioning TESOL through a translanguaging lens: Global perspectives* (pp. 275–292). Springer International Publishing.
Sebbowa, D. K., & Majani, W. P. (2021). Dialogues over decolonisation in East Africa: A case study of History education in Uganda. *Historical Encounters, 8*(2), 34–53. https://www.hej-hermes.net/8-202
Seedhouse, P. (1995). Needs analysis and the general English classroom. *ELT Journal, 49*(1), 59–65. https://doi.org/10.1093/elt/49.1.59
Seidi, A., Samani, S. K., Fallahi, H., & Parseh, F. (2016). A closer look at ideologies embedded in imported English language teaching textbooks in Iran. *Language Education Studies, 2*(4), 1–7. http://langes.ir/index.php/published-papers/volume-2-2016-r/issue-4-december
Selinker, L., & Gass, S. M. (2008). *Second language acquisition: An introductory course* (2nd ed.). Lawrence Erlbaum Associates.
Semali, L., & Kincheloe, J. L. (Eds.). (1999). *What is Indigenous knowledge?: Voices from the academy.* Garland Publishing.
Serafini, E. J., Lake, J. B., & Long, M. H. (2015). Needs analysis for specialized learner populations: Essential methodological improvements. *English for Specific Purposes, 40,* 11–26. https://doi.org/10.1016/j.esp.2015.05.002
Shapiro, S. (2022). *Cultivating critical language awareness in the writing classroom.* Routledge. https://doi.org/10.4324/9781003171751
Shawer, S. F. (2017). Teacher-driven curriculum development at the classroom level: Implications for curriculum, pedagogy and teacher training. *Teaching and Teacher Education, 63,* 296–313. https://doi.org/10.1016/j.tate.2016.12.017
Shimauchi, S. (2018). English-medium instruction in the internationalization of higher education in Japan: Rationales and issues. *Educational Studies in Japan, 12,* 77–90. https://doi.org/10.7571/esjkyoiku.12.77
Shor, I. (2002). Education is politics: Paulo Freire's critical pedagogy. In P. Leonard & P. McLaren (Eds.), *Paulo Freire: A critical encounter* (pp. 24–35). Routledge.
Shor, I., & Freire, P. (1987). What is the "dialogical method" of teaching? *Journal of Education, 169*(3), 11–31. https://doi.org/10.1177/002205748716900303
Siemens, G. (2005). Connectivism: A learning theory for the digital age. *International Journal of Instructional Technology and Distance Learning, 1*(2). http://itdl.org/Journal/Jan_05/index.htm
Simpson, E. J. (1966). *The classification of educational objectives, psychomotor domain.* The U.S. Department of Health, Education, and Welfare, Office of Education.
Siri, A., & Freddano, M. (2011). The use of item analysis for the improvement of objective examinations. *Procedia-Social and Behavioral Sciences, 29,* 188–197. https://doi.org/10.1016/j.sbspro.2011.11.224

Skehan, P. (1991). Individual differences in second language learning. *Studies in Second Language Acquisition*, *13*(2), 275–298. https://doi.org/10.1017/S0272263100009979

Skilbeck, M. (1984). *School-based curriculum development.* Paul Chapman Publishing.

Skinner, B. F. (1938). *The behavior of organisms.* Appleton-Century.

Skinner, B. F. (1965). *Science and human behavior.* Simon and Schuster.

Smith, G. F., Jung, H., & Zenker, F. (2022). From task-based needs analysis to curriculum evaluation: Putting methodological innovations to the test in an English for academic purposes program. *English for Specific Purposes*, *66*, 80–93. https://doi.org/10.1016/j.esp.2022.01.001

Smith, S. (2018). Tools for successfully implementing enacted curricula. *International Journal of Educational Investigations*, *5*(4), 38–56. http://ijeionline.com/attachments/article/68/IJEI.Vol.5.No.4.04.pdf

Smyth, J., Down, B., & McInerney, P. (2014). *The socially just school: Making space for youth to speak back.* Springer.

Snow, M. A. (2001). Content-based and immersion models for second and foreign language teaching. In M., Celce-Murcia (Ed.), *Teaching English as a second or foreign language* (3rd ed., pp. 303–318). Heinle & Heinle.

Snow, M. A., & Brinton, D. M. (1988). Content-based language instruction: Investigating the effectiveness of the adjunct model. *TESOL Quarterly*, *22*(4), 553–574. https://doi.org/10.2307/3587256

Sohn, B. G., dos Santos, P., & Lin, A. M. (2022). Translanguaging and trans-semiotizing for critical integration of content and language in plurilingual educational settings. *RELC Journal*, *53*(2), 355–370. https://doi.org/10.1177/00336882221114480

Soliman, R., & Shaker, H. S. (2022). The embedded ideology in English and history textbooks at the public high schools in Egypt. *Port Said Journal of Educational Research*, *1*(1), 60–112. https://psjer.journals.ekb.eg/article_260704_46f6ee02ad1378cb87f719420c02d16d.pdf

Spada, N. (2007). Communicative language teaching: Current status and future prospects. In J. Cummins & C. Davison (Eds.), *International handbook of English language teaching* (pp. 271–288). Springer International Handbooks of Education. https://doi.org/10.1007/978-0-387-46301-8_20

Ssentanda, M., Southwood, F., & Huddlestone, K. (2019). Curriculum expectations versus teachers' opinions and practices in teaching English in rural primary schools in Uganda. *Language Matters*, *50*(2), 141–163. https://doi.org/10.1080/10228195.2018.1536162

Stabback, P. (2016). *What makes a quality curriculum?* UNESCO's International Bureau of Education. https://unesdoc.unesco.org/ark:/48223/pf0000243975

Staples, S. (2019). Using corpus-based discourse analysis for curriculum development: Creating and evaluating a pronunciation course for internationally educated nurses. *English for Specific Purposes*, *53*, 13–29. https://doi.org/10.1016/j.esp.2018.08.005

Stein, D. (1998). *Situated learning in adult education.* ERIC Clearinghouse on Adult, Career, and Vocational Education. http://www.edpsycinteractive.org/files/sitadlted.html

Stenhouse, L. (1975). *An introduction to curriculum research and development*. Heinemann Educational Books.

Stewart, C. (2023, December 7). How climate change is affecting mental health in some of the Caribbean's Indigenous communities. *Global Voices*. https://globalvoices.org/2023/12/07/how-climate-change-is-affecting-mental-health-in-some-of-the-caribbeans-indigenous-communities/

Stewart, M. (2021). Understanding learning: Theories and critique. In L. Hunt &D. Chalmers (Eds.), *University teaching in focus: A learning-centred approach*(pp. 3–28). Routledge.

Stieglitz, G. J. (1955). The Berlitz method. *The Modern Language Journal, 39*(6), 300–310. https://doi.org/10.1111/j.1540-4781.1955.tb03457.x

Storrs, C. (2017). How poverty affects the brain. *Nature, 547*, 150–152. https://doi.org/10.1038/547150a

Strevens, P. (1977). Special purpose language learning: A perspective. *Language Teaching and Linguistic: Abstracts, 10*(3), 145–163. doi:10.1017/S0261444800003402

Stryker, S. B., & Leaver B. L. (1997). *Content-based instruction in foreign language education: Models and methods*. Georgetown University Press.

Stufflebeam, D. L. (2003). The CIPP model for evaluation. In T. Kellaghan,D. L. Stufflebeam, & L. A. Wingate (Eds.), *International Handbook of Educational Evaluation* (pp. 31–62). Springer. https://doi.org/10.1007/978-94-010-0309-4_4

Swales, J. M. (1990). *Genre analysis: English in academic and research settings*. Cambridge University Press.

Swan, M. (1985). A critical look at the communicative approach (2). *ELT Journal, 39*(2), 76–87. doi:10.1093/elt/39.2.76

Sweller, J. (1988). Cognitive load during problem solving: Effects on learning. *Cognitive Science, 12*, 257–285. https://doi.org/10.1016/0364-0213(88)90023-7

Sweller, J. (1994). Cognitive load theory, learning difficulty, and instructional design. *Learning and Instruction, 4*, 295–312. https://doi.org/10.1016/0959-4752(94)90003-5

Sweller, J. (2022). The role of evolutionary psychology in our understanding of human cognition: Consequences for cognitive load theory and instructional procedures. *Educational Psychology Review, 34*, 2229–2241. https://doi.org/10.1007/s10648-021-09647-0

Taba, H. (1962). *Curriculum development: Theory and practice*. Harcourt College Pub.

Tabari, B. H., & Rahimy, R. (2021). Tailored vs. Standard curriculum and general English achievement: A study of teachers' views. *Latin American Journal of Content & Language Integrated Learning, 14*(1), 123–149. https://doi.org/10.5294/laclil.2021.14.1.5

Tardy, C. (2019). *Genre-based writing: What every ESL teacher needs to know*. University of Michigan Press.

Tarlanialiabadi, H. (2022). Communicative language teaching implementation in Iran: The case of junior high school Iranian state English teachers. *Journal of English Language and Literature Teaching, 1*(2), 81–98. https://elt.cfu.ac.ir/article_2172.html

Terrell, T. D. (1977). A natural approach to language acquisition and learning. *The Modern Language Journal, 61*(7), 325–337. https://www.jstor.org/stable/324551

TESOL International Association. (n.d.). *The 6 principles for exemplary teaching of English learners.* https://www.the6principles.org/the-principles/

The great ideas: The University of Chicago and the ideal of liberal education. (n.d.). The University of Chicago Library. https://www.lib.uchicago.edu/collex/exhibits/exgi/

Thi, P. B., & Cheng, Y. H. (2024). English needs analysis of food & beverage employees: A case study of a 5-star resort in Vietnam. *English for Specific Purposes, 76,* 74–105. https://doi.org/10.1016/j.esp.2024.07.001

Thijs, A., & van den Akker, J. (2009). *Curriculum in development.* Netherlands Institute for Curriculum Development.

Thiong'o, N. W. (1986). *Decolonising the mind: The politics of language in African literature.* Heinemann Educational.

Thompson, P. (2022). Corpus analysis of disciplinary variation and the teaching of ESP/EAP. In R. R. Jablonkai & E. Csomay (Eds.), *The Routledge handbook of corpora and English language teaching and learning.* Routledge. https://doi.org/10.4324/9781003002901

Thorndike, E. L. (1911). *Animal intelligence: Experimental studies.* The Macmillan Company.

Tinning, R. (2002). Toward a "modest pedagogy": Reflections on the problematics of critical pedagogy. *Quest, 54*(3), 224–240. https://doi.org/10.1080/00336297.2002.10491776

Tolman, E. C. (1925). Behaviorism and purpose. *The Journal of Philosophy, 22*(2), 36–41. https://doi.org/10.2307/2015202

Toney, T. (Ed.). (1984). *Curriculum and syllabus design in ELT: Report on the Dunford house seminar.* The British Council.

Trenholm, S., & Peschke, J. (2020). Teaching undergraduate mathematics fully online: a review from the perspective of communities of practice. *International Journal of Educational Technology in Higher Education, 17*(1), 1–18. https://doi.org/10.1186/s41239-020-00215-0

Trimble, L. (1985). *English for science and technology: A discourse approach.* Cambridge University Press.

Tromp, R. E., & Datzberger, S. (2019). Global education policies versus local realities. Insights from Uganda and Mexico. *Compare: A Journal of Comparative and International Education, 51*(3), 356–374. https://doi.org/10.1080/03057925.2019.1616163

Troudi, S. & Alwan, F. (2010). Teachers' feelings during curriculum change in the United Arab Emirates: Opening Pandora's box. *Teacher Development, 14*(1), 107–121. https://doi.org/10.1080/13664531003696659

Tso, A. W. B., Ng, S. K. K., Law, L., & Bai, T. S. (2023). *The post-pandemic landscape of education and beyond: Innovation and transformation: Selected papers from the HKAECT 2022 international conference.* Springer. https://link.springer.com/book/10.1007/978-981-19-9217-9

Turnbull, M. (2001). There is a role for the L1 in second and foreign language teaching, but . . . . *Canadian Modern Language Review, 57*(4), 531–540. https://doi.org/10.3138/cmlr.57.4.531

Tyler, R. W. (1949). *Basic principles of curriculum and instruction.* The University of Chicago Press.

Tyler, R. W. (with Hlebowitsh, P. S.). (2013). *Basic principles of curriculum and instruction.* The University of Chicago Press. (Original work published 1949).

Uluçinar, U. (2021). Findings of qualitative studies on understanding by design: A meta-synthesis. *International Journal of Curriculum and Instructional Studies, 11*(2), 167–194. https://eric.ed.gov/?id=EJ1329091

UNESCO. (2021). *Getting every school climate-ready: How countries are integrating climate change issues in education.* https://doi.org/10.54675/NBHC8523

UNESCO. (2023). *Climate change communication and education country profiles: Approaches to greening education around the world.* https://doi.org/10.54676/XBVG6945

UNESCO's International Bureau of Education. (2012). *General education quality analysis/diagnosis framework.* http://www.ibe.unesco.org/en/activity/general-education-quality-analysis-framework-geqaf-initiative

UNESCO's International Institute for Educational Planning. (2023, March 22). *Using data to improve the quality of education.* https://learningportal.iiep.unesco.org/en/issue-briefs/monitor-learning/using-data-to-improve-the-quality-of-education

United Nations. (2015). *Transforming our world: The 2030 agenda for sustainable development.* https://sdgs.un.org/2030agenda

United Nations. (n.d.). *Goal 4: Ensure inclusive and equitable quality education and promote lifelong learning opportunities for all.* Department of Economic and Social Affairs: Sustainable Development. https://sdgs.un.org/goals/goal4#targets_and_indicators

University of Pennsylvania's English Language Program. (n.d.). *Philosophy of teaching and learning.* Retrieved June 23, 2023, from https://www.elp.upenn.edu/about/layout-group/philosophy-teaching-and-learning

Usher, R., & Edwards, R. (1994). *Postmodernism and education.* Routledge.

Valcke, J. (2020). Beyond English-Medium Education: From Internationalization to Sustainable Education. In H. Bowles, & A. C. Murphy (Eds.), *English-medium instruction and the internationalization of universities* (pp. 259–279). Palgrave Macmillan. https://doi.org/10.1007/978-3-030-47860-5_11

Valdman, A. (1968). Programmed instruction versus guided learning in foreign language acquisition. *Die Unterrichtspraxis/Teaching German, 1*(2), 1–14. https://doi.org/10.2307/3529036

Valdman, A. (1970). Toward a better implementation of the audio-lingual approach. *The Modern Language Journal, 54*(5), 309–319. https://doi.org/10.1111/j.1540-4781.1970.tb02273.x

Valdman, A. (1978). Communicative use of language and syllabus design. *Foreign Language Annals, 11*(5), 567–578. https://doi.org/10.1111/j.1944-9720.1978.tb00728.x

van den Akker, J. (2007). Curriculum research design. In T. Plomp & N. Nieveen (Eds.), *An introduction to educational design research* (pp. 37–50). Netherlands Institute for Curriculum Development.

van der Laan, A., & Bron, J. (2018). *The curriculum negotiation method: Tool on student voice.* Netherlands Institute for Curriculum Development.

Vygotsky, L. S. (1962). *Thought and language* (E. Hanfmann & G. Vakar, Eds.& Trans.). Massachusetts Institute of Technology Press. (Original work published 1934).

Vygotsky, L. S. (1978). *Mind in society: Development of higher psychological processes*(M. Cole, V. John-Steiner, S. Scribner, & E. Souberman, Eds. & Trans.). Harvard University Press. (Original work published 1930).

Wang, H. (2010). Translating policies into practice: The role of middle-level administrators in language curriculum implementation. *Curriculum Journal, 21*(2), 123–140. https://doi.org/10.1080/09585171003802637

Wang, H., & Cheng, L. (2009). Factors affecting teachers' curriculum implementation. *Linguistics Journal, 4*(2). 135–166.

Wang, Q., & Lu, Z. (2012). A case study of using an online community of practice-for teachers' professional development at a secondary school in China. *Learning, Media and Technology, 37*(4), 429–446. https://doi.org/10.1080/17439884.2012.685077

Warren, M. (2014). "Preparation is everything": Meetings in professional contextsin Hong Kong. *English for Specific Purposes, 36*, 12–26. https://doi.org/10.1016/j.esp.2014.03.001

Watson, J. B. (1913). Psychology as the behaviorist views it. *Psychological Review, 20*(2), 158–177. http://psychclassics.yorku.ca/Watson/views.htm

Watson, J. B. (1924). *Behaviorism*. The People's Institute Publishing Company.

Wawrzynski, M. R., & Garton, P. (2023). Language and the cocurriculum: The need for decolonizing out-of-classroom experiences. *Higher Education*, 1–17. https://doi.org/10.1007/s10734-023-01016-w

Weaver, J. (2020, October 27). Posthuman curriculum studies: The twilight of humanism. *Oxford Research Encyclopedia of Education.* https://doi.org/10.1093/acrefore/9780190264093.013.1130

Wedell, M., & Malderez, A. (2013). *Understanding language classroom contexts: The starting point for change*. Bloomsbury Publishing.

Wenger, E. (1998). Communities of practice: Learning, meaning, and identity. Cambridge University Press.

Wesche, M. B. (2010). Content-based second language instruction. In R. B. Kaplan (Ed.), *The Oxford handbook of Applied Linguistics* (2nd ed., pp. 275–293). Oxford Academic. https://doi.org/10.1093/oxfordhb/9780195384253.013.0019

West, M. (1937). The "reading approach" and "the new method system." *The Modern Language Journal, 22*(3), 220–222. https://doi.org/10.1111/j.1540-4781.1937.tb00591.x

West, R. (1994). Needs analysis in language teaching. *Language Teaching, 27*(1), 1–19. https://doi.org/10.1017/S0261444800007527

Wheeler, D. K. (1976). Curricular questions and model answers. *Vestes, 19*(1), 52–55. https://files.eric.ed.gov/fulltext/EJ146774.pdf

Wiggins, G., & McTighe, J. (2005). *Understanding by design* (2nd ed.). Association for Supervision and Curriculum.

Wiles, J. W., & Bondi, J. C. (2014). *Curriculum development: A guide to practice* (9th ed.). Pearson.

Wilkins, D. A. (1973). A communicative approach to syllabus construction in adult language learning. *Symposium on a unit/credit system for modern languages in adult education.* Council of Europe. https://files.eric.ed.gov/fulltext/ED086012.pdf

Wilkins, D. A. (1976). *Notional syllabuses.* Oxford University Press.

Willis, J. (1996). *A framework for task-based learning.* Longman.

Wilson, B. G. (2012). Constructivism in practical and historical context. InR. A. Reiser & J. V. Dempsey (Eds.), *Trends and issues in instructional design and technology* (3rd ed., pp. 45–52). Pearson.

Wingate, U. (2022). Student support and teacher education in English for Academic Purposes and English Medium Instruction: Two sides of the same coin? *Language Teaching*, 1–12. https://doi.org/10.1017/S0261444822000465

Wood, D., Bruner, J. S., & Ross, G. (1976). The role of tutoring in problem solving. *British Journal of Psychology, 66*, 181–191. https://doi.org/10.1111/j.1469-7610.1976.tb00381.x

Wood, L., & Davis, B. G. (1978). *Designing and evaluating higher education curricula: AAHE-ERIC/Higher Education Research Report 8.* The American Association for Higher Education. https://files.eric.ed.gov/fulltext/ED165669.pdf

Wu, X. (2010). Universal design for learning: A collaborative framework for designing inclusive curriculum. *i.e.: inquiry in education, 1*(2), 1–13. http://digitalcommons.nl.edu/ie/vol1/iss2/6

Xiong, T. (2012). Essence or practice? Conflicting cultural values in Chinese EFL textbooks: A discourse approach. *Discourse: Studies in the Cultural Politics of Education, 33*(4), 499–516. https://doi.org/10.1080/01596306.2012.692958

Yan, C., & He, C. (2012). Bridging the implementation gap: An ethnographic study of English teachers' implementation of the curriculum reform in China. *Ethnography and Education, 7*(1), 1–19. https://doi.org/10.1080/17457823.2012.661585

Yan, L., Litts, B. K., & Na, C. (2020). Learning in the more than human world: A conceptual analysis of posthuman pedagogy. In M. Gresalfi, & I. Horn (Eds.), *Proceedings of the 14th International Conference of the Learning Sciences, Vol. 4*, (pp. 2313–2316). International Society of the Learning Sciences.

Yilmaz, K. (2011). The cognitive perspective on learning: Its theoretical underpinnings and implications for classroom practices. *The Clearing House:A Journal of Educational Strategies, Issues and Ideas, 84*(5), 204–212. https://doi.org/10.1080/00098655.2011.568989

Yoon, J., & Casal, J. E. (2020). Rhetorical structure, sequence, and variation: A step-driven move analysis of applied linguistics conference abstracts. *International Journal of Applied Linguistics, 30*(3), 462–478. https://doi.org/10.1111/ijal.12300

Zhang, E. Y. F. (2007). TBLT—Innovation in primary school English language teaching in mainland China. In K. Van den Branden, K. Van Gorp, &M. Verhelst (Eds.), *Tasks in action: Task-based language education from a classroom-based perspective* (pp. 68–91). Cambridge Scholars. https://repository.nie.edu.sg/handle/10497/20463

Zhang, G. (2023). Authorial stance in citations: Variation by writer expertise and research article part-genres. *English for Specific Purposes, 70*, 131–147. https://doi-org.proxy.cc.uic.edu/10.1016/j.esp.2022.12.002

Zhang, X. (2020). Unpacking EFL textbook content: A focus on teachers' role in the textbook-based classroom. *CÍRCULO de Linguística Aplicada a la Comunicación, 83*, 243–250.

Zhang, Y., & Song, H. (2022). Linguistic imperialism and standard language ideology in an English textbook used in China. *Higher Education Studies, 12*(2), 112–125. https://eric.ed.gov/?id=EJ1345161

Zmuda, A., Kuklis, R., & Kline, E. (2004). *Transforming schools: Creating a culture of continuous improvement.* Association for Supervision and Curriculum Development.

Zuidema, L. A. (2005). Myth education: Rationale and strategies for teaching against linguistic prejudice. *Journal of Adolescent & Adult Literacy, 48*(8), 666–675. https://doi.org/10.1598/JAAL.48.8.4